The Practitioner Inquiry Series

Marilyn Cochran-Smith and Susan L. Lytle, *SERIES EDITORS*

THE M-CLASS TEAMS

Boston:
Roberta Logan, Site Coordinator
Joseph W. Check, Supporting Site
   Coordinator
Nancy O'Malley
Eileen Shakespear
Darcelle Walker
James Williams
Walter Wood
Junia Yearwood

Chicago:
Betty Jane Wagner, Site
   Coordinator
Kathy Daniels
Tom Daniels
Stephanie Davenport
Griselle M. Diaz-Gemmati
Brenda Landau McFarland
David O'Neill

New Orleans:
Cynthia Roy, Site
   Coordinator
Karen Alford
Reginald Galley
Sarah Herring
Elena Valenti
Pat Ward
Doris Williams-Smith

San Francisco:
Elizabeth Radin Simons and
   Carol Tateishi, Site
   Coordinators
George Austin
Verda Delp
Deborah Archuleta Juarez
Ann Lew
Susanna Merrimee
Phil Potestio

MAJOR CONTRIBUTORS

Carol Treasure
Catherine Borella

Inside City Schools

INVESTIGATING LITERACY IN MULTICULTURAL CLASSROOMS

Sarah Warshauer Freedman
Elizabeth Radin Simons
Julie Shalhope Kalnin
Alex Casareno
and the M-CLASS **teams**

FOREWORD BY **Sonia Nieto**

Teachers College, Columbia University
New York and London

National Council of
Teachers of English
Urbana, Illinois

Published simultaneously by Teachers College Press, 1234 Amsterdam Avenue, New York, NY 10027 and the National Council of Teachers of English

This project was funded primarily by the U.S. Department of Education, through a grant to the National Center for the Study of Writing and Literacy. The Rockefeller Foundation funded an opening conference for the teacher researchers and also funded residencies for Freedman and Simons at the Bellagio Study and Conference Center. The Spencer foundation funded Delp's and Alford's work on their chapters through the Small Research Grants program.

Library of Congress Cataloging-in-Publication Data

Inside city schools : investigating literacy in multicultural classrooms / Sarah Warshauer Freedman . . . [et al.] ; foreword by Sonia Nieto.
    p.   cm.—(The practitioner inquiry series)
    Includes bibliographical references (p.   ) and index.
    ISBN 0-8077-3840-9 (pbk. : alk. paper).—ISBN 0-8077-3841-7 (cloth : alk. paper)
    1. Language arts (Secondary)—United States. 2. Social sciences—Study and teaching (Secondary)—United States. 3. Multicultural education—United States. 4. Education, Urban—United States. 5. Education, Secondary—United States—Curricula. 6. Action research in education—United States. I. Freedman, Sarah Warshauer. II. National Council of Teachers of English. III. Series.
LB1631.I63   1999
428′.0071′2—dc21   99-11984

ISBN 0-8077-3840-9 (paper)
ISBN 0-8077-3841-7 (cloth)
NCTE Stock No. 23465

In memory of Karen Alford
Teacher and researcher

Contents

Foreword

ALL GOOD TEACHING and learning begins with important questions, and INSIDE CITY SCHOOLS is a good reminder that teachers' questions need to be at the center of educational research. Extraordinary things happen when teachers investigate their own practice in collaboration with students and with university researchers. When their research centers on complex issues of difference and social justice, the results are even more compelling. As I read this book, I was moved to laughter, to tears, and to deep reflection on what happens when teachers work together in considering serious issues that are usually left outside the schoolhouse door.

The chapters in this book were written by members of the Multicultural Collaborative for Literacy and Secondary Schools (the M-CLASS Project), a national teacher-research network of English and social studies teachers and university faculty. They write about classroom-based research on learning, diversity, bias, and inequality. They describe how they had to grapple with difficult and painful issues that often eluded happy endings. Through their research, they confronted—not always willingly at first—the conflict and controversy that are the inevitable consequences of broaching such issues. The result is that courage and daring are woven throughout the fabric of this book, because teachers and university faculty together faced the daunting responsibility that is at the heart of teaching: to create caring and inclusive communities where consequential and worthwhile learning can happen for all students.

There are many lessons to be learned from this book, but I will mention just two: how teacher research that focuses on difference and social justice invariably leads to transformation; and the tremendous impact of this kind of research on relationships in and out of the classroom.

There are numerous examples in these chapters of how teacher research that focuses on difference can lead to the transformation of students, teachers, university researchers, and learning itself. Teachers and students, for instance, undergo change through exposure to knowledge that is traditionally left out of the curriculum, and through having to hear what they may not always want to hear. Because racism and inequality are rarely discussed in school, few teachers know how to handle these issues in classroom discussions. In due course, school becomes a fairyland disconnected from the lives of students; it can be safe but also antiseptic, with few connections to reality.

The poignant question posed by one of Griselle Diaz-Gemmati's students is a case in point. As Diaz-Gemmati writes, "Her question to me in one journal entry will plague me forever: 'Why you have to bring all this garbage into the classroom?'" In spite of her misgivings, by the end of her research project Diaz-Gemmati was convinced that she had been right in pursuing questions of inequality and racism in her literature class. As she concluded, "Ignorance seems to be bliss and safe, but can I truly affect the lives of my students by reciting prerehearsed lines on a make-believe stage? Do I want to defer these discussions of race and prejudice to dark alleys that are constantly punctuated by the sound of gunfire?"

In the same way, the teacher researchers discuss how their curriculum and practice were transformed as a result of their research. They provide specific examples of how focusing on difference helped them to think of multicultural education in a much broader way. No longer simply a question of adding "ethnic" content to the curriculum or putting up posters with the faces of students of diverse backgrounds, multicultural education became for them a philosophy, a way of looking more critically at their own practice and all school policies and practices.

Teacher research that centers on difference changes the nature of the relationships between and among teachers, students, and university faculty. Relationships are at the essence of teaching and learning, and it is only when students define themselves as learners that learning can actually take place. And this self-definition can only take place when students have consistent and unqualified support from their teachers that they are capable of learning in the first place. Yet defining themselves in this way may be difficult for students with experience of feeling culturally dominated and who feel that they have no place in school because they are invisible in the curriculum. One of the teacher researchers, Junia Yearwood, wrote about the impact that the words of Malcolm X had on her thinking: "A people without history or cultural roots also becomes a dead people." Extending this notion to students, she suggested that students who have no cultural roots are also "dead," and that "'dead' students have no desire to learn." Forging relationships with students is one way to promote their desire to learn, and in this book you will see many examples of how caring teachers went about creating and nurturing these connections.

But the impact of relationships extends far beyond the classroom and school. Teachers found many ways to link student learning with relationships outside of school. The moving poem written by Larisa about her grief following her mother's death is an illustration of what her teacher Nancy O'Malley called "the redemptive power of writing." In another example, Elena Valenti writes about the influence of Buddy, a trucker who developed a cross-country communication with the students in her class. Although he struggled with literacy himself, Buddy nevertheless relentlessly urged his young pen pals to "stick with it," and in the process he became an inspiration to students who felt marginalized from school.

The work of these teacher researchers is what might be called "multiculturalism in action" because it concerns real teachers and students in real classrooms. The focus on critical practice, evident here, is missing in much of multicultural education. For all the insights and contributions it has made to the profession, multicultural education is too often either a superficial add-on to the curriculum, or top heavy with critical theory but short on critical practice. In this volume, teacher and university researchers create substantive multicultural classroom communities by asking hard questions and puzzling through some difficult situations. The result of their work is also significant for universities struggling to figure out how to prepare teachers to effectively teach a diverse population of students.

INSIDE CITY SCHOOLS complicates dichotomies in educational discourse: multicultural education versus the canon; separatism versus common culture; heart versus mind; teaching versus learning; learning versus feeling. Such dichotomies are challenged by the talented teachers who have written about their classroom research in this book. They are committed to making the simplistic more complex; they want their students to learn *and* think or, in the words of Paulo Freire, "to read the word *and* the world." There are no easy formulas here; in fact, readers may be surprised at the range of pedagogical strategies these teachers use, or at the philosophies of teaching and learning and life that they express. Their research is not tied up neatly at the end. We are left with even bigger questions that defy easy answers, and this is as it should be when the topics of diversity and bias are included in classroom conversations. But for teachers and university faculty who believe in social justice, there is no other option than to bring these concerns into schools and classrooms. If our goal is to create safe, inclusive, and powerful learning communities that lead all students to high levels of achievement, then differences need to be faced honestly. In the words of Deborah Archuleta Juarez, one of the teacher researchers, "Either we deal with issues of race, culture, and class or the issues will deal with us." In this book, teacher researchers working with their students and with university researchers point out some ways in which we can begin.

Sonia Nieto
University of Massachusetts

Preface

THIS BOOK IS DEDICATED to the memory of teacher researcher Karen Alford. She did not live to see its publication or to see her words in print, but like all of her colleagues on this project, she had important ideas to communicate about teaching and learning. In a talk at the 1994 annual meeting of the American Educational Research Association, Alford reflected on the process of doing teacher research, what it meant to her and to her students. In that talk, as she reflected on why she became a teacher researcher, she explained to the audience, "It all starts with wondering" (Alford, 1994, p. 2). Alford's words were particularly true for the teacher researchers who participated in this project. Each one wanted to do a teacher research project because each was "wondering" about something that wasn't transparent, something that would take thought and digging to figure out. Alford explained:

> My M-CLASS research question led me to wonder what my students in my class would learn about history if they wrote in the voice of people from the past. But now my wondering travels further—I wonder about my students; writing; their work on projects; their relationships with their peers and their teachers; their places in life. I know I do this [wondering] because of my participation in M-CLASS.

Alford also realized that her wonderings had important effects on the way she taught and ultimately on her students:

> While I'm glad that we adults are learning from this process of class-room research, I think the real winners are my students. One of them noticed that I had changed. I had asked my students to reflect on lots of aspects of their writing for their third-quarter writing portfolio. Ann was working on this—papers all over her desk. She said in a frustrated voice, "Ms. Karen, you're different than you were last year."
> "What do you mean? More gray hair?"
> "Well, now you make us think. Thinking's hard!"

Alford's wonderings and her writings about them were much on her mind even after she was diagnosed with breast cancer, even as she bravely faced a bone marrow transplant, and even when she was sent home from the hospital and told that there was nothing more that the doctors could do for her. That she worked on her research until the end dramatized its importance to her, but her commitment was not unique. Most teachers do wonder about a lot of things, but given the day-to-day demands on their time and a general lack of support for teachers to wonder, to think, and to write, many never have a chance to delve into those wonderings, much less communicate their messages to a wider audience. Karen Alford reminds us all that our time here is short; our problems are large; and we wait to solve them at our peril.

Acknowledgments

IN ADDITION TO our funders—U.S. Department of Education, the Rockefeller Foundation, the Spencer Foundation, and the University of California at Berkeley—we thank the National Writing Project (NWP). NWP provided initial help in selecting the M-CLASS sites and teachers, and Writing Project directors and teacher consultants participated actively as site coordinators and informal consultants. The Writing Project's long-time experience with teacher research and their successful university-schools collaborations taught us more than we can begin to acknowledge here.

We also are grateful to many individuals: our families—Bob and Rachel Freedman; Herb, Rachel, and Daniel Simons and Christa Laib; and Peter Kalnin and all the Shalhopes; colleagues in Boston, Chicago, New Orleans, and the San Francisco Bay Area who helped identify potential teacher participants—Rebekah Caplan, Marcia Largent Corcoran, Smokey Daniels, James Gray, Cynthia Greenleaf, George Hillocks, Alice Kawazoe, Nanette Koelsch, Carol Lee, Dan Lindley, Catherine Lucas, Jabari Mahiri, Arguiro Morgan, Miles Myers, Janice Ollarvia, Charlie Suhor, and Shelly Weintraub; those who provided scholarly resources and information about the schools—Richard Alba, Geraldine Clifford, Marcia Farr, Meg Gebhard, Jewell Gould, Paul Holland, Alfred Hess, Josie Landry, Nat Lecour, Carol Lee, Linda Lenz, Herbert Lindenberger, Kevin Marshall, Robert Marston, Pam Masarski, Alex McLeod, Celia Ruiz, Walter Williams, William Taylor, David Tyack, Guadelupe Valdés, Rhona Weinstein, Carolyn Wilson, Helen Ying; those who responded to portions of the manuscript—Courtney Cazden, Elyse Eidman-Aadahl, Robley Hood, Laurie Novak, Ellie O'Sullivan, Lynda Soroka, Richard Sterling, and Berkeley students Esperanza Alcala-Collins, Pamela Fong, Tom Malarkey, Sarah Manyika, Brad Olsen, Debra Schneider, Laura Snyder, and Sharon Wachs and Stanford student Maisha Tulivu Fisher; as well as others who assisted on the project: Maribel Gonzalez, Ayana Hudson, Barbara McClain, and Cristina Santamaria.

We send our heartfelt appreciation for the generosity, special expertise, and invaluable assistance of these many friends and colleagues and of the many others who are too numerous to name.

A Note on Terminology and Transcription

THROUGHOUT THIS BOOK, the term *multicultural* is used in its broadest sense to indicate the coming together of different cultural groups, whose identity may be based on ethnicity, national origin, social class, gender, religion, generation, and the like. Diversity of ethnicity was the primary variable we used to decide whether to consider a classroom multicultural. In the few cases that a single ethnic group dominated a classroom, we made certain that other aspects of cultural variation were present.

In this volume, we use the term *ethnicity* to refer to what are sometimes called racial differences as well as any ethnic differences that are related to country of origin or religion. We use the term *race* to denote ethnic differences that are highly charged politically. We understand that race is purely a social construct, with no biological basis. To refer to particular racial/ethnic groups, we use terms that are preferred by the groups themselves. In the case of *African American* and *Black,* both terms are in common usage. We use these terms interchangeably for the most part; however, for Blacks who are not born in the United States or who are the children of immigrants, we use the term *Black* rather than *African American* or we refer to the country or area of origin (e.g., Afro-Caribbean, Cape Verdean).

For individuals of Mexican and Central and South American origin the terminological issues are more complex. Some people of Mexican origin prefer the term *Chicano* or *Chicana* whereas others prefer *Mexican American,* with the preferences depending on region, generation, and political orientation. We use both terms, with contributors from particular regions generally using terms that are most widely used and accepted in their regions. In particular, to indicate Mexican origin, *Mexican American* is more often the preferred term in Chicago whereas *Chicano* or *Chicana* is more often the preferred term in the San Francisco Bay Area. At times, within a given region, we switch between these terms to be consistent with how individuals self-identify. In the past the term *Latino* or *Latina* was used just to refer to immigrants from Central and South America but now has assumed a broader usage in California, where people of Mexican origin self-identify as Latino, as do those of Central and South American origin (Latino Eligibility Task Force, 1993). This broader usage, which is spreading to other areas of the country, is what we use in this volume. The term *Hispanic* is sometimes used to include people from all Spanish-speaking countries and is commonly used by schools in collecting demographic statistics. We use the term only when referring to such demographic data; in other situations, we tend to avoid it because it technically includes Spanish speakers who are not from the Americas (e.g., Spaniards) and does not include Brazilians who speak Portuguese as their native language.

In the case of *White* and *European American,* we have chosen to use the term *White,* since many people who classify themselves as White are not from Europe and since many people from Europe do not classify themselves as White. Some chapter authors, however, prefer the term *European American* or *Anglo,* and in those cases we have not changed their choice.

Those who straddle cultural and ethnic categories are not easily captured in demographic data. Students of mixed backgrounds may be identified under a single ethnic category, or they may be grouped under the obscuring category "other." When referring to students, chapter authors normally explain the complexity of background or use the identifier preferred by the individuals themselves.

For all transcribed material, original verbatim transcripts were edited for ease of reading. The originals included speech hesitations and repetitions, a period to indicate falling intonation, a comma to indicate rising intonation, a series of three periods for short pauses and four for long pauses. In some cases, phonetic spelling was used to capture pronunciation that deviated from the standard.

The edited transcripts in this volume use standard written spelling and punctuation conventions (to the extent possible without distorting the flavor), do not include speech hesitations or repetitions unless changes would distort the original meaning, do not indicate intonations or pauses, and use a series of three periods to indicate omitted text of less than a sentence and four for omitted text of more than a sentence. Information in brackets is inserted when clarification seems needed.

In addition, in all quoted material in this book, including teachers' writing, pseudonyms are used, with the exception of the names of the M-CLASS teachers and their schools.

PART I

Setting the Context for M-CLASS (Multicultural Collaborative for Literacy and Secondary Schools)

CHAPTER 1

Introducing M-CLASS

Sarah Warshauer Freedman

> I said, "Evelyn, I've never taught . . . any White kids." And she said, "Children are children." . . . And that was a very good thing to say to me because it relaxed me, and it made me more comfortable and not so afraid.
> —Patricia Ward, at Teacher Researcher Meeting, New Orleans, October 31, 1992

> I feel one of the best ways to educate children of color is to examine their cultural background to include socioeconomic, religious, family make-up, and all other factors that could possibly have an impact on their . . . understanding of the world in which they live.
> —Reginald Galley, at Teacher Researcher Meeting, New Orleans, October 31, 1992

WHEN SHOULD TEACHERS focus on what their students have in common and when should they focus on how they differ? African American teachers Patricia Ward and Reginald Galley contemplate this issue in their urban, multicultural English and social studies classrooms. For Ward, Galley, and the many others of varied ethnicities who teach inside city schools, the stakes are high; the students they teach often live in poverty, feel alienated from school, and are at risk of dropping out. How these students are treated and what they learn in school must motivate them to care about learning and provide them with the background and confidence they need to succeed in America's pluralistic society. When it comes to literacy, most teachers who work in city schools agree that ultimately they must provide their students with opportunities to read, write, and learn both about their own cultures and about the wider American experience. What they question is how to understand and then achieve an optimal balance between the cultural differences that cross their students' lives and the commonalities in their experiences.

Ward and Galley were part of M-CLASS (Multicultural Collaborative for Literacy and Secondary Schools), a national network of 24 eighth-, ninth-, and tenth-grade English and social studies teachers in Boston, Chicago, New

Orleans, and the San Francisco Bay Area. This teacher-research network was established by Sarah Warshauer Freedman and Elizabeth Radin Simons through the National Center for the Study of Writing and Literacy at the University of California, Berkeley.[1] The teachers spent the 1992–1993 academic year investigating issues of literacy and learning that were particular to teaching diverse groups of students who came together to create multicultural classrooms.

The concerns of this project, and therefore this book, are twofold: *what* the collaboration of teacher researchers and university researchers found out about literacy learning in multicultural classrooms and *how* teacher researchers learn about these issues, for the purpose both of contributing to knowledge and of developing their practice. Although most books reporting the results of research projects focus mainly on what has been found, in this book we are equally concerned with thinking through what it means to involve teacher researchers in both a professional development effort and a process of knowledge generation.

Just before the M-CLASS teachers began their research, they attended a conference in San Francisco where Troy Duster, Berkeley sociologist and specialist in multiculturalism, explained that the public debates about multiculturalism and literacy offered the teachers little help in understanding their students' needs.[2] Led by academicians and media pundits who are far removed from actual multicultural settings, the debates were characterized by Duster as contentious and mean spirited. He suggested that they polarized the issues; either you are for "ethnic enclaves or you march forward under the banner of universalism" (opening conference, M-CLASS, September 11, 1992). Duster explained that the debates portrayed those on the side of "ethnic enclaves" as wanting to preserve difference, as "separatists" who work to keep ethnic groups apart from one another and from the "mainstream." When these "separatists" consider which curriculum to promote, they argue for a multicultural one, to replace the traditional Anglo-American literary canon (Shakespeare, Dickens, Hawthorne, Twain, Frost, and the like) and to replace the study of Western European history, those subjects that are supposed to provide a common core of knowledge. In their promoting a multicultural curriculum, the separatists also are accused of undermining academic standards, since their opponents consider knowledge of Western history and literature essential to achieving meaningful standards.

Those on the side of "universalism" are portrayed as wanting the opposite of what the separatists want. When the "universalists" consider which curriculum to promote, they argue for knowledge of the traditional literary canon and of Western European history, in the belief that these subjects provide the glue that holds our country together. The universalists, in their efforts to establish commonality, are accused of working to eradicate all ethnic differences and hence all subcultures within the United States. For this reason, their opponents consider them to be racists who believe in denying ethnic groups access to their cultures, their histories, and their literatures.

The M-CLASS teachers, who work daily in multicultural classrooms, saw the issues surrounding multiculturalism and literacy as more complex and multifaceted than revealed in the debates Duster described. Boston teacher Junia Yearwood knows that she must bring her students into the academic world both by honoring and building on what they know and by providing them with access to new ideas and new ways of thinking. Yet she still wondered, "How much of one's own culture does one need . . . to stay connected, to have one's own ethnic identity? And how and in what ways should we share what is American and what we have in common?" (Junia Yearwood, site meeting, Boston, October 31, 1992). Yearwood's colleague Eileen Shakespear explained how Yearwood's quandary complicates the public debates:

> I think a lot of times the justification for multiculturalism in curriculum is that it's the right thing to do. What Junia [Yearwood] does is make the link to the intellectual and say this is how the kid grows intellectually. It's not just that it's right, but there's a product that's beyond the kid just feeling okay about themselves. It's that the kid then goes on and is a better student. He's a smarter kid. . . . having a real intellectual experience with you [Yearwood] and with the books. It's not just a psychological thing, that he's just feeling better. . . . He's growing. He's maturing as a thinker. (Site meeting, Boston, May 23, 1993)

Yearwood used a multicultural curriculum, which the universalists claim denigrates standards, to purposefully promote the high academic standards the universalists argue for. She is concerned not only with what to teach but also with how to teach it. Intellectual growth and maturation is a prerequisite for students' successful engagement in the substantive work of school. Yearwood designed her multicultural curriculum to provide a conduit, a point of access, to this broader intellectual perspective. Yearwood and many of her colleagues used a broad-based curriculum to prepare their students to take an academic frame of reference, to be curious and creative thinkers, to learn how to learn, to come to understand and appreciate books from many different traditions.

Troy Duster provided important motivation for the novice teacher researchers at the M-CLASS conference when he argued that teachers such as Ward, Galley, and Yearwood were in a unique position to break new ground and to help the American public think about issues of curriculum, but also more broadly to reconsider the debates about multiculturalism:

[Teachers] are actually engaged in the living experience of a plural society. . . . [The] pluralistic classroom . . . needs to be part of this debate instead of letting the stage be occupied by the two extreme positions. What's really happening in the society is that people are having experiences across this complex, rich, sometimes conflictual, irritating, angry divide but [also] sometimes [there are] remarkably confluent and inspiring circumstances where students get together across the divide and find enrichment as a function of their differences. That part of the debate is what I think you [teachers] can best contribute because what's thirsted for is an alternative vision where multiculturalism is not just ideologically driven but informed by the experience of the kinds of situations in which most of you are involved. (Opening M-CLASS conference, September 11, 1992)

Teachers, Duster suggests, have the opportunity to document the many positions between the extremes now before the American public and to help Americans understand the complexity of issues, the resolution of which are vital to the health of the nation. Because teachers assume the responsibility for connecting their goals for teaching with their students' interests and learning needs, they find that they must quickly move beyond what seem to them petty quarrels about what books to teach. Rather, they focus on meeting their larger goals, which include encouraging their students to become lifelong readers who can understand and interpret many types of literature, who can write for varied audiences and purposes, who can speak articulately and convincingly in varied situations. What these teachers envision for their students are multicultural literacies—literacies that provide students with an understanding of the variations within these United States but at the same time bring us together as one nation.

ESTABLISHING A MULTICULTURAL TEACHER RESEARCH NETWORK

In the formation of M-CLASS, the goal was to bring together a multicultural group of teacher researchers from cities in different regions of the country. Through their research these teachers would model ways of exploring their practice, and they would provide findings to other teachers who, like themselves, confront every day the multicultural complexities of growing up American.

To locate interested and experienced teachers, Freedman and Simons worked with contacts in cities in the northeastern, southern, midwestern, and western regions of the United States. These contacts included (a) National Writing Project (NWP) directors, particularly those active in the NWP Urban

Sites Network; (b) directors of nationally funded projects focused on literacy and involving large numbers of teachers of students of color (e.g., the members of the Rockefeller Foundation Collaboratives for Humanities and Arts Teaching [CHART] groups); and (c) other prominent educators and teacher educators at the sites. Before making final selections of sites and teachers, Freedman or Simons conducted telephone interviews with over 75 nominated teachers. In these interviews, the teachers were asked about their theories of teaching in multiethnic/multiracial settings, about important issues they confronted in their classrooms, and about their interest in interrogating their practice and thinking together with a group of colleagues about the complexities of literacy learning in multicultural urban schools and classrooms.

Through these conversations, Simons and Freedman selected 24 teachers—6 each in Boston, Chicago, New Orleans, and the San Francisco Bay Area. They also confirmed the availability of at least one site coordinator in each area. The site coordinators were NWP leaders who were also leaders in teacher research and often were affiliated with a local university. They were charged with organizing the local activities and developing a local community where the teachers would feel comfortable working with one another. Without local leadership to direct and guide the local communities, it would not have been possible to sustain and support the teachers' research. The site coordinators were Roberta Logan, supported by Joseph Check in Boston; B. J. Wagner in Chicago; Cynthia Roy in New Orleans; and Elizabeth Simons, supported by Carol Tateishi, in the San Francisco Bay Area.

The teachers who were selected had reputations as successful practitioners in urban, multicultural classrooms and were interested in engaging in a yearlong teacher-research process about literacy and learning as students of varied ethnicities and social classes come together. Members of the group were not selected for their unified views about multicultural curriculum or for a particular ideology about integrated schools. They all looked forward to confronting difficult issues and understanding something of their complexity. Essential to the success of M-CLASS was the choosing of teachers who were committed to making a contribution as a result of engaging in this reflective process.

A diverse group of teachers was also chosen from each site. Table 1.1 lists the 24 M-CLASS teachers and gives information about their experience levels, the subjects they taught, and the schools in which they worked. With respect to ethnicity, 10 were African American or Afro-Caribbean, 9 were White and from varied backgrounds, 3 were Latina (one of Cuban, one of Mexican, and one of Puerto Rican origin), and two were Asian American (one of Chinese and one of Japanese origin); 7 were male and 17 were female. Four were immigrants to the United States, and three of these came not speaking English. Although most were from middle-class backgrounds, at

Table 1.1 Teachers and Schools

Teacher(s)	Years Teaching	Subject	School and Grade Level	School Size	Special School Features
Boston					
Nancy O'Malley	22	English	John D. O'Bryant School of Mathematics and Science (Grades 9–12)	1,077	Examination high school, technical emphasis
Eileen Shakespear	25	English	Fenway Middle College High School (Grades 9–12)	196	Alternative high school on community college campus, for troubled teens, part of Coalition of Essential Schools
Darcelle Walker	20	English	John W. McCormack Middle School (Grades 6–8)	668	Comprehensive middle school, sought after by parents
James Williams	15	Social Studies	Frank V. Thompson Middle School (Grades 6–8)	335	Comprehensive middle school, high concentration African Americans
Walter Wood	25	English	South Boston High School (Grades 9–12)	864	Comprehensive district high school, site of nationally televised riots
Junia Yearwood	14	English	Boston English High School (Grades 9–12)	1,312	Comprehensive district high school
Chicago					
Kathy Daniels and Tom Daniels	24, 31	English	Farragut Career Academy High School (Grades 9–12)	2,325	Comprehensive high school, in neighborhood changing from mostly Black to mostly Mexican American, site of televised riots
Stephanie Davenport and Brenda Landau McFarland	25, 18	English, Social Studies	Lake View High School (Grades 9–12)	1,319	Comprehensive high school in ethnically mixed neighborhood
Griselle Diaz-Gemmati	10	English	Norwood Park School (Grades K–8)	235	Small elementary school in White neighborhood, with busing
David O'Neill	29	English	Lane Technical High School (Grades 9–12)	3,950	Examination school; science, technology, music, and art emphases
New Orleans					
Karen Alford	6	English/ Social Studies	Audubon Montessori (Grades K–8)	480	Montessori and French immersion magnet school; first come, first-served admissions

Name		Subject	School	Enrollment	Description
Reginald Galley	3	Social Studies	Fannie C. Williams Middle School (Grades 6–8)	1,248	Comprehensive high school in ethnically mixed neighborhood
Sarah Herring	23	English	Edna Karr Magnet (Grades 9–12)	1,057	Academic magnet, test scores required for entrance
Elena Valenti	9	Social Studies	Andrew Jackson High School [St. Bernard Parish] (Grades 9–12)	833	Comprehensive high school; blue-collar, mostly White neighborhood and school population
Patricia Ward	28	English	McMain Secondary Magnet School (Grades 9–12)	1,343	Academic magnet, writing test and 2.0 or greater GPA required for entrance
Doris Williams-Smith	17	English	Lusher Extension (Grades 6–8)	888	Arts and gifted multicultural magnet school; first-come, first-served admissions; good-conduct record required
San Francisco Bay Area					
George Austin	7	Social Studies	El Cerrito High School [West Contra Costa] (Grades 9–12)	1,412	Comprehensive high school, mixed ethnically and socio-economically
Verda Delp	20	English	Willard Junior High School [Berkeley] (Grades 6–8)	529	Comprehensive middle school, mixed ethnically and socio-economically
Deborah Archuleta Juarez	4	English	Calvin Simmons Junior High School [Oakland] (Grades 7–9)	1,036	Comprehensive middle school, mostly non-White populations
Ann Lew	20	English	Philip Burton High School [San Francisco] (Grades 9–12)	1,149	Comprehensive high school, large ESL population
Susanna Merimee	18	ESL	George Washington High School [San Francisco] (Grades 9–12)	2,738	Comprehensive high school, large ESL population
Phil Potestio	7	Social Studies	Havenscourt Junior High School [Oakland] (Grades 7–9)	613	Comprehensive middle school, mostly non-White populations

6

ach city was from a working-class family or grew up in
.

her researchers made creating teacher-research commu-
M-CLASS cities particularly complex. Not only were the
up, but for the most part they did not know one another
gan and before they set out to work together to address
substantively and politically difficult and sensitive topics.[3]

This mix of teacher researchers, however, was critical to the goals of
M-CLASS. When lone researchers work on questions about multiculturalism,
they necessarily write from their own experience, as an African American
female (e.g., Delpit, 1988; Foster, 1997; Ladson-Billings, 1994), as a White
male (e.g., Blauner, 1992; Grant, 1988), as an African American male (e.g.,
Banks, 1995; West, 1994), as a Latina female (e.g., Gutierrez, 1992; Valdés,
1996), as a White female (e.g., Sleeter, 1989). Although individuals in M-CLASS
still think and write from their own experiences, the project as a whole aims
to connect these varied voices in ways that combine the multiple points
of view of a mix of researchers, from varied racial and ethnic backgrounds
and socioeconomic classes (see also Nieto, 1992, for a combining of diverse
voices). As a group, the research team had experienced more of the complexities of the lives of students who come together in multicultural classrooms
than any one teacher or researcher or even small research team could experience. A primary goal of the teacher-research process and of this book is for
these multiple voices to play off of and inform one another.

In the United States, teachers work with classes of students from multiple ethnic and cultural backgrounds in many kinds of schools and school
districts. To provide a sense of the M-CLASS settings, Table 1.2 summarizes the
ethnic distribution in each M-CLASS district and school.[4] As is the case for the
great majority of urban school districts in the United States, the M-CLASS
districts were populated mostly by students coming from conditions of poverty, with most of these African Americans and others immigrants and the
children of immigrants. White and middle-class families have often fled from
the cities to the suburbs and to private schools. The demographic anomalies
in M-CLASS are the mostly White, largely working class, suburban St. Bernard
Parish, which borders Orleans Parish; and the San Francisco Unified School
District, where the biggest group is Asian American, not African American.

In New Orleans, with its high concentration of African Americans, the
few multicultural classrooms that exist are in magnet schools. These popular
schools are found in the more affluent areas of the city, offer special programs
in the arts and in particular academic areas, and draw students from the
local neighborhood as well as from across the city. The situation is similar in
Chicago. Although some Chicago schools find themselves with multiethnic
populations because of court-ordered busing aimed at achieving ethnic bal-

Table 1.2. Percentage of Students in Schools and Districts by Ethnicity, 1992–1993

				%			
	N	*White*	*Black*	*Asian*	*Hispanic*	*Other*	*All Minority*
BOSTON							
All Boston	62,407	20.2	47.6	9.1	22.7	0.4	79.8
Boston English High School	1,312	12.8	47.5	3.0	36.5	0.2	87.2
Fenway Middle College High School	196	20.0	54.0	6.0	20.0	—	80.0
John D. O'Bryant School of Mathematics and Science	1,077	9.0	48.9	29.9	11.9	0.3	91.0
John W. McCor-mack Middle School	668	21.9	47.5	4.3	26.0	0.3	78.1
South Boston High School	864	27.5	35.5	12.6	23.6	0.7	72.4
Frank V. Thompson Mid-dle School	335	8.9	83.0	3.0	5.4	0.6	91.1
CHICAGO							
All Chicago	411,582	11.6	56.2	3.0	29.0	0.2	88.4
Farragut Career Academy	2,325	0.2	29.5	0	70.2	0	99.7
Norwood Park School	235	47.7	24.7	2.6	24.7	0.4	52.4
Lake View High School	1,319	17.1	18.2	2.8	61.3	0.5	82.8
Lane Technical High School	3,950	35.0	18.4	17.8	28.3	0.5	65.0
NEW ORLEANS							
All New Orleans	84,444	6.5	89.3	2.8	1.4	—	93.5
Audubon Montes-sori	480	41.0	50.0	3.3	5.4	0.2	59.0

(Cont.)

Table 1.2. (cont.)

				%			
	N	White	Black	Asian	Hispanic	Other	All Minority
Edna Karr Magnet	1,057	32.3	52.2	10.8	4.7	—	67.7
Fannie C. Williams High School	1,248	3.7	76.0	19.8	0.4	—	96.3
Lusher Extension	888	47.1	46.5	2.8	3.6	—	52.9
McMain Secondary Magnet School	1,343	21.3	66.1	8.3	4.2	0	78.7
All St. Bernard Parish	9,076	85.7	9.3	2.8	1.4	0.8	14.3
Andrew Jackson High School	833	92.7	2.5	1.2	3.0	0.6	7.3
SAN FRANCISCO BAY AREA							
All San Francisco	61,882	13.9	18.2	47.5	19.8	0.6	86.1
Burton High School	1,149	4.2	20.2	43.5	16.2	15.8	95.8
George Washington High School	2,738	16.3	12.7	61.3	6.0	3.7	83.7
All Oakland	51,234	7.3	54.9	19.6	17.6	0.5	92.7
Calvin Simmons Junior High School	1,036	1.5	30.3	12.6	50.3	5.2	99.9
Havenscourt Junior High School	613	0.5	54.0	8.8	34.9	1.8	100.0
All Berkeley	7,954	36.5	43.2	8.2	11.0	100.0	63.5
Willard Junior High School	529	31.9	51.8	6.4	9.3	0.6	68.1
All West Contra Costa	31,289	27.0	35.4	12.8	18.6	6.15	73.0
El Cerrito High School	1,412	27.3	45.3	17.0	8.6	1.6	72.7

Sources and notes: Boston school information obtained from Kevin Marshall, Department of Research, Assessment and Evaluation, Boston Public Schools, 5/15/97, (617) 635-9450. Boston Fenway Middle College High School, because of the size of the school and its status as an experimental program, is not included in district record keeping. Statistics are estimates provided by Robert Marston. Chicago school informa-

(Cont.)

Table 1.2. (cont.)

tion obtained from the Chicago Public Schools School Information Database, http://acct.multi1.cps.k12.il.us/download.html. New Orleans data provided by Walter Williams, Student Data Manager, New Orleans Parish, 8/27/97, (504) 365-5301. St. Bernard Parish statistics: personal communication from Josie Landry, Secretary Child Welfare and Attendance, 5/15/97, (504) 271-2533. All California school data were taken from the 1992–1993 California Basic Educational Data System (CBEDS). This report is available from the California Department of Education Internet site (http://goldmine.cde.ca.gov/). San Francisco and Oakland district information was taken from Sietsema and Bose (1995). Berkeley and West Contra Costa district information was taken from the 1992–1993 CBEDS report. The table retains the label for ethnicities used in these documents. For California sites, the CBEDS data include statistics for the following groups: American Indian, Pacific Islander, and Filipino. Those statistics have been summed and are represented in the "Other" category on this chart. The term "Hispanic" is used in this table because this is the term used in all reporting of school demographic data.

ance, and other schools became multiethnic when caught in the shifting demographics of neighborhoods in transition, many have achieved integration as magnet schools. In spite of well-functioning magnet schools in both cities, those schools without magnet programs, which serve by far the majority of students, are mostly all Black and generally offer comparatively weak academic programs.

Unlike in New Orleans and Chicago, in Boston and the San Francisco Bay Area many schools are well integrated. In Boston, court orders abolished all neighborhood schools and a citywide plan assigns students to schools to achieve ethnic balance. In the San Francisco Bay Area, Berkeley integrated voluntarily in the 1960s; West Contra Costa instituted an open enrollment policy; San Francisco's schools are under court orders; and Oakland schools are poorly integrated. In all of these districts, special schools have been created to offset White and middle-class flight from the systems.

The examination school is another type of multicultural senior high school entrenched in each of the M-CLASS urban centers. These schools have become a bastion for the urban middle classes, since many middle-class children score high enough on admissions tests to gain entrance in numbers disproportionate to those of students from lower socioeconomic classes. Exam schools generally have substantial White populations, except in San Francisco, where now over half of the students at the exam school are of Asian origin. It is important to note that the exam schools in Chicago, a city with strong working-class roots, began as vocational schools for the sons and daughters of workers rather than as academic schools designed to prepare the elite for college entrance. They still maintain a distinctly vocational flavor.

Most of the M-CLASS schools sit in multiethnic pockets, where teachers and students are trying to forge safe and harmonious learning communities, often in the face of a larger environment that is not itself well integrated and that may be hostile to varied groups coming together. The M-CLASS teachers were attempting to understand how to better serve our nation's school-children who come together across cultural groups and meet daily in their classrooms.

The M-CLASS schools represent a range of types of multicultural settings, but in all of them, even the magnet schools and the examination schools, 50% or more of the student body come from conditions of poverty. Descriptions of two of the M-CLASS schools provide a more specific sense of the kinds of classrooms the teachers worked in. The schools, which represent the ends of the M-CLASS continuum, are Farragut Career Academy High School in Chicago, where Kathy and Tom Daniels taught, and Lusher Extension in New Orleans, where Doris Williams-Smith taught. Farragut, among the most troubled, is somewhat typical of other Chicago schools; Lusher Extension, with a reputation for academic excellence, is less typical of New Orleans schools but provides a fine view of a well-functioning magnet school.

Farragut draws from the surrounding neighborhood, which is changing from mostly African American to mostly Mexican American. The school is considered undesirable due to entrenched neighborhood gangs and violence in the community and the school. Many parents try to transfer their children to other schools, which they hope will be safer. The principal has had to close the school on several occasions in recent years because of violence between warring African American and Latino gangs both in the school and in the neighborhood. Ninety-two percent of the students were on the federal free or reduced-fee lunch program and came from homes with incomes below the poverty level. The reading scores of 75% of the entering freshmen were below grade level.

At the other end of the continuum is Lusher Extension, a multicultural magnet school for grades 6–8. Lusher is located in New Orleans's upscale, historic Garden District and attracts students from a mix of ethnic groups, socioeconomic classes, and areas within the city. Parents literally camp out on the streets for several days before registration begins in order to enroll their children. Students are admitted on a first-come, first-served basis. About two thirds are classified as academically gifted and 20% as talented in the visual or performing arts. Although the student population includes a wide range of socioeconomic levels, 50.3% are below the poverty level and on free or reduced-fee lunch.

Of the 24 M-CLASS teacher researchers, 9 taught in schools similar to Farragut, with almost all of the students coming from conditions of poverty and the schools suffering the impacts of gangs, violence, and the other tensions of inner city life. Three taught in settings similar to Lusher, where the school serves a true cross section of ethnic groups and socioeconomic classes and is known for a strong, well-functioning school community and excellence in its faculty and academic programs. These schools attract a higher percentage of White and middle-class children than do most others. The other 12 taught in schools that fall somewhere between these extremes.

CONCEPTUALIZING THE RESEARCH

Through research in their schools and classrooms, the 24 teachers searched for answers to their own most pressing questions about literacy and learning in their classrooms. Underlying all of their questions were their dilemmas about balancing what their students had in common with how they differed. The teachers studied how much consideration to give to selecting curricular material that would match their students' experiences, how to make similarities and differences explicit through discussions of sensitive topics about race and ethnicity; how to see and help their students see from the points of view of others; how to teach basic skills to heterogeneous groups; how to coordinate curriculum with what teachers at other grade levels teach, especially when administrative support is lacking; how to handle issues from outside the classroom that affect classroom life, such as violence, poverty, and racism; how to establish an atmosphere of comfort and security for all students. Appendix A contains a list of the teachers' questions.

For M-CLASS to succeed, the teachers had to think together about these issues. If they could not talk comfortably and honestly with their colleagues, M-CLASS would fail. For this reason, the M-CLASS organizers thought about how to engender an open atmosphere where difficult issues could be discussed and where the teachers could help one another push their understandings forward. The teacher-research literature says little about how to create multicultural research communities.

The main tactic in M-CLASS involved explicitly raising difficult issues from the start. The Berkeley team first provided a stimulus for the teachers to begin thinking about such issues privately on their own. The stimulus was a provocative article by Lisa Delpit, "The Silenced Dialogue" (1988), which everyone read before attending the opening conference in San Francisco. Next, issues about race, ethnicity, class, and culture were raised openly at the conference, which began with a panel on multiculturalism, moderated by

Troy Duster, and with presentations by a group who came with a diversity of experiences and perspectives: Barbara Christian, professor of African American studies at the University of California (UC) Berkeley; Wilma Chan, Oakland School Board member; Kris Gutierrez, professor of education at the University of California at Los Angeles; and Jabari Mahiri, professor of education at UC Berkeley.

The panelists primarily helped the teachers clarify their thinking about multiculturalism. They first talked about the shifting meanings of the term, from the time of the civil rights protests of the 1960s when *multiculturalism* meant opening up education and other social institutions to include everybody, to a term that has become increasingly "politicized" to mean the formation of "enclaves" of people of color. Barbara Christian and Jabari Mahiri explained the political force of the term, linking it to notions of power in the society and in the classroom. Christian argued that if the United States were to embrace multiculturalism, there could be a significant change in the power structure, something that frightens people and makes them attempt to hold on to what they have. Moving closer to the teachers' domains, Mahiri linked Christian's notions of changing political power to notions of power in the classroom, explaining, "When you're talking about multicultural education, you're talking about challenging the power structures that exist in the classroom and . . . I think you're also talking about empowering students." He suggested that part of the job of teachers in multicultural settings is to help students gain access to power and that in the process teachers have to "empower" their students by learning to share power with them. Empowered students have a say about what happens in the classroom.

Gutierrez related her research about student talk and teacher talk to issues of empowerment. She found that although excellent teachers often try to engage students in "dialogue" and "conversation," they may inadvertently continue to dominate and control the talk. She demonstrated how difficult it is to break out of well-established but often dysfunctional interactional patterns that depress rather than promote real conversation and student empowerment. Gutierrez further claimed, "Civilization is conversation," a phrase that a number of the teachers remembered and continued to quote long after the conference. In fact, the M-CLASS teacher researchers, in one way or another, wrestled with issues of power for the entire research year.

Following the panel, Duster led a whole-group discussion focused on issues the panel members had raised. He pointed to what he considers the most basic dilemma teachers face in multicultural classrooms:

> We need to be alert to the fact that we either have an image of the shedding of differences or the possibility that students coming together across their differences may perhaps enrich the classroom experience

and maybe ultimately, the society in which they live because of their differences.

During this discussion, the teachers explained in concrete terms some of the everyday concerns they and their students have: the hurtful stereotypes imposed on their students because of their cultures and ways of speaking; the teachers' personal insecurities about teaching children from a cultural background other than their own; the critical need for fostering understanding among students from different cultures; what specifically it means to empower students as learners.

As they had even more time to think and reflect, many of the teachers worried about the magnitude of the tasks ahead. Boston teacher Walter Wood described his classroom realities and his fears:

> How do we bridge what we are talking about as good practices and the realities of my classroom—the lack of furniture, the lack of materials, and sometimes the discipline that we have to deal with? . . . Sometimes I think that we intellectualize and then we go back to the real world and get away from it very quickly. (Small-group discussion, opening M-CLASS conference, September 12, 1992)

By voicing his concerns, Wood pointed out the importance of projects that give teachers a space for respite and reflection, and then provide support so that teachers can figure out how to take their reflections back to the worlds they inhabit and thereby change those worlds.

To deepen the reflections that began in the discussion and to help the teachers delve further into these sensitive issues, the Berkeley team next asked the teachers to write about the ideas the panel raised. The teachers shared their reflections the next day in small groups of four, with teachers from different sites and of varied ethnicities. In these groups, the teachers also shared their responses to Delpit's article. The groups provided a space for the teachers of color to talk about their feelings about White teachers and forced the White teachers to think about what they did and did not know about, as Delpit calls it, "teaching other people's children." White teacher Eileen Shakespear reflected:

> I was so struck [in Delpit's article] with her first page of quotes from the teachers, talking about other teachers who just didn't get it. . . . It was really interesting to think that she described the defensiveness of White teachers. After reading the article I had to say, "I feel really defensive." That was just exactly what she was talking about. It was such a revelation. . . . It comes back to so much of your behavior being sub-

conscious. (Small-group discussion, opening M-CLASS conference, September 12, 1992)

Shakespear came to M-CLASS with a research question that was aimed directly at showing herself and other White teachers how to deal with some of that defensiveness. Delpit helped her to ground her feelings and to better understand them. Shakespear focused on learning about what White female teachers need to know to understand the needs of their Black male students (see Shakespear, this volume).

Latina teacher Deborah Juarez from San Francisco responded differently to the Delpit article. In graduate school she had read an article whose author argued that by teaching standard English, teachers promoted low self-esteem among speakers of other dialects. Delpit, writing as a person of color, made Juarez revisit this argument:

> What makes her [Delpit] different is that she takes the stand of a person of color, a person whose acquisition of the power style begins with school, not with home. How can people of color acquire power without acquiring the particular language and style of those in power? No matter what I personally believe—and I am not sure—I myself have acquired that language. I know that I'm attending a conference on the study of writing because of it. I know what acquisition of a particular language form has done for me as a Hispanic female as far as opportunity is concerned.

As Juarez related these issues to her everyday practices, she concluded that although she may need to teach standard English, she also would need to teach students about social dialects and to teach them not to equate "talking White" with believing that "White is right":

> It seems to me that social theory, linguistics, history, and so on, need to be introduced into the classroom. I want my students to understand, for example, why standard English is the language of power, why they must obtain it to succeed, and why it is not a question of it being a proper form as opposed to it being the form that is imposed upon us. (Reflections on M-CLASS, opening conference, September 12, 1992)

Whereas the conference established the group as a national network, the real work of community-building had to happen at the local sites. Keeping these discussions alive would be a necessary part of that community building. Once the teachers returned home, Freedman or Simons visited each site in the fall to lead a weekend workshop in which the discussion would continue and to attend the teachers' classes. Before these visits, they sent the teachers another article, Robert Blauner's (1992) "Talking Past Each Other: Black and White Languages of Race," and asked them to read it and also to review Delpit's (1988) "The Silenced Dialogue." Freedman opened a discussion with the Chicago group:

> I started musing about the big theme [in Delpit] which was the silencing of dialogues, and I was thinking about this research project [M-CLASS] and that we set it up on purpose to have a multicultural group of teachers and to start dialogues. It's a really tricky business. I just hope that throughout the course of this project that we can keep the dialogues going and that we all really listen carefully to each other because I think that we have a tendency to sit around and agree with each other at meetings, but we really might not always agree with each other. And I think it's important to get all those issues out on the table and for us all to be able to talk from our own perspectives, to allow some of that variety, to see what that means in relation to multicultural teaching. I think we've got a lot to learn from each other. So I hope that we'll have the courage throughout this year to be as open and honest as I think Delpit is in this article. Because it does take a lot of courage to do that, and it's not easy to do. It's especially not easy in a group where there's a lot of variety and where there's a lot of cultural difference among the members of the group. (Site meeting, Chicago, October 18, 1992)

At every site, the conversations that followed were long and rich. They are discussed at some length in the coming chapters.

From the outset, the M-CLASS teachers had multiple opportunities to think alone and with others; to experience ideas through the different channels provided by reading, writing, talking, and listening; to gain distance by responding to the ideas of others; to come closer by sharing their own experiences; to read and hear the points of view of colleagues and experts with different backgrounds and experiences than their own. Not only did these activities lay the groundwork for continued sharing in meetings throughout the year, but they also modeled the kind of multicultural sharing and understandings the teachers might encourage in their classrooms. The M-CLASS community stimulated many of its members to risk dealing explicitly with issues of race, ethnicity, gender, and social class in their teaching and to explore their experiences in their research. Besides supplying a model, M-CLASS provided a safe haven where teachers could figure out how to handle the situations that raising these issues often introduced into their teaching.

In these ways the M-CLASS teams began a conversation that continued throughout the year. Oftentimes the teachers disagreed with one another. As time went on, they raised topics they knew might be unpopular with their peers. They helped one another step outside their own worlds to see the worlds of others. They also sometimes miscommunicated and sometimes did not or could not listen to one another. But they were full of good will and in the end supported one another through a sometimes psychologically draining, sometimes elation-filled, and always labor-intensive research year.

The teacher researchers did not come up with easy answers, but rather explored problems grounded in the realities of their classroom life. They tell about their challenges; they reveal their failures as well as their successes. They were not swept by the tides of political correctness, but rather voiced their concerns for their students and for what they thought would serve them best. They took important steps toward achieving the goal Duster set forth as they provide alternative visions for thinking about multiculturalism, literacy, and learning. Their research aims to inform their own classroom practice as well as the research and practice of other teachers and university researchers. Their research ideally will advance the national debates as well.

THE LARGER PROJECT

At the same time that the teacher researchers were conducting research in their classrooms, they were the subjects in a research study conducted by the Berkeley team. The team audiotaped the teacher-research meetings, collected the teacher researchers' writings, and coded these data for major themes about literacy learning in multicultural settings and about how the teachers went about conducting their teacher research and what they were learning from the collaborative process. Appendix B contains an explanation of how these data were analyzed.

The thematic scaffold for Parts II–IV (Chapters 3–11) of the book is derived from this analysis, with each of the three parts addressing one of three themes about literacy learning in multicultural settings that the M-CLASS teacher researchers wrote and talked about frequently. Part II (Chapters 3–5) focuses on how the teachers learn to see their students, to look beyond stereotypes and across boundaries of race, ethnicity, social class, gender, and generation. Part III (Chapters 6–8) focuses on constructing an inclusive literacy-based curriculum that deals explicitly with issues of race and ethnicity. Part IV (Chapters 9–11) focuses on how the teachers empower their students with a curriculum that upholds high academic standards for literacy and learning and meets the needs of diverse populations.

Each part of the manuscript presents teacher research in two ways—the findings of the teacher researchers and the observations of the Berkeley team.

Each part includes an overview that introduces the section, two chapters by individual teacher researchers, and a synthesis chapter. In the teacher-authored chapters, the teachers speak for themselves and focus solely on their research. These chapters also include concrete suggestions for other teachers about how to solve problems related to the theme for that part. In the synthesis chapter a member of the Berkeley team compiles the thoughts of the 24 M-CLASS teachers about the theme for the part. Appendix B provides information about the methodology for compiling the synthesis chapters. This chapter also highlights the work of several teacher researchers on topics related to the theme. When the teachers have written in some detail about the theme, their writing is included in the form of vignettes. These, and highlighted material, are not necessarily central to the teachers' research questions. The synthesis chapters give examples of how individual teachers used the research process to learn about their settings as well as how they contributed to knowledge.

Each of the three parts of the book focuses primarily on a separate theme, but because the themes are intertwined in everyday life, in the Parts they inevitably mix and overlap. This occurs both in theory and in practice.

Before delving into the major themes about literacy learning in the teachers' multicultural classrooms, we offer in the next chapter, which completes Part I, a description of the M-CLASS teachers' research approach and the collaborative nature of the M-CLASS project.

CHAPTER 2

The M-CLASS Approach to Teacher Research

Sarah Warshauer Freedman

JUST AS TROY DUSTER suggested that teacher researchers are perfectly positioned to provide alternative visions about multiculturalism and literacy, the M-CLASS teachers (by conducting research in their classrooms) were well positioned to provide alternative visions for the educational research enterprise itself. The teachers' visions add a bottom-up perspective to what has traditionally been seen mostly from the top down.

John Elliott explains in his foreword to Jon Nixon's *A Teachers' Guide to Action Research:*

> Whether teacher-based research operates autonomously or collaboratively it marks a radical departure from the traditional view of educational research as a specialist activity, the results of which teachers apply rather than create. (Elliott, 1981, p. 1)

Like Elliott, other leaders in the teacher research movement justify teacher research on the grounds that teachers' knowledge and professional abilities can add significantly to knowledge about teaching and learning (e.g., Cochran-Smith & Lytle, 1993; Gonzalez et al., 1993; Mohr & MacLean, 1987; Nixon, 1981; Stenhouse, 1985). According to Cochran-Smith and Lytle (1993):

> Research by teachers represents a distinctive way of knowing about teaching and learning that will alter—not just add to—what we know in the field. . . . As it accumulates and is more widely disseminated, research by teachers will represent a radical challenge to our current assumptions about the relationships of theory and practice, schools and universities, and inquiry and reform. (p. 85)

Teacher-research communities have varied goals, however. Many have as their primary aim providing growth experiences for teacher researchers, who use their findings to think anew about their teaching and to improve their practice, with some teacher researchers perhaps deciding to publish their work and contribute to a larger dialogue. Winter (1989) writes, "Action research would ideally hope to generate a culture of innovative professional practices, rather than an accumulating corpus of research reports" (pp. 112–113).

In contrast to Winter, M-CLASS's Berkeley-based, university-research team, like Elliott and Cochran-Smith and Lytle, wanted to provide opportunities for teacher researchers to contribute to a larger collection of knowledge about educational practice as well as to grow professionally. The Berkeley team was careful to communicate these goals to the site coordinators in the four cities and to the teacher researchers. Roberta Logan, like the other site coordinators, pushed her Boston group early in the year to think about the dual purpose of their research. She raised the following questions for discussion:

> What's the role of this kind of research? What will it do? How will it inform us as individuals? How can your heightened awareness through teacher research inform all of us? (Site meeting, Boston, October 31, 1992)

Logan's first two questions ask generally about the role of teacher research. She then embeds answers about the dual role of their research in the two questions that follow. She asks the teachers to think first about how the research will inform "us as individuals," that is how it will help teachers grow as professionals. Next, she asks them to think about how their research will inform "all of us," that is, how it will contribute to general knowledge.

TEACHER-UNIVERSITY COLLABORATIONS

In planning M-CLASS, the Berkeley team and the local site coordinators aimed first to create a national network. The goal from the outset was that the national group would work collectively to make a coordinated and nationally relevant intellectual contribution and publish its findings. Gonzalez, Moll, and their colleagues (1993) provide an example of one model for coordinating a project so that collectively a university/school collaborative can contribute knowledge on a focused topic. In their project, the university team involved four elementary school teachers in a study "for the express purpose of identifying and documenting knowledge that exists in students' homes" (p. 1). The teachers were all teaching working-class, Latino students. All followed the same procedures for collecting data, which they then combined into a single data set and analyzed collaboratively with the university team during after-school study-group meetings.

Although M-CLASS had similar goals to those of the Gonzalez project, we decided to structure the research process somewhat differently. In M-CLASS all teachers focused on the same general topic—literacy in urban, multicultural settings—but within that topic, the teachers selected their own individual research questions, designed their own studies, and analyzed their own data. This process, in the end, allowed the teachers to make important individual contributions that clearly came from their unique perspectives; however, it also required that the university team invent structures to support their individualized work, especially in the areas of research design, data collection, and data analysis.

Throughout, the university team carefully considered the nature of the collaboration we wanted to build. In particular, we were concerned that the support from the university be helpful but not overbearing. It was critical to the success of our work together that the individual projects be initiated by the teacher researchers and not by members of the university-based team. Nixon (1981) provided a helpful framework for conceptualizing the structures that university-based faculty could contribute. He first suggests that university-based faculty can help teachers acquire needed information about research techniques, especially about qualitative research. He explains, "One of the blocks to the development of action research in schools is the lack of information concerning the range of research techniques available for use in the classroom. Many teachers, if they think of educational research at all, see it within a narrow tradition of psychometric testing and statistical analysis" (p. 143). Second, according to Nixon, "institutions situated outside the school have a vital role to play in the coordination of isolated initiatives; not only as impersonal clearing houses, but as supportive frameworks which sustain and encourage collaborative research" (p. 144). Finally, he explains, "dissemination is a crucial part of the research process. . . . For dissemination to be effective it must be seen as integral to the research design, not as an optional extra tagged on the end" (p. 144).

Although Nixon's last point is embedded in the goals of M-CLASS in that all of the teacher researchers planned to write for publication, not all teacher-university collaborations have the goal of communicating results to a national audience. Furthermore, even though the M-CLASS teachers planned to write about their findings, they were not comfortable with any concept of dissemination that implied that they would tell other teachers how to run their classrooms. Rather, with their writing they hoped to stimulate other professionals to think in new ways that might help them make decisions appropriate to their own schools and classrooms.

Besides understanding the importance of establishing the national network, we knew it would be crucial to the success of the project to establish strong local communities. As those who have written about teacher research consistently argue, teacher researchers must come together regularly in teacher research groups where they can talk honestly about their teaching and reflect on their actions (e.g., Cochran-Smith & Lytle, 1993; Goswami & Stillman, 1987; McKernan, 1991; Mohr & MacLean, 1987; Nixon, 1981; Stenhouse, 1985; Tafel & Fischer, 1996; and varied groups sponsored by the National Writing Project, including the Urban Sites Network). In these research communities, teachers need to be able to admit their doubts and their difficulties, take risks, and learn. In M-CLASS local groups at each site served this purpose and provided an essential forum for keeping the teachers involved and focused.

In Appendix C we explain how we organized M-CLASS—including the opening conference; three nationally coordinated workshops at each site, which we called site meetings; regular local meetings; and additional frequent interactions between the Berkeley team and the teachers and the Berkeley team and the site coordinators via electronic and regular mail, telephone, and fax.

Within the context of the national network and local M-CLASS communities, two aspects of the research process proved particularly challenging for the teachers: devising credible yet practical research methods for teacher research and deciding on genres for writing about the results. It is to these challenges that the rest of this chapter turns.

METHODS FOR TEACHER RESEARCH

Joseph Check (1997) suggests that methodology is an area where the teacher-research movement is experiencing serious growing pains. The M-CLASS team felt those pains acutely. Although traditional university-based methods often were helpful to the teachers, sometimes the teachers needed to adjust and modify those methods. According to Winter (1989), "What is needed is a set of methodological principles designed specifically for the opportunities and limitations of being *both* a practitioner *and* an investigator of practice" (p. 9). The Berkeley team and the site coordinators worked collaboratively with the teachers to develop what Huberman (1996) calls "a robust yet tailored methodological repertoire," specifically designed for teacher research (p. 138).

Selecting and Refining Research Questions

The teachers' processes for selecting their research questions differed from those of university-based researchers, but their methods for refining their questions were quite similar. With regard to question selection, the teacher researchers, rather than reviewing the literature, looked to their everyday lives. They grounded their questions in their teaching, but the questions also usually had deeper personal roots. Many traced their questions to experiences from their childhoods or to their early years of teaching. The Berkeley team hoped that the teachers would pursue questions leading to unique contributions arising from their special perspective as practitioners. For example, because teachers have ongoing and regular contact with their students, they could potentially draw especially thorough and revealing portraits of student development. Similarly, because of their everyday work in the schools, teachers could potentially make unique contributions to understandings of classroom and school life. Most of the teachers developed initial questions fairly easily, usually during the opening conference or first site meeting.

The main work with questions involved refining them. Griselle Diaz-Gemmati's journey illustrates how, in early letters and telephone discussions with the teacher researchers and during the first meetings, the Berkeley team and the site coordinators worked with individual teachers to help them with this refining. Her experiences also show the roles the other teacher researchers played in helping one another as well as the role the teacher researcher played in thinking through her ideas on her own. Diaz-Gemmati's journey, like the journeys of her colleagues, does not seem particular to teacher researchers. They faced the same issues as does everyone who is learning to do research: how to find space to figure out what they know; when they are floundering, how and when to get help; and how to ensure that guidance does not take away ownership of the research.

Diaz-Gemmati did much of her initial thinking on her own, both in her writing and in her discussions with her colleagues. She formulated her initial question at the conference: "Does parent involvement directly affect student literacy?" This question was related to but was not really what she would ultimately ask. She expected to involve parents as collaborators in her research, and she wanted to see how their attitudes affected those of their children. She also hoped to change these attitudes as she worked with them. Soon after she returned from the M-CLASS conference, however, she decided that her original idea was not practical. She wrote in her research log on September 16, "The parents I particularly wanted to involve are no longer available." She later explained what she meant to her research group:

> I don't want Susie's mother that stays home with [her] baby because Susie's mother is no longer the norm. . . . I wanted the minority parents, and these would not be available to me at all. (Local meeting, Chicago, October 31, 1992)

Diaz-Gemmati realized on her own that, for the most part, these parents were too busy managing the difficulties of day-to-day life to participate in the ways she originally envisioned.

She decided to solve this problem by changing her focus from parents to students and to the ideas that students were bringing into her classroom. In her next log entry, she showed that she was interested in adults only as they influenced her students' prejudices:

> The issue of prejudice is really a burning topic. The minority kids get "passionate"; the White kids watch. Rodney King is a constant reference point; the L. A. riots another.
>
> It is so obvious that many of their statements are echoes of what they've heard from adults.
>
> How can I get them to tell me how they feel, not what they're being taught to feel? What did I get myself into? (Research log, September 17, 1992)

On October 4, Chicago site coordinator B. J. Wagner, in anticipation of Freedman's upcoming visit to Chicago, wrote a letter giving her sense of Diaz-Gemmati's research question:

> Griselle's research question is "How do students relate to racial tension or prejudice in the world around them and their literature [meaning literature representing their varied cultures]?"

In her talks with Diaz-Gemmati, Wagner found that Diaz-Gemmati was thinking about how to integrate her concerns about her students' prejudice and racism into her class's literature curriculum.

At the October 18 site meeting, Diaz-Gemmati explained to her fellow teacher researchers the twist that her question began taking once she realized that it would be impractical to work directly with the parents and once she began to see how her interests related to her literacy curriculum:

> I tackled the idea of having students explore their own feelings and prejudices, sift through what is their conception and what is mimicked in the adult influences in their lives. Finally, I've decided to stay with the issue of prejudice and racism in literature, allowing the students to relate to these issues from personal points of view, through such media as journal writing, letter writing, reports, art, research papers, debates, and personal experiences.

She continued to worry, however, both about maintaining her research focus and about the students' worlds outside school:

Every time I think I got a hold, an ankle, an arm, something, it slipped away, and I don't feel focused. I do think that this is something that has to be addressed, because these kids go back into their own segregated lives, and when they do go to work there's no such thing as going to work in a Mexican factory or a Black office. They have to learn how to get along with other people. I know that it is necessary, and I feel very passionate about it.

Diaz-Gemmati's peers joined her in a long and reflective discussion about the problems at her school resulting from cliques of students from varied ethnic groups. The White clique that had been together since kindergarten did not include others, and Diaz-Gemmati worried that the White students "think that minorities just come and go and you really don't have to deal with the issue." Similarly, the minority cheerleaders kept the Whites off the squad, recently having told three Whites who wanted to try out, "You weren't born with the rhythm; you just can't move the way we do."

Realizing that this discussion was not linked to her other stated point of focus, the literature, she said, "I still want to do this racism in the literature." Here Diaz-Gemmati shows the difficulty she is having separating teaching and research and indirectly asks for help by saying to the group that she has not included everything she wants in her question.

At this point, when the other group members offered no suggestions, Freedman intervened to try to help Diaz-Gemmati focus her thoughts. Freedman suggested that she think about the issues of racism and prejudice as they related to her literacy curriculum, broadly conceived to include literature and other media:

When you started, you said you wanted to have students explore their own prejudices, right? And you want to relate it [their prejudices] to literature and to the response. . . . There are groups of White kids and there are groups of minority kids, and they're shutting each other out. So a big part of the dynamics in the school in terms of their own prejudices has to do with this phenomenon of shutting one another out. So maybe your question could be something like, "What happens when students begin to explore their own prejudices?" You would keep track of the kinds of opportunities you give them to explore their own prejudices through literature, through art, through whatever, through debates, through discussions, through explicitly pointing out things that are going on in the school.

Still focused on the teaching issues, Diaz-Gemmati and the other teacher researchers discussed the ideas, related to themes in *To Kill a Mockingbird,* that her class had been talking about. Once again, Freedman returned the conversation to the research, explaining how she hears Diaz-Gemmati conceptualizing her question. This time Freedman also included Diaz-Gemmati's interests in the community outside school:

> It sounds like you're moving toward something in the area of "What happens when students explore their own prejudices or the theme of prejudice through varied kinds of media?" [You] could look at the evolution of what happens during discussions and how do discussions change; or it could have to do with does it affect their daily lives and the way they interact with other people in their daily lives. I think you could look at it in both venues, in the way they react to things that are distant from them, because sometimes it's easier to deal with it when it's more distant, and it's not day-to-day life. You might not be able to change day-to-day, but you might be able to change the way you're thinking and the way you're talking first. So it seems like it'd be good to look there, because you may not see real action of the type you want, but you may see movement that might make you more hopeful.

Following the October site meetings, Freedman or Simons wrote a letter to the site groups, summarizing each teacher's question, any obvious problems the teachers still had to resolve, and the data they would need to collect in order to answer their questions. In the part of the Chicago letter addressed to Diaz-Gemmati, Freedman stated her understanding of the question and decisions she saw on the horizon:

> What happens when adolescent students begin to explore themes of racism and prejudice as they discuss and write about literature? In particular, how do they separate what they feel and think from what they've heard in their families and communities?
>
> Griselle, your question looks well focused to me. Of your remaining decisions, you'll want to think about how long a time span you will take to collect data for your study. Also, will you focus on the students as they explore themes across varied pieces of literature, or just with *To Kill a Mockingbird*? If you want to include more than one piece of literature, which others will you include and why?

At this point, Freedman took the liberty of writing a question focused narrowly on the literature rather than more broadly on literature and other media. She also reinserted Diaz-Gemmati's interest in linking what she was learning to the students' families. In her letter to the group she was careful to explain:

I was worried that when I left that some of you still felt 'muddled.' . . .
Liz and I have found it helpful to collaborate as we sort out our own research questions, and so it's in a spirit of collaboration that I'm writing
this letter. In some cases I have fiddled with the wording to focus the
question a little more tightly; in some cases I made changes for purposes of discussion. . . . None of what I am writing here is meant to be
directive; I just hope it's in some way helpful. I apologize if I've done
damage to any of your questions. Just let me know, and we'll change it
back if I have." (Letter to Chicago site, October 26, 1992)

At the next local meeting, Diaz-Gemmati remarked to the group:

I like the way that my question reads in Sarah's letter. It seems that
she's sifted through a lot of stuff and left me with what I like. (Local
meeting, Chicago, October 31, 1992)

As time went on, Diaz-Gemmati made only minor modifications to the wording of the question (see Chapter 3).

It was difficult for the teachers to narrow their focus to just one of the
many important issues that concerned them in their daily teaching lives. The
Berkeley team and the site coordinators' interventions were aimed at helping them focus on a sufficiently narrow, but crucial, issue for their research.
The Berkeley team also worked to create a collaborative relationship that
left teachers responsible for deciding on the topic for their research and the
university-based researchers playing a supportive role.

By this point in the process, most of the teachers, like Diaz-Gemmati,
were ready to focus their ideas and were able to move ahead relatively rapidly
with the help of the Berkeley team and site coordinators. There were times
when our attempts at collaboration went less smoothly; a few teachers felt
that their ideas were being tampered with in ways that made them uncomfortable. However, they seemed to feel free to speak up, showing that they maintained ownership of the ideas and that the basic collaborative mode was
working. By the end of October, all of the teachers had developed meaningful
and feasible research questions and were anxious to move forward, something we have been told is unusual for many teacher-research communities.
In M-CLASS the ongoing local discussions and the feedback from the Berkeley
team's letter seemed to move the teachers' thinking along. Naturally, many
continued to refine their questions throughout the research year, but the university collaborations seemed to help them achieve enough initial focus to
get off to a solid start early on. It seemed neither necessary nor desirable to
extend the process of deciding on a question for any of them.

Collecting and Analyzing the Data

Early on, the Berkeley team explained to the teachers that the purpose of collecting and analyzing data was to help them make unconscious activities conscious. After observing the classroom of Boston teacher Eileen Shakespear, who was studying how African American male students interact with White teachers, Simons said:

> It was interesting for me to watch you talk to them [your African American male students] both as a colleague but also as an adult. You change that voice depending on what's happening in the situation. . . . I think it's a lot unconscious. So I'd start taking some notes on the interactions that you have with them and making more conscious, if you can, the kinds of connections that you make with them. . . . Just start looking at what it is that you do with these kids that establishes your relationship with them. (Site meeting, Boston, October 31, 1992)

Also on the topic of making the unconscious conscious, Winter (1989) writes:

> "Experience" is not quite the same as "*learning* from experience." We have all heard the witticism directed at a colleague who is supposed to have had "ten years' experience": "No," comes the reply, "They've had *one* year's experience repeated *ten* times over." The point is that when we learn *significantly* from our experience, we use skills (which can be improved) and methods (which can be described). (p. 8)

To decide on which data to collect in order to answer their questions and thereby to examine their unconscious actions, the teachers brainstormed together, generating long lists of possibilities. Their data lists read like standard lists in university-based studies and included such items as video or audio recordings of interactions in the classroom, samples of student writing, interviews, books and other materials that the students read as part of the curriculum, responses to questionnaires, test scores, classroom materials (handouts, instructions on blackboard), teacher researchers' observations and field notes to capture those observations, teacher researchers' reflective journal entries.

At points in the data collection and analysis processes, the M-CLASS teacher researchers faced obstacles that led them to modify standard methods. They also sometimes found themselves in situations where they had advantages and could collect and analyze data in ways that would have been impossible for an outsider. These adjustments to standard ways of collecting and analyzing data are a significant part of what makes teacher research unique. McKernan (1991) writes in detail about data collection for teachers' research; he culls what he writes, however, from traditional qualitative-methods texts for university-based researchers, without making adjustments for teacher researchers. He seems to assume that teachers can overcome any obstacles they might face and that they can easily use standard methods. Winter (1989), by contrast, acknowledges these obstacles and offers principles to guide the research process. The obstacles include (a) insufficient time, implying the need to "formulate a method of work which is sufficiently *economical* (as regards the amount of data gathering and data processing) for a practitioner to undertake it alongside a normal workload" (p. 35); (b) need for insights above and beyond those that the practitioner gains naturally in the course of teaching, implying the need for "a clear *difference* of procedure between action-research's form of gathering and analyzing the data generated through professional practice, and the procedures of professional practice itself" (p. 35); (c) need to differentiate action-research from university-based research, with methods that "build upon the competences which practitioners already possess" and are "*accessible*" but that are unlike university-based methods (pp. 35–36); and (d) need to "contribute [to the teacher] a *genuine improvement* of understanding and skill. . . in return for time and energy expended" (p. 36).

Although Winter suggests helpful principles, he does not discuss the consequences of particular decisions about methodology, nor does he consider advantages teachers might have when they collect and analyze data. Our observations of the M-CLASS group show some of those consequences as well as some of the advantages full-time teachers enjoy.

Data Collection. With regard to data collection, given the resources available, the M-CLASS teachers faced difficulties in three areas: keeping regular field notes, collecting data while teaching, and transcribing tapes. The Berkeley team had hoped that the teachers would be able to keep regular, ideally daily, field notes in which they recorded and reflected on observations related to their research questions. Given that our goal was for the teachers to complete their project in a year, we expected the teachers to collect data for approximately 3 months, although many extended the time. Consistent with Winter's point about time, most of these teachers could not find time to write field notes regularly. Elena Valenti of New Orleans described her problems: "I am pressed to find time to write two or three sentences when the class is over, while it's fresh in my brain, about what happened that day." Sarah Herring concurred, but Valenti's remark stimulated her to think of solutions. A helpful dialogue ensued during which the group discussed ways to manage keeping field notes:

SARAH HERRING: Remember what one of those speakers [at the opening conference in San Francisco] told us, "You write when you need to." Remember?

DORIS WILLIAMS-SMITH: And there may be some times when you will need to do a lot of writing and other times when you're just doing some reflection. And that reflection can help you develop ideas that you want to write down.

CYNTHIA ROY: And it may be that when you go home, and you've had some dinner and you're having a glass of wine, and you're watching a program, it may come to you what happened in class that day, and you'll get out a notebook and write it. I know it feels better to write immediately after—

ELENA VALENTI: Well so I don't forget. Just the key words that you remember—

CYNTHIA ROY: You may have to give yourself a break and tell yourself that's just impossible because you've got another class walking in the door in 5 seconds. Do it at night when you're relaxed and you can think calmly about it. [*Someone comments sarcastically about being relaxed, and Roy continues*] Oh, relax? That's not a good word? [*laughter*] Teachers are never relaxed? (Local meeting, New Orleans, October 18, 1992)

The group agreed that it is often impossible for teachers to write field notes every day. They came up with three ideas for keeping records. Herring and Williams-Smith discussed writing periodically at strategic times, when there is a lot to record that is pertinent to the research question. Valenti talked about jotting down "key words" so she would not forget important happenings. Roy, the site coordinator, suggested that teachers might write in the evening, after a little time has passed. Although that's not ideal since, as Valenti fears, the teachers will forget some things, Roy's suggestion offered a reasonable compromise. In the end, the teachers' field notes were not always as complete as they would have liked, but because they were in the classroom every day and were full participants in its life, they found that even sparse notes were often very helpful in jogging relatively complete memories of an event.

It was also the case that some teachers managed to write more often than others. Most notably, Tom Daniels in Chicago happened to have a study hall period soon after his class, which gave him "about 20 uninterrupted minutes daily" which he used for writing his field notes. In these notes, he "looked back at each student in the class, noted what he or she did, looked back at interactions between students and teachers. Occasionally I read entries from the last week or month" (Daniels & Daniels, 1994, p. 10). He contrasts this kind of reflective writing with his previous ways of reflecting on his practice and explains his newfound rewards:

> [Before] reflection was always in rather general terms. This time I wrote as specifically as I could. I began to see patterns. When I could recall actual talk, I noted it in the journal. Each student began to emerge as a separate and distinct person in a way that helped me understand general outlook on life, method of operating in school, their view of themselves, and how they thought others saw them. Based on that information, I began treating each one in a way I thought would help them. I always did that before, but now I had much better information. I also noted information gleaned from their own daily journals. (Daniels & Daniels, 1994, p. 10)

Through this experience, Daniels came to realize "I'm the kind of person who really doesn't become conscious of his thinking until he writes it down" (Daniels & Daniels, 1994, p. 10).

The ideal is for teachers to write regularly, but the reality is that, without time specifically designated for writing field notes or other kinds of support, many may not be able to manage. The compromises are not perfect but do not seem to be so problematic as to seriously jeopardize the research.

Another difficulty teachers encountered involved managing some types of classroom data collection while teaching, especially tape recording. George Austin missed an important day of tape recording because he could not take the time to look for his tape recorder. In another case, Walter Wood complained about the interruptions that make data collection problematic:

> I'm just finding there's so many interruptions to what I'm trying to do . . . [it's] very hard for me to keep on track because there's just so many other things that are happening that I have to deal with and that's been tough for me to try to remind myself, "Put something in your notebook," or try to think about what you're doing with the kids in relation to what your research is.

Wood then went on to explain that he was asking students to complete a questionnaire when a fire alarm went off:

> They were writing little things, and I was in the middle of doing that and the alarm goes off. We're outside and then when we get back, I'm in a lousy mood. The kids are in a lousy mood.

Roberta Logan, the site coordinator replied with understanding, "And you can't 're-gather'" (local meeting, Boston, January 21, 1993).

A third difficulty emerged because the teachers did not tape record everything they thought was important to their research, and they had little time to transcribe what they did record. To compensate, they made notes in their research journals, often reconstructing dialogue. As Tom Daniels said, "When I could recall actual talk, I noted it in the journal." Published teacher-research articles often contain constructed dialogue. After the New Orleans group had read several teacher-research articles, Cindy Roy, the site coordinator, initiated the following conversation, which led to considering a process to follow for constructing dialogue:

> CINDY ROY: We call it constructed dialogue because the meaning is still there. You may not have the exact words but the meaning is still there and you can create a dialogue because you know that student and you know yourself. You can create a dialogue that's real and meaningful between the two of you.
> ELENA VALENTI: That's true.
> SARAH HERRING: I know. I wrote a lot in my journal, and I tried to catch things. This is really my most valuable material because sometimes I wouldn't have my tape, and I said, "Wow, I should've gotten that picture or I should've had my tape," but I can jot it down in here and I can go back. (Site meeting, New Orleans, February 25, 1993)

Sarah Herring constructed dialogue when she wrote the following journal entry about her focal student Jamal:

> Jamal is one of the students that I must work with. He lacks self-esteem, so he compensates . . . by being the class comedian. Today I made the comment, "My good student will do an excellent job."
> He stated, "Well, I guess I'd better go sit outside" [*laughter*].
> It was then necessary for me to change the statement again, so I said, "Jamal will be one of my best students."
> Not to be outdone, he recounted, "Not your best student, not me." He hadn't heard the word *one,* so I corrected him.
> "Why not?" I asked.
> "Because I'm not going to apply myself."
> "Why not?" I again asked.
> "Because I'm not," he said. Then he was silent.
> I said, "He did use *apply* so that's a good word."
> Grace stated, "Anyone can use apply."
> "Yeah," Louise interjected. (October 22, 1992)

Here Herring constructed the dialogue from memory although she probably did not remember the students' or her own exact words. Because she wrote the dialogue soon after it occurred and because she knew the speakers well, she was taking steps to avoid distorting the speakers' meanings.

In spite of these difficulties, the teachers sometimes found themselves in a better position to collect data than other researchers. In some cases, the teachers were able to fit the data collection naturally and seamlessly into their teaching process. For example, Doris Williams-Smith wanted to get her students to respond to a number of questions about their revising process. She devised the following questioning technique:

> When I asked them questions, I need to make it as natural as possible, so I give them journal topics to write about. I decided that I will throw a question out as a journal topic every now and then. That way it seems like it's just a part of the regular classroom instruction. . . . If it's a journal topic that's thrown out among the many other journal topics, then they'll answer honestly. . . . If it's a journal topic, they go, "It's just another journal topic. I can say what I really mean." (Local meeting, New Orleans, October 18, 1992)

In other cases, the teachers adjusted the way they were collecting data so that they could get more telling information. Nancy O'Malley found her students to be uncomfortable with the kind of interviewing she had originally planned:

> There was an awkwardness [with the one-on-one interview]. . . . It's . . . "Well she's nice. She's doing this research. She's gonna write something and she's making my ego feel good. But why am I alone in this room with her while she's asking questions?"

O'Malley switched from interviewing students one on one to interviewing them in a group:

> The minute the other kids were in there it was so much better because they were supporting each other, and then it was totally comfortable, and I'm not the interrogator. (Local meeting, Boston, March 16, 1993)

The easiest data for the teachers to collect was student work, especially student writing. There are no questions about the integrity of such data and few issues that arose about either the difficulty or ease of collecting the data. Teachers often collect student writing and may keep it for years, whether they are doing teacher research or not.

Although the teachers collected tape recordings and wrote in research logs, these data often became secondary sources, to provide context for the writing and to help fill in background information. In such cases, although the tape recordings were not always transcribed and the logs not always kept regularly, the teachers had some records. This information served them better than memory alone. In the few cases when the teachers relied on such data as a primary source, they managed to collect it fairly regularly.

Because of the complexities of collecting data while teaching, there were some kinds of studies that the M-CLASS teachers simply could not conduct. Most obviously, they did not collect and systematically transcribe tapes. Also, they could not do studies that involved detailed analyses of teaching-learning interactions.

Data Analysis. In many senses the teachers analyzed their data in traditional ways. The Berkeley team and the site coordinators provided support to help the teachers learn to analyze qualitative data. However, as was the case for data collection, it was sometimes necessary and even desirable for the teachers to adjust university-based methods.

Following usual methods, the teachers first learned to see patterns in their data and code those patterns. During their second visit to the sites, Freedman or Simons' weekend workshop focused on qualitative data analysis. Freedman began her workshop in Chicago by reiterating the main reason that teacher researchers should collect and analyze data rather than just write memories of their experiences:

> The whole reason . . . is to push deeper so that you'll be able to say something that strikes an insight that you wouldn't just get from a more casual look. (Site meeting, Chicago, February 28, 1993)

In preparation for the teachers' first forays into data analysis, Freedman or Simons modeled their own thinking processes and explained their analysis procedures. Simons began by telling the Boston group how she starts:

> Basically I read, reread, and reread until the data begins to make sense to me, until I see patterns which are useful for my question.

She then recounted the precise steps she follows:

> Here are my steps. I think about my question before I start: "What am I looking for?" However, I don't let that deter me from seeing things I'm not looking for. Then usually what I do is I read the whole thing through to get a gestalt, the whole picture. . . . Then I read it through a

second time, making notes in the margin of anything that strikes me as
noteworthy or interesting. Then I look at my marginal notes and see if
there are patterns that emerge. Sometimes I'm aware of them while I'm
in process, and sometimes I see them later on. . . . when I review to see
what patterns seem to be important enough to code. . . . Everybody
has their own system. I tend to color code them [the patterns or catego-
ries] with highlighters. . . . I really do love doing this, and find it intellectually thrilling. . . . Basically, there really are sort of serendipitous
surprises when you do this. Sometimes, after coding, I'll see a new and
a better way to arrange the data. I play with the data until the story it
is telling makes good supportable sense to me. (Site meeting, Boston,
March 27, 1993)

To provide a concrete illustration of how to analyze data, at every site
Freedman or Simons analyzed two logs written by a student in the class of
San Francisco teacher Verda Delp. Simons showed the Boston group how
she connects the analysis of Delp's data to her research question about the
kinds of thinking her students do:

What I find in my analysis of these logs is that there's certain kinds of
logs in which she [Leah, the student] develops theories and certain
kinds of logs in which she does other kinds of thinking. And this is exactly what Verda is interested in—where what kinds of thinking are
happening in the various places of her program. . . . It seems that there
are differences in the types of thinking in the reflection log and the
reading logs. In the reflection log, Leah develops hypotheses or theories. It's also in these logs that she uses metaphor and plays with language. In the reading logs she summarizes and reflects on the content,
but doesn't develop theories. In both types of logs, she uses writing to
solve intellectual problems and questions. It would be interesting to see
if this [finding] holds true across students, or even in another set of her
logs.(Site meeting, Boston, March 27, 1993)

During this site meeting, the teachers also brought their data, and
Freedman or Simons helped them think about how to derive coding categories that would shed light on the questions they were asking. Karen Alford
immediately prepared to apply what she was learning to her data:

I was wishing I had highlighters with me. I'll bring some tomorrow.
'Cause you mentioned highlight things, look for patterns. But it never

made sense until I saw somebody else doing it. It really did help. (Site meeting, New Orleans, February 25, 1993)

Freedman and Simons followed this workshop with individual letters to and conversations with the teachers about the data. The site coordinators organized follow-up local meetings, during which the teachers worked together and with Freedman and Simons on data analysis.

In spite of the support offered by the Berkeley team and the site coordinators, the M-CLASS teachers did not have much time to practice coding their data. Further, they sometimes found themselves with data sets that were not complete, unlike those that university-based researchers normally would compile. Although they coded some of their data and studied them in ways that allowed insight they would not have gained had they merely reflected on their research question, the teachers did not try to get confirmation of their observations through triangulation of data from different sources, and they transcribed actual conversations selectively if at all.

For these reasons, many of the M-CLASS teachers worried about the validity of their results. They expressed three types of concerns: their interpretations of their data might be biased; they were working with small numbers from which they were nervous about drawing conclusions; and when students became subjects of research, they might change their behavior in ways that would affect their findings. During their meetings, they discussed how to handle these very real issues so that their projects would be meaningful both to themselves and to others. According to Winter (1989):

> The practical problem is not so much: "How can we ensure that our findings are valid?" but rather "How can we ensure that our procedures are rigorous?" In making this shift, the action-researcher avoids the unanswerable question as to whether an interpretation "coincides with reality"—unanswerable for the simple reason that we can never perceive reality except by means of one interpretation or another—and adopts instead the . . . assurance that well established principles will be carefully applied. . . . If action-research procedures are systematically grounded in justifiable and coherent principles (i.e., if they are "rigorous") then we shall have grounds for thinking that the conclusions we come to will be more than the result of personalities, emotions, or expediency. . . . To be worth the effort, action-research needs to have a *more* rigorous process for the investigation of affairs than that which characterizes the everyday practices of professional life, and a *different* conception of "rigour" than that which characterizes positivist research." (pp. 36–37)

On the topic of biased interpretations, early in the year Nancy O'Malley expressed her fear to her Boston group that teachers who held values different from her own would interpret her data differently and reach different conclusions from hers. Joe Check, one of the Boston site coordinators, interrupted O'Malley to advise her about how to take seriously counterarguments to her position and also to think carefully about how best to support her position:

> It seems to me that it would really strengthen your case by incorporating your other person here, and asking him or her, "Why do you say this student is illiterate?" I mean don't just tell me the kids are illiterate because they can't spell, but talk to me for a half an hour and on tape about the things you've observed in your interactions with this student that leads you to draw that conclusion. And then make yourself do the same thing. Be honest with yourself. You're saying, "She [the student] has a gift." Well what if I say to you, "I don't think she's got a gift." Convince me that she's got a gift.

O'Malley articulated her new understanding about how to proceed:

> Then I have to be real detailed and look at the details, look at the allegorical language she uses, look at the metaphoric language. . . . Other people can look at the student and say, "She's good; she's not good." You have to tell me not just your conclusion but how you got to your conclusion. (Site meeting, Boston, October 31, 1992)

Later in the year, Check warned about the dangers of not collecting enough data and about the importance of gaining distance from one's data:

> Your mind's editing what you do all the time. And sometimes you end up with the class that you wish you had taught rather than the class that you actually did teach. (Site meeting, Boston, March 27, 1993)

Check suggests that the teachers get other perspectives, perhaps by having "somebody sit in, take notes" or by asking "a couple of students to do that." Although Check was not suggesting formal triangulation, he was trying to push the teachers to offset potential biases in some way.

Deborah Juarez, in San Francisco, raised her concern about another possible source of bias. In thinking about her colleague Ann Lew's research, she wondered whether Lew's focus on a single student influenced the student's writing and therefore the data Lew collected and the kinds of conclusions she could draw: "How much does your [Lew's] focus on her [the case study student] influence her writing? I mean does she know that she's the subject of your focus?" Lew recognized that "that is a good question," and

Simons continued, "It doesn't mean that you can't do the research, but it's a good question, and it's something that you should have in the back of your mind" (local meeting, San Francisco, January 14, 1993). In Lew's case, the question is moot for some of the student's writing, since Lew collected it before the research began. However, for the writing collected after the study began, the question has no obvious answer. Appropriately, members of Lew's teacher-research group offered no solution but did identify the problem and suggest that Lew remain alert to it. Interestingly, this question raises one of the main dilemmas teacher researchers face. It is the teacher's job to influence the writer, to do whatever she can to help her student write better; as a researcher, however, she must cultivate her awareness of how she influences the student so that she can track how, as both teacher and researcher, she affects the results of her research.

Teacher researchers often report that by virtue of doing research they teach better. In the end, the act of doing research, of reflecting in purposeful and systematic ways, informs the teachers' decision making and drives changes in their practice. In these ways, it inevitably influences them and what their students stand to learn. As researchers, an essential job for the teachers is to not only track their influences but also document these changes in influence.

The teachers' concerns about the small numbers in their studies and about influencing the students' behavior and therefore the results of the research were related to their fears about bias and to a misconception that qualitative researchers are expected to produce generalizable findings. Eileen Shakespear expresses these concerns as she wonders if her observations are particular to the group she observed:

> As soon as I start to make an observation that it seems like I can generalize from, I just see all kinds of places where the opposite might be true, or where there's just a whole other story that isn't being told underneath it. So I'm worried about how do I address that issue, the complexity issue. How do you end up with generalizations about something like this when each person, both the student and the teacher [is] so full of complexity and contradictions? (Site meeting, Boston, October 31, 1992)

Shakespear next revealed the source of her worries, her misconceptions that she thinks she must make generalizations from only a few cases when there may be contradictory cases that she has not studied:

> I'm noting a pattern among White women teachers, who are seen as successful [with minority students], as people who have had experi-

ences of being minorities themselves at some point early in their lives, like in their early 20s, late teens. . . . That [the fact that these teachers have experienced being a minority] may be a key, but, how do I know that? I can't really say that because all I've done is observe that these five or six women have all had experiences like that.

Shakespear's colleague Junia Yearwood replied that she need not attempt to generalize but rather should restrict her claims to her observations:

Well you say that: "I can't verify it, but I have observed from my interviews that there seemed to be a pattern."

Yearwood's comment helped Shakespear see the solution to her problem. She understood that she was not expected to produce generalizable findings, something she previously thought she would have to do:

So there's no obligation then as a researcher to find out if that's actually true or not.

Here Shakespear uses the term *true* to mean generalizable or true beyond the confines of her data.

Because the teachers studied their own work settings, they found that they also had some advantages when they began to analyze their data. As complete participants in the settings, they were intimately familiar with what they were studying. Such "complete participation" (Spradley, 1980, p. 61) presents both advantages and disadvantages, but in the end, within the structure of M-CLASS, the advantages seemed to outweigh the disadvantages. Early in the research year, Freedman explained to the Chicago group how she sees the advantages:

As teachers have started doing research in their own classrooms, they bring a very unique perspective to being able to tell the stories of what happens inside classrooms and to be able to draw the portraits, the really rich portraits. Because these are the folks who are with the kids day in, day out, every day. And so there's a unique kind of knowledge that teachers have that somebody else going into the classroom cannot have, because you don't have the relationships with the kids that teachers have. So it seems real important for the dialogue to include the perspectives of classroom teachers. This project is designed to allow that to come to the front. (Site meeting, Chicago, October 18, 1992)

Spradley (1980) reminds us that all participant observers, including complete participants, must remain aware of the dual purpose of participating at the same time as watching oneself and others. Participant observers must figure out how to take the stance of both insider and outsider. As natural insiders, the complication for the M-CLASS teachers was finding ways to get critical distance. In projects such as M-CLASS the teacher-research community provides substantial help in getting the needed distance. Teachers share their data with their peers and with the university-based collaborators who have experience in the analysis of qualitative data. These less involved parties help the teacher researchers get new perspectives and ultimately help them think through their interpretations of their data. Winter (1989) discusses the possibility of creating a similar collaborative resource at a school site, also suggesting that collaboration—and the multiple points of view that it brings—potentially offer a more impartial account than an individual researcher can.

Shakespear pointed out ways that her group, by providing another viewpoint during the data-analysis process, helped her get distance from her data and avoid pitfalls:

> It's been very revealing to . . . have two other readers, Junia and Roberta, both read parts of stuff, and have them comment. I guess that I feel—though we don't all know each other very well—I really appreciate every voice in here because everybody's really smart. That's the way I like it. [*Laughter*] And I'm really interested in what we're talking about. (Site meeting, Boston, March 27, 1993)

In the end, the teachers and university teams provided checks on the teachers' assertions as they continually asked for evidence to back up assertions and remained alert to contradictions in what the teacher researchers said about their observations.

As Winter (1989) says in the quotation reproduced earlier, teacher researchers need methods for data collection and analysis that are designed with both the advantages and limitations of being a teacher in mind. Like most researchers, the M-CLASS teachers provided the most truthful accounts they could of their research findings. These accounts were enriched by the data they collected and analyzed, as well as by their knowledge of their students and of life in their classrooms. By discussing specifically how the M-CLASS teachers collected and analyzed their data, we hope to open a discussion about methodology for teacher research. We offer points for discussion, not answers. Discussions about methodology are essential if the profession is to develop reasonable standards specifically for teacher research, in the end achieving both the rigor and the tailoring for teachers that Winter discusses.

SPECIFYING CREDIBLE GENRES FOR REPORTING RESULTS

Cochran-Smith and Lytle (1993) suggest that educators must broaden what counts as research, observing that teachers' contributions may take the form of logs or journals, transcripts of oral inquiry processes, classroom studies, or essays. They further maintain that these contributions can become "cumulative and accessible to different people over time for a variety of purposes" (p. 25). As they describe the cumulation process, they propose that the end result might be publication but might also include other kinds of archiving (e.g., computer archives of transcripts of oral inquiry). M-CLASS stayed with conventional forms of publication because unlike Cochran-Smith and Lytle, we were not confident that others would change their notions of what counted as research. We found that writing for publication pushed the teachers to reach new levels in the knowledge they gained from their research.

For the most part, the M-CLASS teachers had little or no experience in writing for publication and needed a great deal of support to go though the time-consuming process of completing publishable pieces. We found little guidance in the literature for how to steer them through this process or even how they might write about their results in ways that would enter a national professional dialogue.

As the teachers wrote, genres began to emerge that were both comfortable for the teachers and potentially appealing to a general audience of educators, especially other teachers but also the wider educational community. In the end, the most important consideration was that the teachers' voices are dominant in this book.

The university team worked with the teachers to explore possible genres for writing about their findings. We read teacher-research articles that we admired and that we felt had made an impact. In the end, we carefully studied three articles, all by teachers in the San Francisco Bay Area, that showed some variety in approach and writing style: Joan Cone's "Untracking Advanced Placement English," (1992), Jane Juska's, "The Unteachables," (1989); and Ann Lew's "Raw Fish or Steamed?" (1992).[1] We selected local authors because they were available to speak to the M-CLASS teachers about their writing and research processes. For the opening conference, all the participants had read the articles by Joan Cone and Jane Juska. By the middle of the research year, Ann Lew, a San Francisco member of the M-CLASS group, had agreed to share a draft of her writing with the national network.

As they studied these three pieces, the teams in each city developed a set of guidelines for writing. At the midyear Chicago site meeting, Freedman explained how the team would proceed:[2]

> Read [the teacher-research models] from the point of view of somebody who is going to be writing one of these things and think about

the kinds of techniques that they [the teacher writers] use that are appealing to you as a teacher even to the point, not just of substance but of rhetorical technique—how they use quotations—I mean really down to the nitty-gritty—the kinds of stories they use, how personal is it. (Site meeting, Chicago, February 28, 1993)

Through our analyses of these models and the teacher researchers' writing and discussions, we found three general features that marked the teacher-research genre as distinct from the standard university research report. First, their overall structure was generally a first-person, double narrative that included a research and a teaching strand. Second, the teacher researchers' theories and their rationales for their studies emerged from stories of their personal and professional experiences rather than from the literature. Finally, their tone was personal and conversational.

First-Person, Double Narrative

These teacher-research articles were unlike other research reports, because the dominant genre was the first-person narrative. Cone (1992), in an archetypal example, opens with

> I began the year in Advanced Placement (AP) English with a discussion of *All the King's Men,* a novel my students had read and written papers on over the summer. I thought that first discussion was a success, but my perception was not shared by at least one of my students. (p. 712)

She uses the narrative past tense and sets herself up to follow a chronological organization.

Juska (1989) begins by introducing her main character, her class: "At my school they're called the Bs. After their ninth-grade year, they are tracked into the non-college, terminal classes" (p. 1). She next poses her research question: "What would happen if I turned over my power to them?" Then she writes, "After 25 years of teaching, I decide to find out." Juska eases into a present-tense narrative that contains her answer to her question and her story about her year with her Bs: "September rolls around (it always does), and I get scared. There they are, all Bs and not yet friendly" (p. 2).

Lew (1992) opens, "Our family takes part in both cultures. On New Year's Day we go across the bay to visit my father and stepmother for the traditional Oshogatsu meal." After describing her Japanese family traditions, she turns to her husband's side: "In January or February, we get together with my Chinese in-laws to celebrate the Lunar New Year." She then describes her early memories of embarrassment about speaking "another language" and having to explain that she "ate raw fish." She intertwines these personal narratives with her study of her responses to her students' writing.

The M-CLASS teachers found the narratives appealing, fitting to what they were trying to accomplish, and in contrast to what they considered formal and pompous research reports, which they could not imagine themselves writing:

> KAREN ALFORD: I like that she [Ann Lew] never really says [in a
>   "pompous" voice], "And so I decided to do research to see at least
>   . . ."
> SARAH HERRING: Mm-hmm!
> SARAH FREEDMAN: It's not that kind of a voice.
> SARAH HERRING: She's just talking to you about this student who
>   wanted her paper graded, and that leads into the discussion of
>   why she suddenly realizes that it's important to put structure in a
>   class like hers where the students are going to need their voice.
>   (Site meeting, New Orleans, February 25, 1993)

Doris Williams-Smith especially appreciated the inclusion of feelings and emotional reactions that are appropriate in the narrative genre:

> The idea that they include their personal fears regarding what's going
> to happen makes the classroom teacher really more interested and feel
> like this is something that would be beneficial because this person
> doesn't really know what's going to happen. As opposed to reading
> many research journals where it's like, "This is the answer and we're
> very confident." (Site meeting, New Orleans, February 25, 1993)

Karen Alford summarized the teachers' conclusions about the virtues of the narrative form as she discussed part of Lew's draft report: "The story just makes you want to read it." However, Alford was careful to qualify her point, expressing her impatience with gratuitous stories in which the writer "doesn't talk about her question."

The teachers normally included two narrative lines, with one focusing on their research and the other on their teaching. The research line explains the teacher's research process, procedures, and findings. It consists of one of two types of studies: a case study of one or more students, in which the teacher either traces the student's progress across time or examines how the student responds to instruction (e.g., Lew, 1992; Chapters 4, 7, 9, and 10, this volume), or a study of policy or curricular issues affecting the classroom that generally focuses on findings about teaching the whole class (e.g., Juska, 1989; Cone, 1992; Chapters 3 and 6, this volume). The research line was new to the teachers and proved to be the more difficult of the two lines for them to integrate into their writing.

The teaching narrative weaves through the research narrative. From a university-based research perspective, the teachers would normally provide information about their teaching as background, but the teacher-research articles did something more. By weaving the teaching story into the research story, the writers produced a more complex and elaborate tapestry than they would have by describing the teaching as just contextual background. Doris Williams-Smith explained how she saw the two narrative threads interwoven in Jane Juska's article:

> She [Jane Juska] would blend in, she would talk about something [from the research] and then she'd come back and she would explain what effect it had on her and what she's learned from that incident. I liked the way she went back and forth with what she was actually learning from the experiences. I think Joan [Cone] did the same thing in hers . . . the reflection, the teacher reflections.

Juska, in essence, writes about her teaching and then her research, and then cycles back to how her reflections from her research affect her teaching.

Whereas university-based researchers feel compelled to write about research procedures in detail sufficient for others to be able to judge the merits of the study, the university team and the teacher researchers decided that teacher-research pieces would also need to provide enough information about teaching practices to give helpful ideas to other teachers. Simons concluded with the Boston group, "If our target is teachers and we want them to know what successful practice is, we've got to tell them what we're doing" (site meeting, Boston, March 27, 1993). The development of this second narrative line seems to be a distinguishing feature of the teacher-research genre.

The teaching narrative turned out to be what most interested the M-CLASS teachers, when they read teacher research articles. James Williams in Boston, for example, in reflecting on Jane Juska's "The Unteachables," did not question her findings, but rather considered whether he could teach the way she does:

> What I liked about it was the person [Juska] did have enough sense to say, "Hey, something isn't working. I have to do something different." That was the first thing. The second thing is that they not only made an attempt but they did do something. Now, there's a couple of things that's associated with that. I have a couple of questions. . . . One was the lack of structure. I would be sort of, you know, reserved to try that. Lot of freedom. A lot of chaos. (Site meeting, Boston, March 27, 1993)

The teacher readers wanted sufficient detail in the teaching narrative and became frustrated when information was missing, as the continuing conversation about Juska's article illustrates:

> JOE CHECK: There's a very complex pedagogy here that's not described at all, and it probably took her [Juska] years to develop.
> NANCY O'MALLEY: Because she says things like empowering and the voice and all of that. But you want to know how to do it. (Site meeting, Boston, March 27, 1993)

At the same meeting, the Boston teachers discussed the negative aspects of writing about their teaching. Many were afraid to publish accounts of what they do behind the closed doors of their classrooms. They anticipated the wrath of school administrators who might censure them. Junia Yearwood explained:

> Well, I know sometimes I hesitate to put down exactly [what] I do in the classroom for fear that other people [administrators] may criticize it. . . . That's why I don't put it down. It could cost my job.

In most situations, the M-CLASS teachers decided it was important to risk being honest about their classroom practices, although their anxiety never disappeared. A number of these excellent and dedicated teachers struggled with situations where they not only had little support from their administrations but were actively opposed.

Embedded Beliefs and Explanatory Theories

The second feature that we found to characterize the teacher-research genre is that the authors often embed their beliefs and explanatory theories in engaging personal anecdotes that open their articles. In the New Orleans site meeting, when the teachers discussed the articles, Elena Valenti commented, "I like the personal beginning. I like when you tell a story about yourself that led you to something." Freedman pointed out how teachers' theories may be embedded in these personal openers:

> Those personal beginnings seem to me to work nicely because they told about their personal history and how they got to want to study what it is that they're studying. I think that embedded in that personal history of why it is that you want to study this, that your theories come out and so it seems like that's a really nice way to—

At this point, Karen Alford interrupted, both to concur with Freedman and to say that she already had thought of opening her piece with a personal anecdote that explains why she teaches history as she does:

> I'd already thought to start mine that way because—like an "ah-ha!" I was thinking about, "Why am I wanting to come to study history this way? Oh, I remember!" And so I thought I'd explain why I liked to study history that way.

Alford (Chapter 7, this volume) follows through with her plans. She begins by sharing childhood memories of losing herself in past time while reading historical novels or studying other eras. She uses these memories of personal experience to explain why she works so hard to help her students find their own passionate connections to the past and why for her research she wanted to see what her students would learn about history if they made such connections. Alford's personal experiences also help her decide how she wants to teach and what data she wants to gather for her research project. She knows that, because she will need to craft activities encouraging her students' imagination of life in the past, she will have to help them understand the past from the point of view of the common person. She decides to assign logs in which her students write from the viewpoint of people from the past, and then to study these logs to examine how their historical understanding evolves.

Not all teacher-research articles open with a personal story to frame the research. In some cases, the experiences are more deeply embedded in the writing. For example, well into her chapter, Eileen Shakespear (Chapter 4) writes about her new son and his influence on her vision of her students:

> I saw in their [my students'] eyes the love and the desires I felt for my son. Someone somewhere at some time in their lives cherished each of them and yearned for the best for each of them, probably someone still did. How could I not respond to the power of so much invisible devotion, so much yearning?
>
> What came out of that baby vision was a new dedication and a new standard for me. I started then and continue to say to myself often: "Would today be a good day for my son? Would what happened in this room today be something I'd want my son to experience?"

She elaborates on this theme:

> When I taught junior high in Boston, I had a wonderful principal, Gene Ellis, whose faculty motto was, "Teach the child as if he were

your own." That phrase resonated for me before I had my own and rang like church bells afterwards.

It is these feelings of motherly caring that escalated Shakespear's concern about the school experiences of her African American male students and that drove her desire to conduct research to find out how she and other White female teachers could do better for them.

For other M-CLASS teachers, personal experiences were nowhere in their writing. We found that most of the time, however, the experiences still existed, albeit behind the scenes. In Chapter 9 (this volume), Ann Lew does not include the experiences that shaped her research questions and approach to her research, but these experiences are intertwined in her thinking and decision making. Lew was an immigrant herself and knows well the issues involved in learning to write in English and especially the stigmas of written errors that are common in second-language writing. She discusses these issues in the teacher-research meetings. Lew also writes about her broader cultural experiences explicitly in the earlier "Raw Fish" draft, which we used as a model. Although there she reflected on the dynamic movement of cultures coming together, noting that her home is different from the one she grew up in, in the end she chose to drop these explicit references to her own experiences in favor of getting more quickly to the specific issues of her paper. Although these general experiences motivated her research, her memories were at too high a level of generality to move her quickly enough to her topic of the development of standard usage and the role of error correction.

Whether the teachers wrote about their beliefs and explanatory theories explicitly and up front, embedded them later on in their writing, or left them out altogether, Alford's, Shakespear's and Lew's decisions in their classrooms and research emerged from these sources. In this sense their personal beliefs and theories are part of the M-CLASS teacher-research genre, always in its process and often in its product as well.

Personal Voice

The third feature of the teacher-research articles is the personal voice, accompanied by a conversational style. As Doris Williams-Smith says, "You can hear the person's voice. They sound as though they're talking to you" (site meeting, New Orleans, February 25, 1993). In thinking about the techniques the writers use to achieve this personal voice, Patricia Ward in New Orleans pointed out the use of dialogue. Sarah Herring noticed the metaphors that come from personal experience. She was particularly taken with Lew's use of stir-fry as a description of multiculturalism, with all its intact and distinct colors and flavors. Herring was inspired to use a gumbo metaphor for her writing. Elena Valenti noticed that the writers reveal their feelings about what they are finding out; emotion is written in rather than edited out. The teacher researchers also use the first-person pronoun. Karen Alford appreciated Jane Juska's sense of humor: "One of the things I like about Jane's is that it's so funny."

The teacher writers live close to the experiences of other teachers and can convey their ideas to this audience meaningfully. Doris Williams-Smith explains how the teacher researchers bring alive the students they write about:

> When they describe the students or they give us a look at the students, we can identify some of the things that are mentioned about these students with some students that we've taught, and so it makes it seem very real, and it brings the message home to teachers who read the articles.

MOVING ON

At the end of the year, Patricia Ward told the cautionary tale of the long process Harper Lee went through in writing *To Kill a Mockingbird,* changing a short story into a novel. Little did the teachers or the Berkeley team realize that those who continued to work for publication would experience something close to what Harper Lee had. In the end, 6 of the 24 teacher researchers, most working for 3 or 4 years beyond the 1992–1993 research year, completed manuscripts that we now include as chapters in this book. The rest completed substantive drafts, many of which are part of those chapters that synthesize the M-CLASS community's thinking about key themes about literacy and learning in multicultural classrooms.

The voices of the 24 teachers permeate this book. They are powerful and moving, intelligent and insightful. They tell of carefully crafted research that leads them to offer alternative visions for literacy and learning in urban, multicultural classrooms.

Seeing Beyond Stereotypes: Looking Across Boundaries of Race, Ethnicity, Gender, Class, and Generation

WHEN WE LISTENED to the tape recordings of the M-CLASS meetings and read the teachers' writing, we found that the teachers were preoccupied by the topic of Part II: seeing beyond stereotypes. They wanted to get to know their students, to see beneath their surfaces; and they wanted to create communities of learners in their classrooms, in which their students got to know one another. They considered their ability to see their students and their students' abilities to see one another as intimately intertwined with teaching their subject matter. They may have been preoccupied by seeing because in multicultural classrooms the job of seeing was not a straightforward task. Rather, it was often fraught with emotional conflict. This conflict emerged as teachers and students began to cross many difficult-to-cross boundaries, including those of social class, race, ethnicity, gender, and generation as well as those caused by the school's institutional labels, which promote unfortunate stereotypes, and those that emerge from students' surface behaviors, which oftentimes do not reflect their true intentions.

In Part II, six M-CLASS teachers explore the complexities of "seeing" in multicultural classrooms—from both their points of view and those of their students. These six teachers look at different aspects of "seeing." Some describe techniques for seeing their students and discuss the new insights they gain; others explore what's involved in helping their students see one another; still others connect their new knowledge with their efforts to help their students see better, working to turn new insights into academically and socially constructive action.

In Chapter 3 Griselle Diaz-Gemmati describes her sixth-grade classroom, where the potential for culture clash and misunderstanding was great. White, working-class students from the surrounding neighborhood were together with African American and Latino students, most of whom were bused in from poverty-level neighborhoods in the heart of Chicago. To help her students see one another more clearly, Diaz-Gemmati used frequent writing as part of a multicultural literature curriculum to encourage students to think and talk about many potentially divisive issues they commonly avoided, especially those surrounding race and racism. During the research process, Diaz-Gemmati and her young students often experienced fear, loss of control, and pain. Diaz-Gemmati discusses her internal struggles as she dealt with the consequences of encouraging her eighth-graders to take a careful look at one another's very different lives:

> It's real painful to commit it [my research] to paper, and I have a lot of mixed emotions about taking this last year of childhood away from these kids and forcing them to look at social issues that are going to be bombarding them for the rest of their lives. That bothers me. It bothers me that they cannot look at each other one more time in my classroom without thinking, "What are you really thinking? Are you really a bigot? Or do your parents' influences really run deep in your heart?". . . . They [my students] still trust each other, but they're more intense. They're a lot more intense. (Site meeting, Chicago, February 29, 1993)

Until the time she finished her chapter, Diaz-Gemmati had worried that emotionally it would be impossible for her to complete it.

The author of Chapter 4, Eileen Shakespear, faced her own challenges. As a veteran with more than 20 years of experience in Boston schools, Shakespear had taught increasingly large populations of African American students. For a number of years, she had wanted to learn more about these students, particularly males with a history of difficulties in school. As a White female, she especially wanted to write for other White females, the predominant group teaching in these schools.

When she began her research, Shakespear already knew a great deal about her Black male students because of her years of teaching experience and the close relationships she had developed with many of them across the years. However, she also knew that she had more to learn. As she once said, "If our goal is to see our students, we have to know where our sight is weak."

Shakespear enlisted André, one of her African American former students, to help interview some of her Black male current students who had experienced difficulty in school. André felt that for Shakespear to get useful information, he would have to conduct and tape record the interviews privately, without her presence. In this way, Shakespear gained access to feelings, opinions, and points of view that are often kept from outsiders. As one of the interviewees commented, the information he and his fellow students revealed was "straight up and raw." Although Shakespear directs her writing to White female teachers, her results are relevant for anyone who teaches similar populations.

Chapter 5 brings together writings about boundary crossings by Walter

Wood, George Austin, Brenda Landau McFarland, and Phil Potestio. These teachers alternatively look across gaps in social class, generation, and political orientation as well as consider the blinders that come from institutional stereotyping. Like Diaz-Gemmati and Shakespear, they write on controversial topics and take risks. They find that crossing boundaries involves exploring the consequences of differentials in social status and power that affect us all and that underlie many of the different life experiences and sensitivities that we bring to our considerations of these often painful issues.

The six teachers who have contributed to Part II came to their research with good will and a genuine desire to be helpful to others by communicating what they had learned. Though they purposefully tried to learn and write about students whose experiences were unlike their own, their insights, inevitably, were shaped by their own experiences. The insights they gained, in some cases, were dramatic; but more often they were small shifts in perspective. Their improved vision, however, did lead the teachers to understand their students better and in many cases to try to solve rather than deny problems, to turn destructive interactions into productive ones, and ultimately to work toward reshaping not only their classrooms but sometimes their schools as well.

—Sarah Warshauer Freedman

CHAPTER 3

"And Justice for All": Using Writing and Literature to Confront Racism

Griselle M. Diaz-Gemmati

I WAS BEGINNING my 10th year as an educator. I smile as I remember entering this school for the first time; my very first teaching assignment. I recall my apprehension. A Latina teacher in an Anglo neighborhood, hired to teach a handful of bused kids in a Spanish bilingual program that spanned grades one through eight. The school's community is in a White neighborhood at the edge of the Chicago city limits. It is a place that borders and looks like the suburbs, but is within the city limits and gives the city's police and fire-fighters the job's required city address. I was insecure and inexperienced, but determined.

I overlooked the often inadequate and sometimes nonexistent materials, the makeshift classroom, and the school clerk's bigoted rudeness. Resourcefulness soon replaced my fears. My bilingual program became a working reality of a multiage, student-directed curriculum.

I dreaded the moment when my kids left my classroom and entered the mainstream student population; it was then that I saw a rekindled look of apprehension and fear in their eyes. I taught them how to stand, but I could not follow through to watch them run.

Three years after I first walked into the school, I told the principal that I would be interested in the newly vacated eighth-grade teaching position, and he agreed to place me in a regular classroom. But the old feelings of uneasiness assaulted me once more. What would the community think? What would they say about a Latina teacher taking over the eighth-grade class? Surprisingly, it was not the community that had misgivings about my ability, but my own faculty, the people I considered my colleagues. They were a group of very traditional Anglo teachers who had about 100 years of teaching experience among them. Some were bold enough to ask me outright if I was qualified to teach typical subjects in a "regular" classroom.

My apprehension developed into a passion for success. Their trepidation became my motivation. That was 6 years, twelve teachers, and three principals ago. Again I had withstood challenge and did not fail.

I was awakened from my ruminations by my eighth graders sauntering into the classroom. Although it was the 2nd day of the new school year, I knew each of them well. I had been their seventh-grade teacher the previous year. My new principal and I were concerned about this group. They had been subjected to a parade of teachers during their fifth and sixth grades. They were not cooperative; they lacked motivation, and they took no initiative. We decided that I should follow them for 2 years to see what impact, if any, I could have on them academically and emotionally. The risk paid off. This class was becoming a cohesive group of adolescents who were well liked by the entire faculty. I had grown attached to them and was glad that my opportunity to embark on a research project included this particular group.

I began my research by asking a specific, and I thought noncontroversial, question: What happens when adolescent students begin to explore the themes of racism and prejudice as they discuss and write about literature? Specifically, can they separate how they feel from what they have heard from their family, friends, and communities?

Before I relate our story, I would like to share some information about my kids. My class consisted of 33 students—19 girls and 14 boys. Of this total, 21 were bused from inner-city schools. The class's median age was 13.8. The ethnic demographics of my group were 15 African Americans (of these, one had a Latino parent and another had a European American parent), 10 European Americans, 6 Latinos, 1 Asian-American (who had one European-American parent), and 1 student of East Indian heritage. I used a combination of school records and student's self-labels to identify them ethnically. The class's reading abilities, according to standardized test scores, ranged from the latter part of 4th grade to the beginning of 11th grade.

My class was part of a unique school of 260 students, with one grade per class and one class per grade. The school is a microcosm of the idealistically integrated community of the future. Our realm encompasses students in a beautiful blend of colors and cultures, including a small number of special education and physically challenged students.

We are an urban school set in an open nine-acre campus on the northwest edge of the city. All of our students love the sprawling grass playgrounds where softball, soccer, football, and basketball games are played simultaneously. For our bused children, who make up about 48% of the school population, the setting contrasts sharply with the black-topped, gang-ridden, fenced-in playgrounds of many schools in their neighborhoods. I enjoy the opportunity to watch the students play with their schoolmates on self-chosen teams during the daily 15-minute morning recess or 45-minute lunch break.

Of three neighborhood public schools in this northwest area of the city, ours is the only one that is truly, and according to federal law, desegregated. The immediate neighborhood at first did not look at our integration with favor. Yet our nine acres were our sheltered zone, our paradise. It seemed to work. The kids were getting along. Their fights seemed to be the minor rumblings of dubiously scored points, ignored rules, or rowdy games of "Johnny Tackle" rather than directed racial instances.

As the eighth-grade teacher, I relish the task of putting the finishing touches on all who graduate from our school. I try to assure my students that their final year of elementary school will be not only enlightening and challenging, but memorable. It's a teacher's utopia. I consider it an advantage to be able to work with these ethnically diverse children from varying socioeconomic levels, with different children brought together in one place to work, study, play, and coexist during their grammar school years.

I embarked on my journey of teacher research with a single focus. I wanted to showcase my kids—a group of 33 fabulous adolescents who had responded enthusiastically to a literature-based, student-directed curriculum. Before me, I had all the ingredients of a thousand success stories. I initiated my research certain that it was going to be effortless. I actually believed that all I would need to do was state what I thought was the obvious. I held fast to the belief that all children can overlook their physical, ethnic, and cultural differences, if all the conditions for learning are just so. I truly believed that if they were provided with a nonpartisan, caring, and safe environment anything was possible. As I look back to the beginning of my study, I wonder, was this my reality, or was it all an illusion?

The rude awakening that my students and I experienced as a result of my research caused havoc in our classroom, on our playground, in our homes, in our communities. I find it difficult and agonizing to talk about our transition. Truthfully, the mere thought of committing the story to paper leaves me raw and emotionally depleted. I could not begin to narrate our experience without first admitting to feeling like an imbecile. How could I not have detected the snags in this magical, imaginary fabric I had woven? What was I thinking? Seeing? Ignoring?

I'll begin by providing some information about how my classes work. First, to establish a student-directed reading environment, I organize an individualized literature program. All students are responsible for selecting their own novels. They keep a log of what they have read and a journal in which they react to and critique what they are reading. They also are responsible for reporting their reading progress to the members of their literature group. Because our school offers its teachers extended class periods, I can provide a daily 20- to 25-minute sustained silent reading time. We have a reading rug where students can sit or lie down on throw pillows they have brought from home, as they read silently. I want them to get comfortable and relaxed when they read. I believe that this atmosphere fosters a pleasant and inviting attitude toward what the students once believed was a tedious task.

Literature discussions usually take place two to three times a week. The literature groups consist of five to seven members of varying reading abilities. I make sure that the members of each literature circle contain both boys and girls, from different ethnic groups, with varied reading skills and interests. Sometimes I choose their groups, and sometimes I help them with their choice. Each circle is responsible for selecting a scribe and a leader. The scribe records in the group's journal what each of the members is reading and the group members' reactions to each piece of literature. The leader prompts each member to talk about different literary aspects of the book, such as character analysis, setting, plot, and the like.

The literature leader keeps everyone's comments to a specific time limit, usually no more than 3 to 5 minutes, and briefs the entire class on the discussions that have taken place during his or her meeting. Responsibilities shift every 2 weeks or so to assure that everyone gets an opportunity to be a leader and a scribe. Since five literature circles meet at once, I go from one to the next as an observer and as a member, not as a supervisor. I really get a charge from listening to my students discuss literature from different perspectives and watching them attempt to substantiate their opinions with passages from their novels. When I am part of the group, I share my reactions to whatever novel I happen to be reading and relate my reactions to the author's writing. My students feel empowered by the ability to choose what they read.

Once the independent reading workshop becomes part of our daily routine, I initiate class novels into the program. The routine for reading a class novel is the same as for independent reading, except that now everyone reads the same novel. Reading the same piece of literature helps the class build an intellectual community as we share common reading experiences. We get to know and discuss characters we all are familiar with. Together we interpret the same dialogues and discuss the structure of a commonly known plot. I still assign independent reading for homework. The record keeping for both readings remains entirely the responsibility of the individual student.

To assist the students with the choice of a class novel, I present them with a list of prospective paperbacks on the same general theme as well as a brief synopsis of each of the suggested titles. The students then select the novel by a majority vote. Usually they elect to read something I recommend, but there are times when they negotiate with me to select a book they've heard about that isn't on my list.

To understand what happens when my adolescent students explore themes of racism and prejudice as they discuss and write about literature, I wanted my class to read two novels, *To Kill a Mockingbird* (Lee, 1960) and *Roll of Thunder, Hear My Cry* (Taylor, 1978), both of which deal with racial prejudice, but from different perspectives. I had read *To Kill a Mockingbird* years before and was haunted for weeks by its poignancy. Scout, the main character and narrator, is a prepubescent girl who is not afraid to speak her mind. Her relationship with her father is unique, and at several junctures in the novel, she flagrantly opposes her father's opinions. Scout is one of two children in a one-parent family, something I felt many of my students could relate to. I was also intrigued by the subtle understanding that the nucleus and mother figure in this White family was their Black maid, Calpurnia. I planned to use class discussions, student journals, audio recordings of literature circle discussions, student writing assignments, and written reflections of what I observed in class as the data for my research.

I first initiated a strong campaign to kindle interest in *To Kill a Mockingbird*. I lobbied for my choice by announcing to the class, "There's this novel I've read about a man who gets accused of rape. At his trial, all evidence points to his innocence. It becomes increasingly obvious to the reader that this accused man is physically incapable of committing this horrendous act of violence."

"What happens to him?" asked Nick.

"Well," I answered, "I'd rather you read the book to find out."

The class emitted a mixture of moans and chuckles.

"Mrs. Gemmati!" smiled Melissa, "Why do you do us like that? OK, I'm curious, where's this book?"

After 2 years with the same class, I felt that I had a good understanding of their group dynamics. Still, I did not want the students to feel as if they were forced into reading the novel, so I had an alternate plan. Had I felt strong resistance, I planned to organize a group of interested students to read the novel and derive my research data from their responses and reactions. I knew that the ideal situation was to have the entire class participate, but I would not have compromised my integrity or risked the students' trust. Fortunately, though, the whole group was eager to begin with *To Kill a Mockingbird*. After the paperbacks were distributed, I let the kids skim through them for a while, encouraging them to read the back cover. Some asked me questions about the time in history when this story takes place. We talked informally about the South, especially after the Civil War. We discussed mockingbirds. We reviewed and shared our general knowledge about Alabama.

I deliberately focused at first on injustice rather than on racial prejudice. I wanted my students to arrive, if they ever did, at the topic of racism by themselves.

After their initial reading assignments, the students' enthusiasm to read *To Kill a Mockingbird* varied. Some were hesitant to start such a "fat" book; others waded through its heavy metaphoric descriptions as if trying to sprint through water, but ultimately, the animated discussions that started coming from the literature circles were well worth these early difficulties.

Initially, everyone was on equal footing. Everyone seemed to pick apart the literal meaning of the words and phrases in the reading assignments. During class discussions, we explained the descriptions of Maycomb to each other. Some of the metaphors Lee uses were taken quite literally by some students. When we discussed the description "tired old town," I was amused to discover that some children envisioned a town of elderly people.

Then something altered the discussions. I happened to be sitting in on a circle discussion when a major disagreement erupted between two of my top students. The word *nigger* offended the White students in the circle much more than the Black students. Shelly, who is White, brought up this point in the discussion. In not so many words, she let her circle know that it was one of those words everyone knew, but did not use. Nancy, who is Black, resented Shelly's taking offense.

"I don't see what your problem is," she sarcastically responded to Shelly. "No one ever called you guys nothing but 'Master.'"

Shelly insisted, "Doesn't it bother you to see that vulgarity in print?"

"No, why should it?" retorted Nancy. "We know where we come from."

At this point I asked Nancy if she or people she knew addressed each other by the term *nigger* and how she felt about it.

"It don't bother us. We know we mean no harm by it."

"Then why does it tick you off when I get offended by it?" Shelly persisted.

"It takes on a different meaning coming from you," Nancy snapped.

I was perplexed. I felt that it was one of those things that many people wondered about, yet never vocalized for fear of being misinterpreted. Shelly did not possess the inhibition I felt. I asked Nancy to explain what she meant by her remark, "It takes on a different meaning coming from you."

She thought for a moment before she replied, "Mrs. Gemmati, it's like different. If my mama is complaining about her boyfriend and calls him an ass, that's OK. But if I call him an ass, she gets all over me. It's like that."

Still, Shelly refused to give ground. "It's like using a swear word."

"It depends who's doing the swearing!" Nancy shot back.

The battle lines were drawn. Others joined the fray. Soon the group was talking at rather than to each other. The rest of the discussion volleyed back and forth around the conjecture that the word *nigger* was a White man's way of ensuring the imposed lower status of the Black man. It also touched upon how some Blacks refer to each other as *nigger* without offense because they share common ground. I sat back dumbfounded. Being neither Black nor White, I felt inept at defusing the mounting tension. Yet I knew exactly what Nancy was talking about. I too used nuances with relatives and close friends that would take on an abrasive tone if used by someone other than a Puerto Rican.

The bell reverberated in the hallway, but no one paid attention. The discussion was becoming a heated argument. I felt that I had to intervene. I knew the issue was unresolved, but there was no getting them past this one point without appearing to side with one person or the other. I uneasily shooed them out to recess. A heavy tension lingered in the room for the rest of the morning. The final entry in my journal that day was, "God, what have I gotten us into?"

My drive home felt unusually long that evening. The discussion from Nancy and Shelly's literature circle was on constant replay in my mind. I couldn't drown it out. My resolve to do something about it was overwhelming. A strong part of my personality consists of being nonconfrontational. This was uncomfortable territory, and I didn't enjoy finding myself in this predicament. I wanted to discuss my situation with someone and thought of contacting some of my teacher friends but was apprehensive about their reactions. After quite a bit of deliberation, I decided to keep this incident to myself.

I arrived at school early the next morning. The previous night's fitful sleep did nothing to enhance my usual grouchy morning disposition. I listened to my voice making the morning announcements. It sounded terse. The students seemed edgy. Was I imagining this tension, or was it really still there?

The morning's opening activities went on as usual. Larry collected the lunch orders, Maria passed out journals, José took attendance, Freddy watered the plants, Shelly vacuumed the reading rug. The rest of the students talked among themselves as is their custom. When the chores were done, we quieted down to start writing in our personal journals. Twice I attempted to write. Nothing came. The stark white page dared me to write about my inner turmoil. I couldn't. I said a silent prayer and stood up to start the class.

"Today I'd like you to help me do a word cluster." The exercise was not new to the class. I often use this procedure to introduce new vocabulary. I find it can help the kids understand words or phrases in context and individually. The students' stirrings told me that they were fishing in their desks for their thesauruses and dictionaries. "Put them away," I announced over my shoulder as I turned toward the blackboard, "You'll only need your honest opinions and beliefs for this cluster." I printed the word "stereotype" on the board. The class sat strangely still for a few moments. The members of Nancy and Shelly's literature group silently stared at the word. Other hands around them shot up.

"A belief about something."

"A notion."

"A judgment."

The chalk in my hand tap-danced as I hurriedly wrote their responses on the blackboard.

"Is a stereotype good or bad?" I prompted.

"Bad!" was their chorused reply.

"Why?" I attempted to look directly at each of them in turn as I spoke.

"Because," Nancy spoke for the first time that morning, "it's like saying all blondes are dumb." Shelly's head flew up and her icy blue glare bore into Nancy's face.

Fearing a repeat of yesterday's heated discussion, I quickly wrote the word *prejudice* next to our first cluster.

"OK, now let's cluster this word." Did my voice sound as tense as I felt?

"White."

"Black."

"Hispanic."

"Hindu."

"Chinese."

Again I hurriedly wrote on the board. After a moment, I stood still, with my back toward the class. I ignored the names of the other ethnic groups that were shouted out. Ultimately, the room settled into an uneasy silence.

"What," I asked, still facing the blackboard, "do any of these ethnic groups have to do with the meaning of the word *prejudice*?" I slowly turned to face a group of kids I thought I knew.

"Blacks hate Whites."

"Whites hate everyone," someone abruptly countered.

"The word in question is not hate!" I snapped harshly. Again I tried to look directly into each of their faces. The strained tone of my voice did not elicit any other comments or responses. I felt they had plenty to say, yet I knew that the general tone of their answers was not conducive to a productive discussion.

Thinking I might be able to diffuse some of the tension by stopping the whole-class discussion, I said automatically, "Get in your literature circles, and cluster the word *prejudice* with your groups." Divide and conquer. Was that what I wanted to do?

As was my usual practice for my teacher research when students worked in groups, I went around to each group to set up tape recorders. The last thing I wanted to do was interfere or disrupt their discussions. I did not want my presence to infuse their answers with whatever responses they'd think I would want. As I later listened to the tapes of their circle discussions, I felt like an intruder. I felt as if I were eavesdropping on something confidential, something personal.

Their discussions that morning bounced back and forth for nearly half an hour. I asked each group to instruct its scribe on precisely what the members wanted to report to the whole class. I hoped that this impromptu system of channeled reporting would harness some of the negative energy that threatened to ignite my classroom.

Issues on the prejudice of gender, age, religion, race, and roles surfaced in these class reports. In a fervent circle discussion, Allen, a Black student, helped everyone realize a very important truth.

"Today's society," he reasoned, "makes us be prejudiced against each other." He stood up to emphasize his point when the others in the circle told him he was way off base.

"If you see a big guy," he directed his comments to the girls in his circle, "with a black, bulky leather jacket, face not shaved, funny-looking eyes, earrings on, hands in his pockets, walking over in you direction when you on a street, and it's getting dark and you alone, don't tell me you ain't going to be scared. You going to imagine the worse, and you going to try to get out of his way. Right?"

The group did not respond.

"Hell," he continued, "even the cops say we should report stuff like that . . . call if we see anybody suspicious. Who gets to define suspicious? Our prejudices!"

Not one person countered Allen's argument. They felt he had a valid point.

For a while the scribes, holding true to our literature-circle procedure, kept personal attacks at bay. Although the intensity of the students' convictions ebbed slightly during our attempts at proper classroom etiquette, it flowed just as profusely beneath the surface of our decaying facade.

In *To Kill a Mockingbird,* the attitude of White townspeople toward Blacks and those who helped Blacks sparked heated exchanges in literature circles. I tried to put everything in a historic perspective by having my students research the Jim Crow practices. I also attempted to explain the social, economic, and moral climate of the South after Reconstruction. I by no means tried to assuage the feelings of frustration the class felt when they realized the way the Blacks were regarded and treated. The students could not comprehend the flagrant disregard for human dignity the White townspeople displayed toward the Blacks.

Alas, common ground! Everyone agreed that the treatment of Blacks in the South during that period of history was deplorable. The students of color felt angry and vengeful. Their journals and writings reflected one common underlying theme—pent-up resentment. The White students felt defensive and their writings told me that they were angered and confused about their feelings.

I convinced myself that if I prompted my students to channel their energies into their reading logs and journals, I could help them deal with their anger. My strategy helped, and I watched their writings take on a new, sharper hue. They exposed themselves to me in a way that was personal, sad, and confidential. They shared dismal chunks of their lives through the silent monologue of their pens. They pressed their secrets between the sacred pages of their personal writings.

Mary, an African American girl, confessed to being afraid of fights, arguments, and confrontations. She related that her literature circle forced her to take stands on issues through combinations of unrelenting stares and uncomfortable silences. Her opinions were carefully neutral; she was afraid of being wrong. Her pent-up rage exploded several times during circle discussions, and she completely lost control. Her question to me in one journal entry will plague me forever: "Why you have to bring all this garbage into the classroom? This was the only place I could be without being made to think about stuff like who don't like who. Why you doing this to us?"

Her question pelted me with regrets. "Why was I doing this to one of the best classes I had ever had? What was I doing to them? What was I doing to me?" I wanted to cancel my commitment to the research at this juncture. After long periods of reflection, I knew I couldn't. I had pushed too far. We had heard too much. The students and I would never—could never—go back to the place we were before the project started. We needed to finish what I had started to obtain some sort of closure. It would have been cruel of me to evoke these feelings in my students and then abruptly try to reestablish the relationships we had before the research began. I continued the research, but was anxious about it.

The accusation of rape in the novel was another burning issue during circle discussions. Once again my class divided itself into separate camps—this time the dividing factor was gender.

The issue was not whether the character Luella was raped. Obviously she wasn't. The problem was the attitude of several males in the classroom:

"If she wanted Robinson that bad, he should have done it. After all, he was convicted of the crime anyway."

This viewpoint made me seethe. The girls were angrier still. It was difficult to keep my emotions from interfering in their discussions. Many times I abruptly left a circle whenever a comment I passionately disagreed with was made. The girls brought up the issue of prejudice again.

"If a girl talks or dresses a certain way, it's your belief that she's asking to be raped if she doesn't agree to a man's advances?" Nancy was livid.

A student with a police officer in his family brought in a graphic description of a rape from an actual police report. Slowly and carefully, I tried to steer these boys clear of the ignorant, but generally accepted, assumption that rape is a crime of passion. I quietly reminded the class of the number of innocent children, including boys of all ages, who are violated or molested every year. Some male students defended their belief that the punishment for rape depended on who the victim was.

Discussions continued to volley back and forth. Shelly sarcastically reminded the boys that all female victims were someone's mother, sister, daughter. "Pray it never happens to anyone you love." Her words were tainted with acid. Some boys started mumbling among themselves.

Nancy commented that Black men in the old days were done away with for looking at a White woman, and those stupid ones who went with White women were "killed like dogs in the street." But any White man could do what he wanted to a Black woman.

I don't know what prompted Larry to say, "Joe's mother's White."

Before I knew it Larry and Joe were exchanging blows in the middle of the classroom. I watched frozen with shock as they rolled over each other on the floor. Once I could get to where the melee was taking place, I found myself incapable of separating them. Nancy appeared, as if from nowhere, and grabbed one boy from behind. They got to their feet and continued exchanging blows. Nancy somehow got one of the boys into a full Nelson while I pressed the other to the wall with all my strength.

"Go ahead," she yelled, "Kill each other off. Isn't that what we doing to ourselves? Isn't that why we have no Black brothers hanging around? How many of you got your daddy home? Black men can't discuss nothing without killing each other. No wonder we in such a sorry state."

A hush fell over the classroom. I was shocked. No one except Nancy had tried to stop the fight. I was so disappointed. Holding back tears, I barked commands at the students. Everyone was to sit absolutely still at their own seats until the bell rang. In a choked voice I told the students to ask themselves why they did nothing to help Nancy and me intervene. During the final 15 minutes of that day not one student met my furious gaze.

In the quiet aftermath of a classroom left in utter disarray, long after I heard the buses pull away from the curb, I wrote in my journal: "The violence of today's society has permeated our classroom."

The novel was finished, much to my relief. I sat and pondered the ramifications of our discussions on our class. I knew that the kids' feelings were still raw. Yet they seemed hesitant to let the issue go. I asked the class if there was some unresolved sentiment about the novel that we had not explored. One question that stirred up an animated discussion was "Were the children in the novel prejudiced?"

All in the class agreed that they were not. The students observed that the kids in the book saw the town recluse more as a mystery than anyone to be shunned. They also realized that the children believed in Robinson's innocence and supported their father's defense of him.

"Why then," I asked, "do you think that these particular children in the

novel were not prejudiced when most of their neighbors and school friends
were?" Subsequently, most agreed that it had to do with the children's father
and upbringing. I prompted their circle discussions with questions such as
"Have you ever been discriminated against?" "If so, when and why?" The
obvious responses of color, nationality, and religion surfaced. When I suggested they write whatever they did not feel comfortable talking about, other
responses started to trickle in.

"Some people don't like me on their team, I'm kind of slow when I run."

"Some kids say I'm ugly, my brothers do too. When they have their
camera in school they don't want me in the pictures."

"Some of my friends make fun of me cause I go to LD [learning disabili-
ties] classes. They think I'm dumb and don't want me on their science team."

Kathy, a child of White South American and Black Caribbean heritage,
usually sat inert and despondent during class discussions about racial issues.
No matter what type of peer pressure was exerted, she refused to comment
and countered the group's questions with stony silence and hostile glares.
She also wrote journal entries that carefully skirted the issue of racism, but
concentrated frequently on injustice. It wasn't until I asked for this writing
that I was to find out the source of Kathy's misery:

> My aunt had all the family over for Easter a few years ago. When it
> came time to take pictures of the kids with their baskets, she asked me,
> my brother and my sister to step out of the way. She don't like my dad
> 'cause he's Black. I guess she don't like us 'cause we're not White. My
> cousins on my dad's side say he had to marry my mom. They make fun
> of me too. My mom's always depressed. My stupid sister is going with
> a White boy. I guess I don't ever feel like if I'm going to fit anywhere,
> and it's not my fault. It's not fair.

"I can't be part of their group," another student wrote. "Everything they
do costs money. My parents can't just hand over money for the movies or the
mall. So I make believe I'm not interested in their activities. They'd make fun
of me if they thought I was poor. My mom and dad would kill me if I said
to someone we had to count our money twice before spending it. No one in
this neighborhood is supposed to be poor."

Another student who has an Asian father and a White mother tells me,
"My mom acts real cool when I have my friends come over. She even drives
them home. But afterwards she says, 'Why don't you have more White friends
from our own neighborhood?'"

It surprised me that this particular student checked "White" on his high
school application form. I never had the courage to ask him why. Later that

semester, I proofread a description of himself in a letter he wrote to a prospective mentor. He stated that he looks "slightly Asian."

I read the students' comments and saw the ugly shreds of our social
fabric that are woven into their personal lives and that destroy their self-
confidence. That day I saw my students as vulnerable children, carrying on
their shoulders the ills of our civilized world.

The class concluded the novel with new insight and raw feelings. The
general consensus was that people are taught to be prejudiced and that racism and injustice have their roots in the home. Our frank discussions and
open writing, I think, helped them air some of their previously hidden feelings and helped them begin to separate their opinions from those of their
parents. Some of the students told me about a commercial that they had seen
on television. In it, the first scene is of bassinets with newborns of different
ethnic origins. Then the camera fades into a panorama of a graveyard. The
narrator at this point says: "In our world, these shouldn't be the only two
places where people don't care who's next door. Stop racism now." The students continued to worry, however, that there really were few cures. To quote
Kathy, "Words are cheap. Actions come too late after the hurt has been
done."

I asked the children to explain if affirmative action and civil rights have
helped ease the division of the races. All agreed they had to a great extent,
but that there is still much to accomplish. Most concluded, however, that
they were just kids and were subjected to following rules and not making
them. They had no choice but to accept the fact that their parents and the
adults in their lives constantly exposed them to preconceived beliefs about
racism and prejudice.

One journal entry states: "It is not easy to tell my dad not to call some
of my friends Spics. He's my dad. He gets mad when I tell him not to say
things like that. He's the boss. What he says goes."

I knew that I would never be able to answer their questions, or assuage
their fears. Their pain was real and intense. They were hesitant to drop the
issue, and I was terrified to continue. Yet I wanted this decision to be their
call. I felt as if I no longer was directing the orchestra, but that the music
was directing us.

The next novel I had in mind, Mildred Taylor's *Roll of Thunder, Hear
My Cry,* was a mirror image of *To Kill a Mockingbird.* It was set at approximately the same time and also dealt with racial conflicts. *Roll of Thunder,*
however, presents the racial conflict from the point of view of a Black child
subjected to the horrors of racism in the South during the Depression, not
from the point of view of White children. Taylor is a wonderful children's
writer and her stories reflect the realism of an historical perspective. I pro-

ceeded with the same selection process as before, only this time the students immediately voted unanimously in favor of reading *Roll of Thunder.*

Again we started the literature circles by redefining the words *prejudice* and *racism.* This time the students' answers were not so hostile, not so combustible. I think the initial shock and reaction of talking about something that's always present, yet avoided, had worn off. They logically concluded, in one circle, that prejudice "is the result of preconceived judgments dictated by certain behaviors in the home and society." I was not only impressed, I was proud.

Issues of discrimination again surfaced, catapulted by certain issues in the novel. One of these issues surfaced when the Black children in the novel received used textbooks from the White schools; the textbooks were tattered and torn. One of the Black children in the story questioned why they had to learn from these old used-up books. We learned that it was the accepted practice in the South to give unusable materials to the "Nigra" schools. This fact brought on a new discussion of the "separate but equal" ruling.

We researched and examined the *Brown v. Board of Education* case and dissected and discarded the separate-but-equal practice as a Band-Aid cure for a social malignancy. We reviewed and applauded Rosa Parks's courageous and nonviolent stand against bigoted laws.

Some children asked older relatives if they remembered the "Whites Only" drinking fountains and rest rooms. Recollections of these times lived by grandparents and great-aunts were the topic of discussion for the entire morning. Horror stories of midnight lynchings and cross burnings were told again and again. Allen told a story he had heard about a neighbor of his great-aunt's in Mississippi who had been set on fire for supposedly stealing something from a White man's field. Allen's story made *Roll of Thunder* more real, more atrocious.

One part of the novel graphically describes the physical condition of a Black man set on fire by a posse of Klan members because he had allegedly looked at a White woman with a "degree of undisguised lust." The students compared this incident with Tom Robinson's trial in *To Kill a Mockingbird.* The circumstances and outcomes were similar, but as Allen put it, "Robinson had a White lawyer protecting him. It did nothing but buy him some time. This guy here had nothing but his words, and a Black man's word ain't worth nothing."

Nancy continued, "He was set on fire to set an example and make others afraid. I'm sure that if they wanted him dead they would have lynched him in the woods. They needed to send a message to the other Black folk that this could also happen to you. They had to spread fear, to intimidate."

All my students were disturbed by the fact that the Black children in the novel were expected to walk miles each day to school, while daily they were passed by a bus full of White kids going in the same direction. Their walks to school included being the object of humiliation as the White bus driver tried to run the children off the road and into muddy embankments.

At this point I asked the students to try to identify the improvements that they felt have occurred in public education since that time. I asked them how they would try to insure that all children received a similarly effective public education. The majority of their answers revolved around the need for the improvement of school facilities and the communities that surround them. Busing and integration, however, were the issues that reopened the proverbial can of worms. I was once again faced with an explosive issue with my classroom of both bused and neighborhood kids.

"Now minorities can get into colleges and jobs first just because of what they are." Shelly spoke without malice. The bused students, I detected, took offense at her statement.

"And if they are the token, they better watch their back, and they got to work twice as hard as their White peers." Nancy's words were spat out like rounds from a machine gun. Their target was obvious. Shelly seemed to gear up for another confrontation.

"Whites are just trying to play catch-up for all the years of inequality. They owe us." Kathy reasoned out loud, before Shelly could answer.

Larry commented next, "Who's kidding who? Yeah, so we come to this nice clean school in a White neighborhood. Who are the ones standing on a street corner in the early morning, in the rain and the snow and in the cold to catch the bus while most of the kids from around here are still in bed? You ever heard of a White kid being bused to our neighborhood? The Whites gave us rides to school all right, away from our own. Every time we try to get a piece of what the Whites got, it backfires on us. They fix it so we are pissed, and then they can say, 'Hey, ain't this what you wanted?' We always gonna be wrong, no matter what we get."

All the bused kids nodded their heads in agreement with Larry's comment. Not one of them had been spared the frustration of waiting for late buses during inclement weather.

Allen spoke slowly, deliberately, "Yeah, we come here and see all the stuff our neighborhood ain't. It's just like the textbooks that the Black kids got in the book. Our neighborhood's like that. We get the leftovers, the areas no one else wants."

I asked the group, "Do you feel that the environment here or the environment of your home school is more comfortable for you?" I wanted them to be specific, and I wanted substantiated answers. I did not want the class discussion to turn into an "Oh I'm so grateful I'm here" testimony. I asked the class to name specific examples of the pros and cons of busing, on the students' being bused and on the schools' receiving them. As I expected, the cons outweighed the pros. Some of the most indisputable reasons were the following:

"All our neighborhood friends are scattered all over. We all go to different receiving schools. The kids from here stay together. They grow together."

"I leave this place at 3:15, so I guess this place is integrated from 9:00 to 3:15, Monday to Friday, September to June, excluding all holidays."

"If the neighborhood kids want to stay for the after school programs and social center, they just walk back to school. If we want to stay we need an act of Congress, a way to get home after dark, a White family that will take us home with them until the activities start and three notes from our momma. It ain't worth all that."

"It is fine if one of the neighborhood kids learns to speak Spanish. Wow, how smart! How intelligent! But we're expected to learn English. Our Spanish ain't so smart. If we don't learn to speak like them, we're dumb."

One of the neighborhood kids asked if the bused kids felt just a little safer here, rather than in their neighborhood schools.

"Sure, but you better run like hell when those buses let you off in front of the home school. Then we got to walk the rest of the way to our house. Sometimes the gangs are there waiting for us to beat us up. At times it's like we're delivered right to them. It ain't all the time but it happens often enough."

The issues they mentioned as pros were touching:

"I've made some good friends."

"I see the kind of neighborhood I want my kids to grow in."

"I met Mrs. Gemmati."

"We do stuff like this—reading novels that kids in other schools don't do. We kinda have a say in things here."

One neighborhood student spoke up. "We don't have it all so great here. Some of the kids from this neighborhood that go to private schools won't talk to us because we talk to you."

Another neighborhood kid continued. "Yeah, they chase us and throw rocks at us, and if we are caught around their house, they try to beat us up because we go to this school. Because there's minorities at this school."

"The people around here don't care how good you are or what you do, and it ain't only the kids; they'd hate Mrs. Gemmati too because she's Puerto Rican."

The moment this was said, a hush permeated the classroom. All eyes turned toward me. I tried to remain unfazed but I felt yanked out of my neutral zone. I now was categorized, labeled, seen differently. I was no longer just the teacher. I was now one of the "sides" I had so desperately tried to stay out of. I hoped that this was the wedge necessary for me to help them realize that they needed to look at a person's qualities first and foremost.

I tried to ask for reasons for their persecution other than being members of our school. None were offered. The bused kids promised to help the neighborhood kids "show these bigots a lesson." I saw a subtle change in the kids toward the end of that particular discussion. I saw them bond, if only temporarily, against a common enemy.

The theme of inequality again was analyzed and cast as a result of racial prejudice. They discussed the fact that in *Roll of Thunder,* Cassie's family was targeted more than others because they had the distinction of being landowners. The students arrived at the conclusion that the Whites were uncomfortable with Blacks who had the potential for material equality—especially as landowners. Ultimately, at the end of the book, the students felt torn. They realized that Cassie's father had deliberately set his crop on fire to distract and ultimately stop the lynching of a neighbor's son. They knew that this crop was the only thing the family counted on to pay the taxes on their land. The students concluded that the family would either have to sell part of their land or lose it outright. They also knew that the boy who was saved from the lynching would now stand trial for the murder of a White man and would be convicted because of the improbability of a fair trial due to his color.

The children had a hard time dealing with the author's decision at this juncture. They compared the ending of *To Kill a Mockingbird* to this one and agreed that it was possible in *Roll of Thunder* for the Black family to keep the land their White neighbors so desperately wanted. "Their decision was a poor one," most maintained. "The kid couldn't be saved anyhow. What was the point?"

"Cassie's dad was faced with choosing between his beliefs and convictions, and the land that had been his since birth. He chose what he believed in," I announced quietly.

"Is that what you want from us, Mrs. Gemmati?"

"What's that?" I asked Shelly.

"You know, to let go of the stuff we see at home and make up our own minds about prejudice?"

Shelly's assumption took me by surprise. I literally had no idea that this was what I had unknowingly conveyed. I smiled at this group of students that I loved unconditionally.

"No," I responded. "What I want is not the issue. It's what you feel is right that's important. If I ask you to follow my convictions, I am doing no better than the person who tells you to believe that all Blacks are bad, that all Whites are racists or that all Hispanics are ignorant and loud. I strongly believe that the way to end prejudice is to stop taking another's judgment as your own. Don't let someone else prejudge for you."

The abrupt ending to the novel left them wanting answers and solutions to the problems we discussed. The novel tied no loose ends.

I attempted to explain that society's ills nowadays were the same yet different. One of the kids brought up the case of the Rodney King beating, and the subsequent beating of the truck driver during the ensuing riots in Los Angeles. Another student brought up the Jeffrey Dahmer case. All his victims were minorities.

"I wonder if the police would have returned that last Asian boy to Dahmer if the kid was White and Dahmer was the minority." Larry's comment surprised everyone.

An animated discussion on many "what ifs" followed. I sat back and listened. Their logic was, I thought, beyond their years.

My eighth graders have read their novels. The discussions, writings, and responses to literature in the format I established for the research dramatically changed our class.

Our feelings are still somewhat coarse, our nerves still exposed. These kids no longer tiptoe around issues of race. In many cases, the issue of race became the stated reason for even the most inconsequential verbal exchanges. Unfortunately, the following type of conversation became quite common in our classroom:

"Let me have a pen."

"Don't have another one."

"You won't let me have one 'cause I'm White. You think I should have my own pen. If I were Black, you'd lend me one. You're a racist."

"I don't care what color you are, girlfriend, I ain't got another pen."

"Why," I asked Nancy's literature circle a few days later, "haven't you ever discussed how these racial differences bothered you before?"

"They always were there, Mrs. Gemmati," she answered, "we just never acted on what we thought."

"Explain."

"It's like how do you act in church? Or in a library? Or when your mamma has company over? You don't act the same as when someone's there watching you, or when you're home and your mamma ain't there."

I knew exactly what she meant. I've become very sensitive about bringing up issues in class that could eventually lead to further rifts among what I once thought was a close-knit group of kids. Ignorance seems to be bliss and safe, but can I truly affect the lives of my students by reciting pre-rehearsed lines on a make-believe stage? Do I want to defer these discussions of race and prejudice to dark alleys that are constantly punctuated by the sound of gunfire? Do I let the neighborhood children continue to be steeped in the smog of superiority that is so choking and prevalent? It was an armor of racism that my students had been dressed in during their years of upbringing, one that was difficult to dent. I did find clues, hints maybe, that the confusion, frustration, and ordeal of adolescence was bleeding into another issue—the questioning of their parents' beliefs about different nationalities, races, and religions. As the year progressed, they wrote in their journals:

"I don't know how long he's (Dad's) felt that way [about others], but lots of things he grew up with ain't even around anymore. The movies ain't a dollar, and damn ain't considered a swear word."

"So what if I bring home someone who isn't Black. If that person loves me and respects me and doesn't do me wrong, why should I refuse him for a Brother who sells on the corner and is a player?"

"Why does she (Mom) call them rag heads? God, that pisses me off. How would she of felt if her Jewish grandfather married another Jew instead of her grandma? She isn't the puritanical Protestant she acts on Sunday all the rest of the week."

"I don't care if my dad says we have to stick to our own. If someone doesn't try to move into more decent places and show other people we ain't the loud and dirty Spics they say we are, how are they going to know different? Someone has to cross over to other neighborhoods and show that we want the same things they do."

The year was ending and I still did not feel closure with my students on these issues of prejudice. Their attitudes were shifting but their sense of one another was still fragile. I believed that the children felt this way too.

We were slated to go on the eighth-grade school trip to Washington, and after our difficult year, the trip began to seem more of a necessity than an option. A few days away from school, parents, teachers, books, and students in other grades seemed like the perfect cure for what felt like a nagging cough. I figured if we didn't bond after being on a bus for umpteen hours and sharing sleeping quarters, there would be no hope.

Interestingly, the tension seemed to dissipate the farther we got from Chicago. As some kids dozed off, others left their groups to form new ones with those who remained awake. We talked about everything and nothing. The boundaries that identified us as people from specific places and with distinct roles got fuzzier and fuzzier. By the time we reached Philadelphia, we seemed to be one group of people, from Chicago, eager to spend uncurfewed time with one another. We cared about each other's luggage, comfort, and likes. We cared.

The tours of Washington were important, yes, and of course educational. But what I was looking at was more than the monuments that mark our country's growth. I was seeing in my students the behavior that is displayed when children are allowed to follow their basic friendly instincts—without worrying about approval or criticisms of who they speak to or who they hang around with.

On the last night before our long bus ride back to Chicago, my student teacher came banging on my door late at night. She was on the verge of hysteria, and it was a good long minute before she could inform me that a group of the kids had not returned to their rooms yet. She had fallen asleep and some of the kids had sneaked out. Just as I was about to dial the hotel security, Melissa ran into my room yelling that Nancy wouldn't answer the door, no matter how hard she banged on it. I dropped the phone and hurried down the hall. I yelled, I screamed, I kicked, but no one answered the door. I had my student teacher run down to the lobby to get a master key. I shuddered as the security guard opened the door.

The scene inside the room was incredible. Pop cans and popcorn were scattered everywhere, the TV was blaring, and about 15 of my students were asleep fully clothed, minus their shoes, which were piled up in a corner, fermenting. The kids were in an array of sleeping positions. Multicolored legs and arms were tangled everywhere. Nancy slowly opened her eyes and saw Shelly, Larry, Joe, and Maria sleeping on the same bed she had happened to crash on. Slowly they started to waken. They looked around and seemed surprised to find themselves in such a noisy, overcrowded room, with their teacher and a security guard standing in the doorway. I started laughing. Freddy took one look at my faded Garfield sleeping shirt, my one sockless foot and tangle of hair and he started laughing. Pretty soon everyone was giggling at someone's sock, pointing at whomever with their thumb in their mouth, the drool coming from a half-open mouth, the weird look of half-closed eyes or disheveled hair.

The security guard looked at us as if we were truly nuts. "These your kids, Miss?"

"Yep," I answered. "Each and every one of them."

I would be lying to myself if I pretended to be the teacher I was before I had initiated this project. If anything, this research has taught me that hard talk on candid issues can take place within the safety of classroom walls. I know that a society that is free of prejudice is many, many years away, but it's something I hope to keep striving for—even if it's only in the microcosm of life that constitutes my classroom.

CHAPTER 4

What I'd Tell a White Gal: What My Black Male Students Taught Me About Race and Schooling

Eileen Shakespear

DEE: I mean just in general, you know what I'm saying . . . I got to get this out. I was on the train, you know what I'm saying, coming to school. I was hooded up, had on my sunglasses, and stuff like that. You know what I'm saying. And the train was crowded, and this old White lady got on the train. So everybody just looking at her, you know what I'm saying, and nobody ain't offering to give up their seats or nothing. So me, having respect for my elders, I'm a get up and let her sit down. When I get up and let her sit down, she going to get up? No, she gonna say, "No I'm not going for it." She gonna say, "I don't want your seat, you can sit back down." And I thought *I* was stupid because everybody looking at me on the train like *I* did something wrong, because I was the only Black man on the train. So everybody was all, you know what I'm saying. That's when they stop conversating. And she's going to tell me that I don't want your seat.

ANDRÉ: What do you think she meant by "I ain't going for it?"

DEE: I think she meant, like, I don't know, to be honest, I don't know. I think she was just discriminating against me because of my color. Because this other White man had got up, and he offered to give her a seat, you know what I'm saying, and she took that. But when I offered it to her, she didn't.

What do I, Dee's teacher, take from this simple story? First, I think about what Dee's day at school must have been like. Could he hear me that day in humanities class? Could he hear me any day? Was his experience of White people hostile enough that learning from me, having a close productive relationship with a White teacher, was impossible? Second, I think about the other people on the train. What were they communicating to him by their sudden silence, by their failure to ally with this young Black man? What were they teaching him, what were they teaching each other? Third, I think about myself. Would I have said the comforting word? Would I have just looked back down at my newspaper? Fourth, I think about the influence on my life of many young Black men like Dee. What have I taught them? What have I learned from them?

I offer Dee's story because it pushes into the central issue of my study. What can I observe about the relationship between Black male students and White female teachers that can inform classroom practice? When I tell other educators about my research question, I get responses that range from "Excellent" to "Hmmm . . .?" to "Who gave you *that* question?" I say of course, "Well, me, I picked it myself." They make me wonder, however, why I did pick that question. Usually I respond to myself, "Because it's there; it's so plainly there," and that satisfies me.

I can enumerate other reasons too. First, education happens in relationships, so shouldn't we study those relationships? Teachers intuitively know that. Second, I ask, For whose sake are we engaged in this thinking and in this practice of teaching? It is primarily for our students' sake. The intellectual welfare of kids is, I think, mainly what schools are for, and it is what I have chosen as my life work. I need to know what's good for my students and what's not, even if the answers shed harsh light on my own hard work.

Questions about teaching people well who are "not like you" are contained for me in a deeper but simpler question about valuing, what I like to call seeing someone: peering into his or her eyes and feeling a touch of human affirmation, very sweet and clear; thinking, yes, I see you in there; yes, I like that; it's a pleasure to see you in there.

Holocaust survivor and biblical scholar Elie Wiesel inspired me to think about seeing better in my own work in a speech he gave in 1985 at Boston University. In explaining why he opened his lecture with a local rabbi, Rabbi Pollack, telling his own childhood story, he said:

> I wanted you students to realize that there are in your midst people
> and you see them and say, "Well they are people just like other people
> who smile, who laugh, who tell jokes, who teach, who drive home, who
> eat bread, chocolate, or candy; and you don't realize that they have sto-
> ries to tell, such stories, that if they were to be known, people would
> tremble." Therefore, when you look at them, think twice what ques-
> tions to ask, what stories you would like them to tell, why certain ges-
> tures appear clumsy, why certain words carry special meaning . . .
> *Look better.* The idea of teaching this subject, of telling these stories, is
> to *sensitize* people that you should become more sensitive to yourself,
> to your parents, to your friends, to strangers. (Wiesel, speech at Boston
> University, April 22, 1985)

How does Wiesel's story relate to my subject here? In more than two decades of teaching, I have heard over and over again from African American kids stories of painful early years in school, of insults, of childhood isolation, of being too much noticed for their color, of being left unchallenged intellectually, of being followed in stores, of being cursed at and pushed by police, of having their mothers embarrassed by store clerks, of being stopped for no cause while driving, of not being waited on at department stores or car dealers, of others being intimidated by their presence in an enclosed space or even on the sidewalk, and on and on.

These common everyday experiences of racism my students have related to me are important to listen to for the underlying suspicion and distrust they suggest. These are some of the "White" experiences kids may have in their heads when they meet me. I need to hear these stories so I know where I'm starting from with individual kids. It is also important for White teachers to recognize how free we are from those negative experiences and thus how different our experience of "color" is from that of our non-White students.

In the op-ed page in any city newspaper, anti-Black anecdotes like those I listed above will be detailed and dutifully criticized by a columnist every few weeks. However, because of their drama, front-page stories about inner-urban thuggery will probably predominate in the newspaper and in our imaginations. I believe that White people are influenced by the media, by their own upbringing, by their peers, by their education, and by our nation's history toward racist feelings and attitudes. These feelings are deep and hidden, and no White teacher should be surprised to have them. Teachers won't comfort their students of color by telling them they are not racist. Any White teacher who reads this and says, "Well, I'm *not* a racist," should utter as her next sentence, "Well, I'm not a realist." White teachers don't have to feel guilty about being influenced by thousands of years of history and conditioning, but we do have to accept the importance of that influence to both ourselves and to our students and we have an obligation to be as honest and as self-reflective as possible around issues of race. The point of all this listening and watching, as Wiesel says, is to sensitize us so that we can really see our individual kids.

MY TEACHING

I've been teaching in the Boston public schools for 25 years. I am of Irish descent. My very British last name comes from my husband, who is Argentine. In my career I have taught over 2,000 students. In the beginning of my career, before court-ordered desegregation in Boston, most of my students were Whites of Irish, Italian, and Greek descent. Gradually, across the years, my classes have become increasingly African American, and Caribbean/Hispanic American.

I spent my first 13 years teaching sixth to eighth graders; now I teach in a pilot school called Fenway High School, which at the time of my research was called Fenway Middle High School College and was on the campus of Bunker Hill Community College in Boston. Fenway is part of the Boston public school system and is a member of the Coalition of Essential Schools. The 250 kids who come to Fenway come for 250 different reasons—because of failure elsewhere, because they want to escape schools that they feel are too large and impersonal, because they are seeking our unusual brand of academic challenge.

Routine discipline problems are less pronounced than they would be in other larger, more impersonal high schools. Problems that do arise are also easier to confront because Fenway is so small and because the community college setting removes a lot of the pressure to be bad that a large high school can create.

The college also has rich, well-supervised facilities that allow me to harness some of the natural restlessness of youth by offering variety, choice, and independence in students' intellectual work. What this really means is that I don't have to keep my students quiet, orderly, and inside a room all period, every day. Having flexibility with support is a great relief for most kids, but it's difficult to provide in many junior high and high school settings, especially in schools that use rigidity as an antidote to disorder.

I also want to note that, though the focus of my research is heavy with heart, the ultimate result has to push through to the mind. Teaching urban kids is an intellectual mission. No one else will ever again teach our students ninth-grade English, or health, or woodworking, or algebra. Teachers must achieve personal relationships with students that are healthy. But we can't do only that. We have to teach our discipline well, too, because we are the only ones who are assigned that job.

When I taught junior high I had a wonderful principal, Gene Ellis, whose faculty motto was "Teach the child as if he were your own." That phrase resonated for me before I had my own son and rang like church bells afterwards. Returning to Fenway after more than a year of maternity leave, I stood to speak, perched high over a sea of grown-up children, all sitting murmuring, heads bobbing, below me on the spotless carpets in our chairless new classroom. When they came to order and all together looked up at me with first-day-of-school silence, I thought exactly this: "My God, look at all these babies!" They were so young, and their faces were each so fragile and full of hope and babylike beauty.

I started then and continue to say to myself often: "Would today be a good day for my son? Would what happened in this room today be something I'd want my son to experience?" This standard makes me ask the hard questions with kids, to expose the emotion and the complexity in issues that I sometimes want to present quickly and simplistically. It makes me push my students to respect the difficulty of a worthy task, so that they do what I would want my son to do: read, write, and research a lot, accumulate knowledge, reason well, make interesting things, and find beauty. I wouldn't want my boy to experience a day on racism or even volcanoes when everything is wrapped up in a few hours with a short-answer test at the end. I wouldn't want my son to go to a school that isn't clean or peaceful. I wouldn't want my son's skills to develop to less than his potential. So too I don't want that for my students.

For me, then, teaching well means that I ask, "Is this good enough for my child?" For certain classes and students in some years, I will answer no too often. But in other years I'll regularly answer yes. That is the way that serious and honest teaching goes. Some kids will not grow with me because of work I'm not doing well enough; or I will enrich the intellectual lives of others because of work I'm doing very well. But I can't step up to do any of it unless I see and love the individual child and expect great things from each of them. Conducting this research project gave me another lens through which I could see my students, another way to gain the knowledge I need to reach this standard with my students more often.

MY RESEARCH METHODS

To answer my research question, which was originally focused on relationships between Black male students and White female teachers, I took notes and wrote journal entries to reflect on my own day-to-day practice. I also interviewed André, a Black male student whom I believed to be particularly insightful. André conducted group interviews with five other Black male students, all of whom I knew would do some strong thinking about this topic. Then, I interviewed two White female teachers who I and others thought were particularly successful with their Black male students.

In the end, I focused my analysis on my own journal reflections, my interview with André, and André's interviews with the other Black male students, because I felt that these data were simply extraordinary. These interviews, where the young men sat down together and talked freely about race and schooling, changed my research. I had not originally planned for the students to meet independently to discuss these issues, but André convinced me that this was necessary. He explained that when he and other African American students met on their own and discussed issues of race, he had observed that they often vented their anger toward Whites before they analyzed the issues. He reflects on his feelings and the group conversation at a meeting with the other Black males he interviewed for this research:

> ANDRÉ: I have a lot of anger in me but . . . I'm not vicious with it. . . .
> There's time when we [Black kids] get around each other that we
> really get vicious [toward Whites], but then by the end of the meeting, we calm down, and we really start to shape that and say, "OK,
> we're mad. We're pissed off. And no, it's not all their [Whites']
> fault." But in the beginning it's like, "Yeah, look at this. Look at
> that." I mean really serious, bringing down facts, bringing books,
> and saying, "Here, look at this, look at this; this is what they've
> done." Then we draw away from that and say, "Yeah, we accepted
> the drugs. We started doing this. We started doing that." And then
> taking some of that blame for ourselves. And then by the end of
> the meeting, we start to shape it.
> EILEEN: And you think that has to be kind of a family thing?
> ANDRÉ: It has to because if you're there, we can't . . . because we respect you, and that's why you can have someone who is such a rebel, like B in your class, and she doesn't come off like she does
> when we have our own meetings in our home. Because she gets vicious. And in your class, because she respects you, she doesn't
> blow off like she usually does. That's out of respect. So if we had
> you there, we couldn't really get out all of our feelings, and we
> need to get out all our feelings, but then we must shape them at
> the end.

André's point about respect gave me a new angle from which to view my students' hesitancy to talk with me about these issues. In a sense they don't want to share with me because I'm White, and I wouldn't get it, but they also don't want to insult me because, though I'm White, I am also *me* and I might be hurt.

Through André's influence, then, I was afforded the rare opportunity to listen in on an open and uninhibited exchange among Black male students. Their conversation—because it explores more general issues of race as well as relationships between teachers and students of color—broadened the focus of my study beyond the scope of my original research question. In this chapter I identify patterns that I saw in these conversations and reflect on their meaning, but essentially, my goal is to invite others to eavesdrop with me—and, in so doing, to gain insight from the experiences these young men relate. My hope is that their conversation might spark a larger conversation about how to make schooling work for young African American men that I think should be going on across the country.

WHAT I LEARNED

In my 25 years of teaching, I have known dozens and dozens of Black boys who say they don't care about school and thinking and learning; who say they don't care about a friend who betrayed them or about an enemy who was killed, or a girl who rejected them, or a baby they don't see anymore; who say they don't care about the soul or love or anything. I have known virtually no one who really meant it. I always believed that these students' pride and posturing held them back from showing emotion and from asking for the help that they really did want. André's interview with the five young men, which was "straight up and raw," as one student dubbed it, confirmed my belief. The interview revealed their rich humor, their anger, their well-told memories, and their advice. These young Black men whom André interviewed all yearned to be seen as normal and worthy people who could do work with caring adults from any background. They also yearned for positive experiences with each other and with other African American adults, especially with grown men.

From all the interviews, my first finding was that these students believe that schools and teachers, both Black and White but especially White, will "mess you up," one way or the other. The interviewed Black male students' experiences of elementary school were overwhelmingly negative. André told of one such experience in his interview with me:

> I was there and I was real ill, because this lady, she was a substitute teacher. . . snatched something from me. And we was all tugging at it. I went to school with all the Castlegates [powerful local gang] and we was all tugging. And she fell. And when she got up, everyone pushed her, and she fell over the other banister. Then it was in my records that I did it. So every teacher that came there, they were afraid of me. So they wouldn't teach me at all. They *would not* teach me. It was like, "Don't worry about it. Here's your seat in the back. You can lounge, do whatever you want to, and when the bell rings, we'll march you on." It was like I never missed a day of school, and I didn't learn anything [*laughter*].
>
> I still tried and tried, and then I just gave up. I hated to write, and I hated to read because I read too slow, so forget it. Then I went to middle school, and I was in Project Promote. I went to school on Saturday. That's when I really started to come out a little. I had a White

teacher, Mr. X, who really started helping me. Also I think too that was where, "Okay, he's deprived. Let me help him too." It was always that. Whenever White people help me, I feel that a lot of times it's because either they're trying to get rid of me, or, "He's poor, underprivileged youth, Black youth, and he's not going to do anything, so I can help him right now." Either they feel sorry for you or they don't deal with you. . . . In elementary school they teach you that two letters come together and it makes a different sound, and I never learned that. So, I would learn words before I learned how to spell them. I could use everything, but I just couldn't spell it, so I couldn't write it. So I never learned that. I just skipped over it. The writing process, I just skipped over it. In elementary school I felt that I was the dumbest kid there was ever going to be. I never realized it [my intelligence] and it took pimps and pushers to tell me because I didn't respect anyone else. I was hanging out with them. . . . It got to the point where they were saying, "Man it's time to grow. Stop hanging with us man. I hear you talk to people. You're good." And they were the old men. That meant something to me, that they thought I was intelligent. . . . I started to believe them a little.

I am often shocked to find that a very sharp student like André, who has no apparent learning disability, spent several years in separate special education classrooms in elementary school, and learned more from street hustlers than teachers. Several interviewed students remembered harried, mainly White adults, coping with their early disassociation and their acting out by getting rid of them, not by counseling them or pushing them to cope with their anger or their rambunctiousness.

Moreover, several students harbored deep resentment about the inaction of elementary school White adults when they acted out or were hurt. They were saddened by the lack of Black teachers; most often these young males missed older Black men in their elementary school lives. They were saddened as well by the lack of protection from the Black teachers they had had and by the distance they felt between their own experiences and those of these teachers. Marcus describes his understanding of the attitudes of his past Black teachers: "It's like, 'I made my PhD. I spent four years, and if I can do it, you can do it too.'" He then exclaims, "Don't even give me that nonsense!" According to Marcus, these teachers had little idea of what would be involved for someone like him to reach their level.

My second finding was that my Black male students felt that their knowledge was not honored and that useful history was not taught to them in school. Schools "mess you up," these young men believed, by closing them off from knowledge and dialogue. In one of the group discussions with

André, Kino told about the time his cousin Dakar, who lived in Boston, came to visit him when he lived in Virginia. Dakar attended Kino's history class and challenged the White male teacher's knowledge; he was dismissed as a liar and troublemaker. The history teacher, said Kino,

> made it seem like the White man was everything, and I was sitting there just listening. I never thought twice about it. But then my cousin Dakar came down from Boston, and he had knowledge. We were sitting side by side, and the teacher starts talking about the Egyptians, and he said there was slaves and slavery even before the Egyptians. The Egyptians enslaved their people and everything. So Dakar raises his hand and he says, "Sir, I think you're giving false information."
>
> He [the teacher] says, "What are you saying?"
>
> Dakar says, "You're making it seem like the way the Egyptians slaved was the same way that the White man slaved." He said, "First of all they [Egyptian slaves] didn't get slashed across their backs like the Whites [in the United States slashed their slaves], like they show on the movies and everything. They [Egyptian slaves] got paid, with food, whatever, and when the pyramids were built, they were set free, so that's not really slavery."
>
> So he [the teacher] was saying, "No, I think you have false information."
>
> Dakar says, "No, I can bring in documents and everything to prove what I'm saying right now."
>
> He said, "Are you trying to act up? What are you trying to say? Get out of my classroom."
>
> When I seen that, I was like, "Oh my God." . . .
>
> Then after class everybody wanted to talk to Dakar about what he was talking about. So when we was talking about it, he says, "You've got to watch out for these White teachers." He really hipped me to the fact that these White teachers ain't out there for me.

Two important points come up in this excerpt. One is the challenge in Dakar's assertion; he—a visitor to the class—is challenging the authority of the teacher to claim he has the right knowledge. Dakar's challenge is posed publicly and accusingly, so the teacher's defensiveness is disappointing but not surprising. The incident shows Dakar essentially bursting in on the teacher's party, perhaps because he found no avenue for intellectual inquiry, no place to pose his question, or add his knowledge. Kids don't have to do that when they're used to thinking along with a teacher and when they're encouraged to ask divergent questions. I can't imagine a history class that is open to inquiry in which a student isn't at some point going either to say something with which I disagree, or to claim to have evidence to dispute my thinking. I assume from the start that that's going to happen. Then, when it does, my role is to help my students explore their thinking by helping them gather scholarly evidence to support their points. My role is not to shoot the student down even if I know I can. Dakar's idea is disputable and may be wrong. That's not the point. Even as a visitor to this classroom, Dakar needed his idea to be responded to intellectually, not personally. To respond to his contribution doesn't mean the teacher would say, "Oh yeah, you're right, and I'm wrong." Rather, the teacher might say, "What you say is interesting. Let's check it out. How do you know that?"

The other point is the way Kino uses the word *knowledge*. When Kino says about Dakar, "And he had knowledge," he means both that Dakar is knowledgeable in general and that he had specific knowledge about the richness of African experience, a kind of secret knowledge that is left out of school and schoolbooks. All of the young Black men interviewed talk about this latter "knowledge" with extreme respect, almost awe. It's a knowledge that has, as André expresses, the power to transform his life. It's not a knowledge that he wants examined by outsider White people or unenlightened Black people. There's a sense that this knowledge will get him into trouble and that exposing it in school will somehow taint it. In the same vein, some of the interviewed Black male students voiced concern that there was a White conspiracy to keep them ignorant.

My third finding is that the interviewed students felt that Black and White teachers thought about them differently. Here André reflects on those differences:

ANDRÉ: To really be honest a lot of times Black teachers do [push us more] but we as Black students don't see. We always see them as being harder on us. I had a Black teacher named Miss Z over at B High. She was a science teacher she was really tough, but she really respected what you said. And we always thought that she was the mean woman, and we could never get along with her. But right down the hall we had White teachers who didn't really respect our thinking. It was just like, "You do it because I say that it's right." And in some way we gave them more respect than we did Miss Z.

EILEEN: Can you say why that might have been?

ANDRÉ: On one level it's because there's no threat there, where Miss Z she's trying to get us to respect ourselves and stimulate us to think about things, and we see that as her just trying to come down hard on us. . . . A lot of times I see Black teachers push Black people more than a White teacher will. . . . If it's someone I can do okay with, and it seems like I'm doing good, then I'll like them.

EILEEN: Can you reflect a little bit on why the White teacher might not push?

ANDRÉ: Some just don't care, and that's just the ones who are burnt out. A lot of them feel like the students are not going to do anything. "I'm doing my job for now, and then they're gone and that's it." Some of them who really don't push because they think . . . "I'm putting them where they can be. I'm following them and not thinking that they're more intelligent than what they're doing." Last year I remember reading three books tops the whole year. I think our teachers were like, "This is all that they can handle." And really that isn't. . . . I think that sometimes White teachers just think that Black students, "We gotta look at them differently." I mean you don't get that at Don Bosco [a local Catholic boy's school]. That's like the difference.

EILEEN: Do you think that White teachers might think the kids are too delicate, that if you push too hard they might fall apart whereas a Black teacher would have more sense of like she has a child herself and . . . ?

ANDRÉ: Definitely. A Black teacher says they must be pushed because they're going to be pushed all their lives, and they'll just get them ready for that. Where a White teacher says that well I don't want to push because they may break, or they might rebel, or they might just leave. Not really thinking like . . . They're being pushed every day. . . . They're having more pressure on them than you can ever apply on them in school right at home. You couldn't push them any harder than the streets are pushing them. I think Black teachers realize that.

Several of the other young men told stories of neglect caused by low expectations. André described his vision of what he would want from teachers for his twin baby boys as they enter school:

You must teach them. They're not going to skip the basic things like I did. My mother grew up in the South, and her parents taught her whatever they were given. That was good enough, and that's what she got. . . . I think my sons should go in there asking for the world.

Someday, any one of us may teach André's children when they are young men. It is crucial that we accept our responsibility for seeing and nurturing them as loved children. I wouldn't expect less from any adult working with my son. Even given all the complex pressures on teenagers, I wouldn't want my son's teachers to accept inadequate intellectual work. Indeed, if he faced dilemmas as complex as those some of my young Black male students confront, I would want him to do even better intellectual work, so he would be better equipped to conquer the difficulties of his life.

Our ability to understand issues of race and to "look better," especially to see through the cloud of fear and negativity that surrounds young Black men such as André, Kino, Dakar, and Dee, to illuminate the core, the highly valuable self inside, is a difficult but essential ability if we are going to be strong teachers for all our students. We are not unaffected by the stories that form this cloud of negativity, but we can be vigilant in our resistance to generalizing from them. Ultimately, these stories need not prevent us from seeing each of our African American male students, or from hearing the other stories, the other side, "my" side, the kids might say, a side that is largely hidden. The Black male students in this study gave me a glimpse into this other side, and, having learned from them, I realize how I need to continue to find creative ways to hear my students' stories, to see them more fully. As teachers, we can't give students the world, but we can use what we learn about our students to work with them as they sculpt for themselves intellectual lives that are solid and full, strong and constructive.

CHAPTER 5

What Teacher Researchers Say About Seeing Beyond Stereotypes

Sarah Warshauer Freedman, with Walter Wood, George Austin, Brenda Landau McFarland, and Phil Potestio

LIKE DIAZ-GEMMATI AND Shakespear in Chapters 3 and 4, the four M-CLASS teachers featured in this chapter used teacher research to see their students, themselves, their classrooms, or all of these in new and unexpected ways. Walter Wood interviewed students with frequent absences to determine why they missed so much school. In the process he saw how distant his stable, White, middle-class upbringing and assumptions were from the worlds his students inhabited. Wood also learned about his students' pressing needs for recognition, positive attention, and understanding.

George Austin, himself an African American, took a new look at his African American student Lateisha, who was stereotyped by the tracking system for the history classes at Austin's school. Although Austin began his research opposed to tracking and knowledgeable about its deleterious effects on students, he found that even his vision was clouded by its stereotyping. Using his research findings as a basis for action, Austin was pushed through his experience with Lateisha to confront the effects of tracking and to challenge this deeply entrenched institutional structure.

History teacher Brenda Landau McFarland examined her students' relationships to the power structures that undergird this country. Through her research, she came to understand why her students felt disenfranchised in ways that she never felt as a young African American coming of age during the civil rights movement of the 1960s. She crossed both generational and political boundaries as she reshaped her curriculum to teach her students what they might gain by participating in rather than isolating themselves from the power structures that affected their current lives as well as their future social and academic choices.

In a different kind of setting, Phil Potestio, also a history teacher, is a White male working in a school that is less than 1% White. Ironically, however, Potestio had an advantage over the other teachers in this chapter with respect to getting to know his students; he was in his 2nd year of teaching most of them and thus had had more opportunity to learn about them and their social and academic needs. He began his research already understanding a great deal about the pressures his students faced. Thus, for his research he was able to work with them to design a curriculum tailored specifically to their interests and needs. Through this process, he learned even more about them and was able to reshape his teaching ideas in response to what he learned. Potestio shows how teachers need not only to see at specific moments, but to continue to look, and to do classroom research that will help them re-see, from varied angles and points of view.

SEEING BEYOND STEREOTYPES OF SOCIAL CLASS: WALTER WOOD

In an effort to gain information about his students' attendance problems, Walter Wood interviewed six students who were in danger of failing because of high absenteeism. He was puzzled because he felt that all six of these students were competent and capable of doing passing work and because he did not understand why they did not attend school.

The Boston school district tried to deal with absenteeism by requiring homeroom teachers to call students' parents or guardians when they were absent. These telephone calls were intended to encourage better attendance. Although his calls made little difference, they gave Wood a glimpse into how different his students' lives were from his own:

> I met many dead ends. Phones were disconnected. Numbers were changed to unlisted numbers. Sometimes there was no answer at home, whether I called during the day or in the evening. One time I called a student's home and found out that I had reached a homeless shelter. The person at the shelter told me that she had not seen that student or any member of his family for more than 2 weeks. This number, however, was the only number that the school had. When the student finally returned to school, I got the number of a grandmother. Later, when the student was absent again, I called the grandmother. The grandmother told me that she had no way to contact her daughter, the student's mother, but if the daughter called in the next few days she would relay the message.

Wood's other way of seeing across social-class boundaries into his students' lives, the one-on-one interviews, taught him even more. The power of his students' stories showed him the complexity of their lives. Although he was aware of the troubles of students, having taught for many years, he was shaken when confronted with the concrete details that the students described as keeping them from attending school. These included unstable or difficult housing situations (overcrowding, frequent moves, parents unable to cope and kicking children out, placement in shelters), difficulty in getting transportation to school, troubles with the law resulting from past gang involvement.

STUDENTS' STORIES

By Walter Wood

Diana has to share a room with her 3-year-old sister, who doesn't sleep much at night. Diana said, "My little sister acts as if she has termites. She is always moving." Her other brothers and sisters play stereos and watch TV, and the walls are very thin. Diana said, "I'm not going to get up at 5:30 a.m. every day. Teachers don't understand. I can't fall asleep at 9:30. Also, we have to wait in line to take a shower and I can't get out of the house."

Marlon explained to me that he was on probation for assault and battery and armed robbery. The incident took place 3 years ago. Marlon told me that he was a gang member back then and that he and four other members were arrested and received probation. He still has 6 more months to go on his probation.

Marlon also had a problem in school that upset his probation officer. Marlon brought a knife to school, and it fell out of his pocket. He had to spend two weeks at the Barron Counseling Center for possession of a weapon in school. This incident also caused his mother to kick him out of her home.

The Department of Social Services has found Marlon a shelter to live in temporarily in Hyde Park. He plans to live there for about a month and a half. He does not plan to go back to his mother. Marlon's father lives in another city, Brockton, with his new wife and her two daughters. His father is trying to get custody of Marlon so that Marlon can live with him.

Marlon's mother is trying to prevent his father from getting custody. She doesn't want Marlon to return to her home, but she is in court trying to prevent her ex-husband from getting custody because of alleged abuse some years back. Marlon has been trying to deal with this while living in a shelter. Marlon's attendance is suffering because he is living across town and is frustrated trying to get to South Boston from Hyde Park. Marlon seems to be losing the year at this point.

Many of Yolanda's absences had to do with her family moving to Boston from New York City. Two weeks after Yolanda enrolled, she and her family drove back to New York to pick up some furniture that they had left behind. Their car broke down, and they were stuck in New York for a week while the car was being repaired. In addition to this disruption, Yolanda moved from Dorchester to Roxbury and back to Dorchester again during the first term. She even had trouble finding the right buses to get to school because of all these moves.

Wood learned that his students desperately wanted to succeed in school. All of those he interviewed told him that they wanted to graduate from high school, and all the girls expressed a desire to go to college. However, in every case, the forces working against them were too powerful for them to will away, although most continued to fight. By the next year, of the six students he had interviewed, two had dropped out of school. The other four remained, including Diana, Marlon, and Yolanda. These three, however, showed no improvement in school attendance, although they all kept the hope that their lives would change, and they all said they believed that they would somehow find a way to come to school more often in the future.

By doing his research, Wood realized how much there was to learn about his students' lives:

> Before I did this investigation I had a vague idea that my students had difficulties at home and in the neighborhood and that this affected their attendance and attitudes about school. Now, because I listened to each of their stories in detail, I have a better understanding of the obstacles that they have to overcome to be successful in school. These obstacles are great and, for some, insurmountable. What was simple and straightforward to me growing up, that is, coming to school every day on time, is not as simple and straightforward to them.

Wood also saw how anxious his students were to talk to him, and was reminded how much it mattered to them that a teacher cared and understood: "This exercise also brought home to me something that I already knew; but I needed a reminder. It is important for the teacher to make a personal connection to the student."

Wood vowed in the coming school year to focus on building personal connections with his students, both in homeroom and in his English classes. He concluded his writing with his hope that "if that connection is made early enough, maybe I can make a difference to someone." A vague knowledge of their difficulties was not enough; seeing his students' lives in detail, he felt, could provide some keys to helping them. Wood knew his work was only a first step, something he could do as a teacher. He also knew what he could do, although something, would be inadequate. To be really effective, teachers like Wood ideally would serve as one link in a coordinated network of social support, based both within the school and the community. Wood's research did point out quite clearly the woeful inadequacy of the school's current response to absenteeism, merely mandatory phone calls from homeroom teachers to families.

SEEING BEYOND INSTITUTIONAL STEREOTYPES: GEORGE AUSTIN

Unexpected circumstances allowed George Austin to see how his schools' tracking policies obscured his vision of his students. Lateisha, who is African American, moved from Austin's mostly non-White average-tracked history class to his mostly White accelerated class. Through his research, Austin closely observed her changing behavior, his changing reactions, and their changing interactions. He explains: "I first met her in the fall of 1992, but it has taken me nearly a year and a half to view our relationship within the context of tracking."

LATEISHA SWITCHES TRACKS

By George Austin

On the first day of school, in my average-tracked class, I went around the room asking students to identify themselves and say a few words. When I got to Lateisha, an African American female, she volunteered an unsolicited, "I don't want to study about no White people's history."

Time froze as the eyes of all the other students seemed to focus on me and just how I was going to respond to Lateisha's opening challenge. My reply was, "History belongs to no one group of people." I didn't particularly want to engage in an open debate of the teaching of history from a Eurocentric versus an Afrocentric perspective on the first day of class.

Over the next few months, my relationship with Lateisha could best be described as antagonistic. We clashed over nearly everything. She frequently came to class after the tardy bell rang. She held ancillary conversations with other students while I talked. My impression was that Lateisha was disrespectful to me and all that she thought that I represented. She let me know that I was just another middle-class Black man to whom she couldn't relate, while I saw her as an intentionally belligerent and disruptive student.

I began to get a different sense of Lateisha near the end of the first semester. It began with a conversation I had with Carol, Lateisha's homeroom teacher. Carol explained that her analysis of Lateisha's defiant attitude was that she was extremely bright, but that she was dealing with some self-esteem issues. She further explained that Lateisha was going to be placed in honors English and that she probably should have been placed in a high-tracked history class. On this latter point I had some disagreement, but I kept silent and listened further as the germ of an idea began to take shape.

I became intrigued with the idea of getting Lateisha out of my class. I decided to pay her counselor a visit to lobby for Lateisha to be transferred to a higher level history class. My main goal was getting her moved; I didn't care where they moved her as long as it was out of my second-period class. In retrospect, I know that I should have tried some intervention strategy to reach Lateisha. But I didn't. Perhaps I found her too intimidating. Whatever the reason, the die was cast.

I was truly ill prepared for what was to happen about a week later when Lateisha walked into my third-period (high-tracked) class midway through the period. She had a smile on her face that lit up the whole room. "I'm here, Mr. Austin," she announced.

I honestly don't know what my facial expression revealed, but I certainly had a sinking feeling in the pit of my stomach as visions of Lateisha totally destroying the harmony of the class crept into my thoughts. Those thoughts turned out to be unfounded. Lateisha, at the end of her first day in the class, made a point of lingering after the bell to inquire about what specifically I had asked for in the homework.

I couldn't believe that these words were coming from a person who had previously told me, "I don't have to do the work if I don't want to. Calling my mother won't make me do it if I don't want to. It's my decision if I want to learn or not."

Lateisha settled easily in the class by quickly developing relationships with several other students. In comparison to how she had previously behaved, she became a model student. She raised her hand to participate in discussions and completed her assignments on time. The first time that she raised her hand and I called on her, I did experience a bit of déjà vu. We had just begun a unit on the Holocaust. Lateisha asked, "How come everybody always want to talk about how bad the Holocaust was, but they never say anything about slavery?" She was deadly earnest and got everyone's attention. I quickly surveyed the room and saw that a red-haired girl named Amy, sitting toward the back, was visibly upset.

Amy, one of the more outspoken people in the class, responded, "We're talking about the Holocaust, not slavery."

Lateisha, stubbornly undeterred, said, "Well, we should be talking about it."

"Let's deal with what's on the floor," I said, quickly jumping in to put out the fire. "What was the root cause of the Jewish Holocaust? U.S. slavery?"

"Hate," responded one student. "Greed," said another.

What followed was an honest comparison of slavery with the Jewish Holocaust, spurred by Lateisha's challenge.

Another example of how Lateisha added to the richness of the class occurred during a current events presentation by a fellow student, Daniel. Daniel, a White 15-year-old, lives with his mother and his stepfather. His father lives in Reno, Nevada, where he runs a casino. Daniel is close to his father and visits him regularly. Lateisha, responding to Daniel's presentation about the growing phenomenon of unwed mothers, blurted out, "All men are dogs, and they run away from their responsibilities and abandon their wives and children." She explained that this was the situation that she sees most of the time.

Daniel took offense. He related how much he respects his father, even though his parents got divorced. He also explained that his father takes an active interest in his welfare, both financially and otherwise. I don't know whether he convinced Lateisha to change her opinion, but I do know that she heard the pain and anger in his response. I certainly heard it.

Lateisha, as the one Black student in the class who was not used to traveling in the sheltered universe of the high tracks, added a new and different voice to the class, one that previously had not been heard. She spoke of personal experiences that were different from those of her classmates. Issues touching on race and culture and class now found a concrete context instead of appearing only in the abstract.

Lateisha, in turn, saw and heard things that she had previously been closed off from. She attended a class where students were supportive and practiced good academic skills. The very notion that she was going into a class where she was being valued as a student had a direct bearing on her self-perception and resultant behavior. She in as much as told me this directly in a recent conversation.

Perhaps best of all, my relationship with Lateisha began to change. I began to see her as outspoken rather than disruptive. Though we still disagreed in our opinions about some issues, such as the minister Farrakhan (she liked him; I didn't), we enjoyed a mutual respect that had been missing before.

Lateisha began spending time in my classroom at lunchtime and sometimes immediately after school and even asked me to write a letter recommending her to attend an after-school program. When I asked her if she was sure she wanted me to write the letter, she responded, "It's OK, Mr. Austin. We're cool now." We not only ended the year with a good feeling, but we continue to have a relationship even today.

In retrospect, I believe that Lateisha's change was directly related to issues of self-esteem. Initially being tracked into the average world history class added to her negative self-perception. I recently asked Lateisha to reflect on her experience of the past 2 years. She described how her transformation from a "straight-A student" to a "rebel" actually began to reach a crisis stage when she first arrived at El Cerrito. What I concluded from my experience with Lateisha is that she resented not being considered worthy enough to be placed into high-tracked classes; consequently, she acted out her frustration in the average-tracked class.

Lateisha's story led Austin to think about the other students he knows who have been harmed by the tracking system, particularly students of color. Lateisha, as one of only three African Americans in his high-tracked class, reminded Austin that the negative effects of tracking are distributed mostly to students of color, something that has been persistently well-documented in the academic literature (e.g., Brown, Carter, & Harris, 1978; England, Meier, & Fraga, 1988; Hilliard, 1988; Natriello, 1994; Oakes, 1985, 1995). In looking at his students' school records, Austin found that many students in his average class, usually students of color, met the same criteria for being placed in the accelerated class that justified White students' inclusion. At one point, the counseling office wanted to add a White student to his already overenrolled accelerated class. When Austin suggested that the student be placed in his underenrolled average class, just as so many of the students of color had been, the counselor replied, "Well, she needs an accelerated class." Austin concluded, "Unequivocally race was an issue." He describes the racial inequities in the different tracks at his school:

> The classes mirror each other in terms of ethnic representation (3
> Whites in a class of 33 in the average tracked class and 3 Blacks in a
> class of 37 in the high tracked class). In talking to my colleagues, I
> found this to be the overall pattern throughout the school in terms of
> tracked classes. While the school as a whole reflects the ethnic diversity
> of the area [approximately 55% African American, 30% White, 10%
> Asian American, and 5% Latino/Chicano], individual classrooms do
> not.

Tracking has been entrenched at Austin's school for many years, but teachers recently have begun to question the practice publicly and work to change it. El Cerrito English teacher Joan Cone has written several articles describing these efforts (see Cone, 1990, 1992, 1993). Austin hears the following belief expressed frequently around the school: "What quote unquote keeps our school its high standards are the kids who kinda float down from Kensington and El Cerrito hills." These kids are mostly middle class and White. If El Cerrito abolished tracking, the fear is that the affluent "hill kids" would leave. Austin notes, however, that this fear seems largely unfounded; the English department has significantly weakened its tracking system, and the school has not experienced changes in enrollment patterns. Because of the El Cerrito English department's strong and successful campaign against tracking, Austin concludes, "I think our English department is probably the most exciting department on campus" (site meeting, San Francisco, October 24, 1992).

Parents and teachers of students in the higher tracks generally argue that mixed-ability classes jeopardize the progress of the most gifted students, even though research indicates that gifted secondary students do equally well in tracked and nontracked classes (e.g., Slavin, 1990). Generally, these parents, mostly White and sometimes Asian and mostly middle class, and these teachers, mostly those with seniority and a record of success, have the strongest voices in the power hierarchy. Austin reports that these teachers fear, in spite of research to the contrary, that the needs of "higher ability" students cannot be met in mixed-ability classes. He finds that those in favor of tracking see only part of the picture, the "upper end"; they do not seem to see or care about the students on the "lower end," who are mostly students of color and whose needs are ill served in low-tracked classes. Austin's research suggests that all concerned must begin to look broadly at the whole picture.

In part because of Austin's research, his department began to experiment with abolishing tracking the following year. Austin was first in line to volunteer to teach one of the experimental, heterogeneously grouped, ninth-grade classes.

SEEING BEYOND POLITICAL, SOCIOECONOMIC, AND GENERATIONAL BOUNDARIES: BRENDA LANDAU McFARLAND

Brenda Landau McFarland came to see that many students in her African American history class, most of whom lived below the poverty level, were uninterested in exercising their democratic, political rights. They had no faith in the American power structure, including its news media and its political system. With her Black, middle-class orientation, she was surprised to learn how committed many of her African American students were to Black separatist ideologies. They felt none of the hope that Landau McFarland still felt, a hope nurtured by her 1960s political experiences in the civil rights movement and by her own life opportunities. Landau McFarland learned about her students' political leanings first through her analysis of their writing in their journals and then by listening carefully to classroom discussions. Her increased understanding of their points of view ultimately led her to reshape her curriculum.

Landau McFarland's journey began in mid-October of 1992, when 7-year-old Dantrell Davis, walking to school holding his mother's hand, was murdered by a sniper's bullet. The event took place in a Chicago housing project, Cabrini-Green, near Lake View High School on the North Side of Chicago, where Landau McFarland taught. Right after the murder, one of her Latino students, who did not live in the projects himself but who was angered by the media's response, wrote in his journal:

> As I got off the bus at Kimball and Lawrence, I saw these two ladies reading the front page of the *Sun Times*. I glanced at what it said, and to see what was in there. There was a picture of Cabrini Green with the headline that read "The Killing Ground" . . . I thought to myself, why

is it now the media makes a big deal about a killing of a boy? Little kids get killed everyday, and there aren't any big headlines! I thought why now, why not earlier?

In an ensuing class discussion, other students said that they thought Dantrell's murder and other similar events were only "isolated incidents," that "the press had just jumped on this," and that Cabrini was "not as bad as it's depicted to be [by the press]" (site meeting, Chicago, October 18, 1992). Although the press may have played up Dantrell's death, the event was far from isolated, and Landau McFarland, who had been a social worker and whose work had taken her to Cabrini, knew that the press was not exaggerating. In fact, Dantrell was the third child from his elementary school to be murdered within a year and the fifth child killed in Chicago in the past month (Nickerson, 1992, p. 1). Landau McFarland feared that many of her students seemed "almost immune" to the violence: "It's like you go to the movies, and you see so many monster movies until you sit and laugh through the scariest parts and in essence deny its horrors" (site meeting, Chicago, October 18, 1992).

Her students' responses to Dantrell's death also led Landau McFarland to open her eyes to how little her students knew about the Chicago housing projects, even though a number of them lived there:

> One young man asked me, "You say 'Project'?" And I said "Yeah."
> And he said "Why is it called the 'Project'?" (Site meeting, Chicago, October 18, 1992)

Landau McFarland took it as her first job to teach her students about the history and politics of the projects. She thought that if they learned this political history, they might come to understand the depth of the problem and the importance of becoming involved in a solution. She began by explaining the establishment of the projects by the WPA in the 1930s. She told how the original projects "isolated these people [the residents] from their relatives who were in the 'Black Belt,'" making it difficult for families to keep in touch with one another. The Black Belt of 1930s Chicago was on the South Side. These first housing projects were just south of downtown. Wealthy, South Side, White neighborhoods sat between the projects and the Black Belt. City politicians, careful not to place such housing developments too near the wealthy White areas, began what became a long history of creating something akin to reservations for poor Blacks, culminating in the construction in the mid 1950s and early 1960s of many large, high-rise projects around the city, including the 23 additional buildings of the North Side project of Cabrini-Green. These newer projects were designed to provide internal courtyards that were to serve as playyards for children and places for community gatherings. Without exception, the closed-off courtyards, which can only be reached on foot, now have turned into battlegrounds, replete with frequent sniper fire. Even the police are afraid to enter them. The Cabrini courtyard is where Dantrell was murdered.

In presenting this history of the projects, Landau McFarland emphasized the planned isolation of African Americans from the surrounding White communities and concluded that it was important to fight what were essentially segregationist policies. However, Landau McFarland was concerned when one of her African American students concluded angrily: "They're trying to get rid of all the Black people." This student, along with several others, went on to argue passionately that Blacks must band together to fight White plots to destroy the Black race, as evidenced in the creation of such projects. They felt that the best solution for Blacks was to deal on their own with their own problems and in the end to create their own all-Black society. That day Landau McFarland learned just how angry many of her students were, and she realized that the Cabrini incident and the conditions in the housing projects were part of what attracted many of them to Black separatist ideology. She concluded, "I learned a lot in that one session. And my role is to attempt to counteract this [separatist ideology] because what it is, it's total dropping out . . . it was amazing that they felt that way" (site meeting, Chicago, October, 18, 1992).

Landau McFarland felt strongly that a separatist stance was not productive for them. Although she understood their rationale for their ideas and their lack of desire to participate in a society that they felt systematically worked to shut them out, she worried that their ideas could narrow their opportunities and in the end would weaken the society at large. She at least wanted them to question their stance. With her new understanding of her students' reasoning, Landau McFarland interpreted the separatist response, at least in part, as defensive—a refusal to interact with Whites because of past experiences of rejection. She put it this way: "My goal is to get them to the point where they realize that the only way they *can* make a difference is that they have to participate to a certain point. They have to." With her goal set, Landau McFarland decided to change her entire curriculum to show her students possibilities for participating in the larger society.

She first attempted to use the example of the evolution of the housing projects as a lesson on the importance of voting to exercise political power, to influence decisions affecting one's life. Not surprisingly, she found that her Black students with separatist leanings argued that it would be senseless to vote "because it's not going to change anything in the Black community. It's not going to change the poverty. It's not going to change the crime. It's not going to change the drugs. It's not going to change the gangs." Landau

McFarland persisted, "One of the ways that you have to [participate] is that you have to exercise that voting right." She told her fellow teacher researchers, "If I don't [teach] anything more than that [the importance of voting], then I will have accomplished something" (site meeting, Chicago, October 18, 1992).

However, Landau McFarland knew that she needed to do more than say that voting is important, so she began acting on her beliefs. She began modeling participatory democracy in the way that she ran her class. Soon after the class discussions of Dantrell and the projects, one student commented in her journal: "This class is not long enough. I need more time to express myself and for the rest of the students to express themselves. We have some pretty important stuff to say." Landau McFarland discussed this remark with the class, and the group decided democratically that the class needed at least one class period per week to discuss whatever they wanted. They also decided to watch the evening news daily and to take 15 minutes of each class period to discuss current events. In her classroom, then, Landau McFarland illustrated how her students could use their voices to make change.

As the discussions continued, Landau McFarland worried about the responses of her White students:

> I feel sort of sorry for the White kids that are in the classroom because the Blacks want to pounce. And I can't allow that to happen. I can't, because if I do, then I have a terrible situation. So I can't allow that to happen.

Landau McFarland encouraged her students to use journal writing to help them solve this classroom dilemma: "What I'm using the journal for, is to write that frustration out." Like many of the M-CLASS teachers, Landau McFarland used writing as a way of dealing with strong and sometimes volatile opinions, to help students think rationally about emotionally charged issues, to help them work through their anger at the injustices they face, to help them handle inevitable conflicts, and to help them explore new ideas and possibilities.

Landau McFarland created a place where her students could safely discuss and write about how their political decisions related to their lives and to African American history. She organized her classroom so that students could think carefully about their separatist ideologies and also hear the contributions of other voices from within and across cultural groups. Toward this end, she brought in a series of outside speakers, including African American professionals, business people, and entrepreneurs. These speakers did not subscribe to separatist ideology and were contributing to the greater society and reaping the benefits.

Landau McFarland came to her African American history class assuming that her students possessed at least some of the political sensitivities and commitments that she had when she was their age in the 1960s. When she saw past the lens of her generation and social class, she found that many of her students had different ideas than she did about participatory democracy. As she saw her students better, she began a process with them of thinking through ideas, and she worked to broaden the options they might imagine for dealing with the difficulties they faced.

CYCLES OF SEEING: PHIL POTESTIO

Somewhat like Landau McFarland, Phil Potestio, who teaches social studies in an Oakland middle school, watched his students in ways that led him to modify his curriculum. Through cycles of seeing, with each cycle leading to new insights, he tailored classroom work to meet his students' changing interests and needs. Potestio began with his concern that many of his students were attracted to gangs and guns. Given the pervasiveness of gangs in the neighborhood surrounding his school, he was aware that many of his students were facing difficult decisions concerning gang affiliation. He understood their attraction but feared that they did not. He wanted to address this issue explicitly, in ways that would help his students take a new look at their choices and that would help him deepen his understanding of their needs. Potestio, who comes from a middle-class, White background, writes about the setting in which he teaches:

> Most people likely would consider this neck of Oakland a scary place. The school is situated on a pivotal corner of a street known as Murderer's Row. There are three large housing projects within four blocks of the school. Turf has been divided up by the gangs for years, and recent immigration patterns have intensified this battle. Four students from the junior high have died in the past 2 years. They are looked upon as martyrs to some nebulous cause. Their names and "RIP" are written on T-shirts worn by some kids.

Potestio explains his decision to teach a unit on gangs:

> The students were very familiar with gangs and their behaviors. There were probably 10 legitimate gang members in this class, and there were a number of kids who didn't seem afraid to speak out about them. This sociological issue brought out dichotomous opinions and sometimes emotions ran high. The feeling of community was already being

tested, because in this neighborhood, gangs are a life-and-death issue, secreted in turf battles and revenge. As an instructor, I saw the need for providing a way in which kids wouldn't have to put themselves on the spot quite so much, essentially defusing the potential for the eroding of community through factionalization. I felt that this class was too precious a combination of positive factors to be jeopardized by blind anger.

Potestio's goal was to give his students an opportunity to reflect on their choices and on the pressures that might lead them to choose gang membership, and also to help them better understand the choices others make.

He began the gang unit by trying to help his students gain some emotional distance from the gangs of their everyday lives, so that they could think rationally about issues surrounding gang membership. He asked students to sort lists of words to see which ones they would identify as social groups. Through this activity they defined social groups as "people who bond together because of a common purpose or trait." They came to realize that gangs were a "social group," and fell into a class with "smokers, musicians, 2-year-old children, and left-handed people." The value of this activity, according to Potestio, was "in providing students with a common, desensitized vocabulary and a deeper grasp of concepts."

Using this academic, distancing vocabulary, Potestio then asked the students to figure out why people decide to join gangs and to evaluate their reasons:

> I tried to balance what one might call justifiable reasons for gang behavior against reasons that exist more for the flash. For instance, I consider "protection" a necessary evil whereas "revenge" has less-noble motives. The kids are given the opportunity to see the many sides of the issue. Those who were adamantly opposed to gangs were reminded of some compelling reasons people might have for joining them, whereas those who were involved in them (and especially those "wannabes") saw some of the risks.

In order to help his students achieve still more emotional distance, Potestio, like Landau McFarland, decided that it was important to place gangs in a historical context—from the Vikings of the 9th century to the Black Panthers of the 1960s, whose roots were in the neighborhood surrounding Potestio's school. In fact, many of his students knew about the Black Panthers "because relatives, family friends, and neighbors were involved." Further, the students had experienced Huey Newton's funeral, which had been held only a few blocks from the school. Potestio explained that he wanted to use this historical material to help his students stretch the concept of gangs beyond their immediate experiences and show some of the reasons people are attracted to gang affiliation: "Some of the impetus for joining gangs comes from the human need to belong, some comes from the need for protection, some comes from the power generated by numbers."

Potestio introduced literature and films to help his students achieve still more distance. They read S. E. Hinton's *Rumble Fish* and watched Francis Ford Coppola's movie based on the novel. The issues they faced in their own lives were similar to ones the characters in *Rumble Fish* faced, "even though the protagonists were White, midwestern, and from another era."

Throughout this process, Potestio's students were expressing their thoughts about gang affiliation. He describes a dialogue between Sam and Suzy that provides one example:

> Sam, a Cambodian student who doesn't often speak, suddenly became vocal: "A group has more power than one person. Sometimes people need help in protecting themselves."
>
> Suzy, a Latina whom I've taught for 3 years, responded, "Well, maybe some people need help but that kind of help [gangs] is just going to get you into more trouble." She said this bravely, considering the fact that all around her sat members of a "minimob," many of them her friends.

During this study of gangs, Potestio encouraged his students to talk in small groups about what they feared most about gangs. Over and over they said that they feared indiscriminate shooting, such as the drive-by shootings that had killed several students from their school.

Once Potestio saw how much the shootings were on his students' minds, he devised an assignment that focused on guns. He asked the students to explain how a gun travels to the hands of a teenager in Oakland, starting with when it is manufactured. Potestio also asked his students to reflect on the consequences of the gun's journey. The students could choose any form for their writing, and Potestio suggested five ways they might approach the assignment: a cartoon; a fictional story, a nonfictional analytic description, a play, or a poem or rap.

Through this writing, Potestio wanted his students to think about the consequences of their actions and their responsibility for them:

> First thing I want them to take in from this is to go outside and realize that there are consequences to actions. . . . Too [often] kids don't do that. . . . The kids'll argue in the class. They'll start talking about it.
> "Nah! That was a firecracker!"

"No it wasn't. It was 9-millimeter."

You know they argue about what the weapon was. And it's just such a fact of their life that I think expressing themselves about it, and understanding that some guy doesn't appear on the corner with a gun. There's a bunch of actions and behaviors and attitudes and a lot of dead ends the kids deal with before getting that gun. (Local meeting, San Francisco, December 17, 1992)

Potestio was pleased that his students wrote seriously and with commitment. Many chose to do this writing at home, which Potestio says "was really amazing" since his students often have difficulty completing even brief homework assignments. He also noted that everyone wrote, the work was of uniformly high quality, and students used every approach he suggested. Through this writing, Potestio was able to see the students' thinking about issues of responsibility and the consequences of their actions.

Potestio read one piece to his teacher-research group, a poem by a young Latina who is a powerful presence in the classroom and is admired by girls from Black, Latino, and Asian backgrounds. Potestio described her as someone who was always an underachiever but whom he thought was gifted. She wrote from the point of view of a gun, portraying people as ultimately responsible for what happens with guns:

I lay hidden in the back of drawer,
Then the sounds of screaming and loud roar.
Sounds like a fight
Then they take me out, to be used tonight
They hold me, with sweaty, quavery hands
and in a second the bullet lands.
They throw me in a bush to hide the evidence
So they'll wonder, "Was it just a coincidence?"
No, I know what really went on.
Even though the ones who did it, is already gone.
So now I'm laying here without my will
So someone else could use me to kill.

Interestingly, the gun is all-knowing but has no will. People, who are responsible for the killing, are out of control; they sweat, their hands quaver, they scream, they roar. They also carelessly discard the gun, which lies in wait for some other person to use for killing.

Through writing, Potestio's students worked through complex issues about guns and gangs and responsibility, issues that they were facing every day in their worlds. Potestio told how this curriculum led one of his Asian students to confide in him about how he was trying to disentangle himself from a gang:

> We had a beautiful discussion today about that. A couple times this week I've talked to him about it. He got jumped. He's been trying to get out of it [the gang]. . . . He doesn't want to go to [a certain high school] which has two gangs.

Potestio worried that "unless you've got some way to get out of Oakland to go to high school," the pressures could become too great. This student was "marked because he's trying to quit . . . even got jumped because of things that were in the past." Potestio reported that the student ended up having to stay in Oakland and was jumped again in high school. One time the student was pulled out of a classroom and beaten so badly with a baseball bat that his arms were broken. Potestio does not know what has happened to this student. He did know of another similar student who managed to escape through Upward Bound and eventually graduated from high school, but he remarked with sadness that few students are so fortunate.

By recognizing his students' concerns and addressing them through his curriculum, Potestio found himself in a position where his students continued to open up to him in ways that allowed him to see them increasingly clearly as the year went on and that stimulated him to continue to adjust his teaching to meet their evolving needs. However, he also had to face the consequences of raising difficult issues and supporting students in their decisions to make changes, since the unfortunate reality was that in the end he had no way to provide a safety net to protect or further assist most of them as they tried to make those changes.

CONCLUSIONS

Through their research, these M-CLASS teachers shifted their angles of vision and began to see their students in new and often unexpected ways. They saw it as their duty to use their insights to prepare young people to use their literacy in ways that will give them the tools to confront social injustices and proceed responsibly as they make choices that will shape the world of tomorrow. They interviewed their students, they observed their classroom behaviors in varied settings and under varied conditions, they watched their own interactions with their students, they considered their students' understandings of what they read, and they analyzed their students' writing. As the students came to see that their teachers were interested and could be trusted, the students revealed parts of their lives that made it possible for the teachers to understand their behaviors and teach them more effectively. Slowly the teachers began to see beyond stereotypes and across boundaries of race, class, generation, and gender. In the end, just as these teachers saw their students anew, they learned that their job as teachers involved helping their students see anew as well. They also learned that they have an obligation to move beyond seeing to take action themselves. They saw the importance of changing their classrooms and their schools and of helping their students take actions that would improve their life chances.

PART III

Constructing an Inclusive Curriculum:
Talking Explicitly About Race and Ethnicity

READING THROUGH THE growing literature in multicultural curriculum (Banks, 1979, 1992, 1995; Sleeter & Grant, 1987) inner-city teachers can at once be inspired, be validated, and get a severe migraine. Banks (1979) suggests that modifying curricula to make them more multicultural "provides a tremendous opportunity to reexamine the assumptions, purposes, and nature of the curriculum and to formulate a curriculum with new assumptions and goals" (p. 9). Banks's observation, although accurate, obscures the monumental task facing teachers attempting to reexamine most aspects of their teaching while facing 150 students and five classes daily. Nonetheless, with the exception of two teachers—Walter Wood and Eileen Shakespear, whose research was not focused on curriculum—all M-CLASS teachers changed either their curriculum, their pedagogy, or both, and often their goals in the course of their research.

This part presents the work of five teacher researchers who either diversified their curriculum to make it more multicultural or refocused their teaching of the existing curriculum to directly address racial and ethnic concerns. How does the work of these teacher researchers apply to the larger educational landscape? Educational research often questions the value of teacher research; what can be learned from isolated teachers toiling away at personally generated research questions? In the work of Deborah Juarez and Karen Alford, whose chapters, 6 and 7, open this section, and the work of Kathy Daniels, Junia Yearwood, and Darcelle Walker in Chapter 8, we see interesting answers to this question.

A major study and often cited source for understanding multicultural curriculum is Sleeter and Grant's (1987) review of books and articles on multicultural education published in the United States, in which they examine the many definitions of multicultural education and evaluate the literature. Identifying a major gap, they write:

We have not been able to locate research studies of any kind on multicultural education in the classroom for grades K–12. So far, most of the literature in this category stresses advocacy, discusses issues, and recommends courses of action. It must move beyond this. There needs to be research on what happens when teachers work with multicultural education in their classrooms, what forms it takes and why, how students respond, and what barriers are encountered. (p. 438)

Within this book, M-CLASS teachers offer their observations about what is involved in implementing multicultural education in their classrooms, responding to the specific contexts in which they teach.

In Chapter 6 Deborah Juarez of Oakland explores what happens in her class when she makes issues of race, ethnicity, and prejudice more explicit in her teaching. Juarez welcomes this challenge and says of herself, "I think that discomfort has to happen . . . before people do get comfortable" (site meeting, San Francisco, October 24, 1992). For that reason, Juarez made race the first topic of the year. The importance of context becomes clear in a comparison of Juarez to Diaz-Gemmati (Chapter 3). Both teachers are Latinas, ask similar questions in their research, and teach eighth grade. But their contexts differ. Juarez's class, set in the poorer flatlands of Oakland, was 51% Latino and 31% African American, with one white student. Diaz-Gemmati's class was 45% African American and 31% White, with most of the African Americans bused to the school, which was situated in a conservative and primarily White working- and middle-class neighborhood. Whereas Juarez welcomed the challenge of teaching potentially volatile topics, Diaz-Gemmati describes her teaching style as "nonconfrontational," especially in her potentially volatile context. Whereas Juarez made race the first explicit topic of the year, Diaz-Gemmati wanted students to discover the topic of race themselves while reading the literature she provided—and they did.

In Chapter 7, New Orleans social studies teacher Karen Alford writes about how, during her research, she realized that "race as an issue lurked beneath a facade of brotherhood at Audubon Montessori," where she taught. Although she had originally planned to focus her research on the more general question of how students learn history through creating voices of people from the past, when Alford saw that the subject of slavery brought forth the most compelling student writing, she narrowed her research. In her chapter, she describes how personalizing the study of slavery, although difficult for her students and for herself, deepened students' understanding both of America's slaveholding history and of their own diverse classmates.

Chapter 8 presents the research of Kathy Daniels of Chicago, and of Junia Yearwood and Darcelle Walker, both from Boston, three inner-city teachers teaching different multiethnic populations in different settings. Their research shows that effective multicultural education is dependent on how a teacher intertwines the complexities of diversifying curriculum and demonstrating caring for students. These three teachers develop multicultural curriculum especially designed to suit the students in their particular settings.

What can be learned from these teacher researchers working alone in their classrooms but in concert with the M-CLASS project? In Part III they reveal what they have learned about developing a diversified curriculum and about what happens when they change their focuses and goals, as well as the questions that remain unanswered for them. The finely nuanced, close observation that underlies their work is only possible through the eyes of the teacher in the classroom daily, year in and year out.

—Elizabeth Radin Simons

A Question of Fairness: Using Writing and Literature to Expand Ethnic Identity and Understand Marginality

Deborah Archuleta Juarez

MY FATHER WAS ALWAYS big on lectures, mainly anecdotal lessons meant to guide me in my life struggle. On one particular occasion in my young-girl years, my dad provided a view of the real world, a world to which I was not yet exposed. So serious in tone, he began by telling me of a job promotion he did not get, given to someone with less seniority, someone he was in the position of training. The "gabacho" (the White man), my father said, "will try to hold you down. You'll have to work twice as hard to be equal." So young, I didn't have the background to understand my father's words. Instead, I saw meaning in his tired expression. Why had my father passed this information on to me? Having been born and raised in New Mexico, where all ancestral generations preceded him, he came out of a historical background of colonialism. His preoccupation with his place in society was a matter of culture and custom, something to be passed down to future generations, in this case me. In later years he repeated his warning, its meaning clear as a fact of life. I never thought to question this "fact of life." Instead I took the information and stored it away.

It wasn't until my "coming of age" in the 1970s that my father's words took on real significance. It was the age of social consciousness, of Black Power, Red Power, Brown Power, and so I had to focus inward. Who was I culturally, and how did I fit into this society? Like others examining their cultural identity, I discarded my White-bred Americanisms and focused on the group identity and culture I had long since discarded with the advent of school and color TV. I'm Chicano, but what does that mean? During my high school years I attended Chicano Power rallies, cut school on *Cinco de Mayo* and wore "Viva la Raza!" badges of pride. In my room hung cultural icons, posters of Ché Guevara, Pancho Villa and Geronimo, yet I knew nothing of Chicano history, and thus nothing of the relevance of revolutionary symbols.

Believing in education as "the great equalizer," my father spoon-fed me his hopes, insisting that I be "better" than he was. Thinking big, I landed at

UC Berkeley—believe me, a strange country to a girl from the flatlands of East Oakland, but nevertheless the "Big Bang" of my social understanding. Whereas my father had stated the obvious about marginality, my ethnic studies and sociology courses provided a source of explanation. Whereas family, friends, and community had reinforced an "us" versus "them" way of viewing White people, my courses at UC Berkeley invited analysis. I didn't realize how much I needed to know the "why" of marginality until the "why" was introduced as an academic topic. Like Clark Kent changing into Superman—that's how I felt knowing, finally knowing. The class notes I took threaded into my life, into my father's life, into the lives of marginal Americans. As I watched other students taking notes, I felt that the information must be falling on deaf ears. What relevance could it possibly have to the sea of White faces around me? Shortsighted, I didn't see their stake in this discussion. Instead, I questioned the absence of these issues in lower grade settings, where ethnic background was tied to a drop-out rate. It wasn't fair to keep a discussion of race, culture, and class from those who needed it, as I had needed it. It wasn't fair to provide the history of one at the exclusion of another. It wasn't fair to the marginalized in our society. What I didn't realize then was that it wasn't fair to mainstream kids either.

In my senior year at UC Berkeley, a White student made a comment to the professor teaching a seminar on Richard Wright: "Racism like that doesn't exist today, does it?" She had spent the entire semester intent and interested, raising her hand to offer insight to text, yet when she asked that question, I knew reality for her was less accessible than fiction. No, keeping anyone ignorant, even those in the mainstream, is not fair.

Fifteen years later, 4 years after I became a teacher, fairness remains an ideal for me, an objective in everyday practice. Personal experience has inspired my teaching, and I can't help but recall how a journey of social consciousness provided a sense of empowerment for me. Through my research I looked for a way to infuse social awareness into an English-class curriculum. Thus my question: What happens when race, culture, and class become explicit topics in the classroom?

I conducted my research at Calvin Simmons Junior High, a Chapter I school, located in Oakland, California. Simmons is located in a primarily lower-middle-class area, its community affected by its share of inner-city problems: crime, joblessness, and poverty. Born and raised in this community, I've witnessed its growth, its decay, and its change of population as various ethnic groups change ownership. In an area with a large Latino population, the school's student body is 51% Latino, 31% African American, 12% Asian American, 2% White, and 4% "other." In Oakland, Simmons is known as a "flatland school"; this is the opposite of a "hill school," where students are more often affluent and White.

It was in this flatland community that I conducted my research as a teacher of eighth-grade English students. For my research I needed to construct an English curriculum that would focus on issues of race, culture, and class. I planned to study how I would implement the curriculum as well as how students would respond to it. Idealistic from the onset, I envisioned student empowerment through a critical exploration of race, culture, and class. Unfortunately, I hadn't considered the lack of appropriate materials in our school book room. Our anthology offered only token selections by writers of color, and its standardized assignment guides did not explicitly address themes of race, culture, or class. There were a number of novels that focused on the African American experience yet none with an Asian American or Latino perspective. Thus, on my own, I selected from my own reading repertoire, made bookstore purchases, and solicited suggestions from colleagues. I regularly scanned my environment, finding appropriate pieces in my daughter's high school newspaper, in the *Oakland Tribune,* or in the *English Journal.* Though lacking in initial resources, I was driven to do the research, and thus to develop curriculum from day to day. Though this approach made me anxious, it had its benefits; it enabled me to continually reenvision the curriculum as more and more I allowed student responses to guide the selection of materials. This co-construction of curriculum was not my original intent; rather, it happened as a consequence of my situation. As if in a dance with my students, I led but also shifted to follow their steps.

Relying on past teaching practice, I presented ideas through reading, writing, and then discussion. The readings included short stories, poetry, articles, and film, providing a context for writing assignments that included both creative and expository response. Writings preceded discussion, allowing students to reflect, to develop thought, and ultimately to think critically in discussion. For the most part, this particular structure remained constant, allowing for some predictability in the implementation of curriculum.

What was not predictable was whether I would be able to replicate my own college enlightenment for my eighth-grade students. My intent was to affirm student reality through an academic focus, eliciting their response in the process. But would this be enough to generate empowerment? I wanted to help students develop critical thinking skills so they could assess social issues more critically. But how prepared was I to face the challenge of controversy? Willing, I moved forward, but not without caution.

Providing an arena where student thought could be safely expressed and challenged became a guiding principle in my approach. I conducted my research during one school semester, during which students focused extensively on issues of race, culture, and to a small extent, class. Student writings as well as my personal journal documenting classroom situations were my data, as were the various texts I used and activities I created. Because my research question is broad and the data extensive, in this chapter, I present a segment of a unit focusing on culture, which I titled "Immigration and Biculturalism." Although the unit by itself does not give a complete picture, it illustrates my methods in the delivery of the curriculum, some underlying values in my teaching approach, as well as the dynamics of the classroom community, giving a sense of the research experience as a whole.

It is important to note that the immigration unit developed as a consequence of the race unit that preceded it. Overall the race unit was productive; through writings and oral exchange students expressed a wealth of opinions on a number of topics such as media stereotyping, the social significance of skin color, and the pros and cons of separatism. In the end, they developed a more critical awareness of how racism functions in society. Still, I did not feel that the race unit was entirely inclusive. My African American students were far more impassioned than were my Latino or Asian American students, whose comments generally focused on personal experience or recent media events. My Latino students related to being objects of suspicion, but none could provide historical data of their ethnic group's struggles in this country, as some African American students were able to do. Asian students discussed their personal struggles with other ethnic groups and the "Ching-Chong Chinaman" chants they had to endure, but seemed to have little information on Asian-White encounters. I concluded that our schools were providing some information on the African American experience but little on the particular histories or cultural experiences of the Asian and Latino groups. Because I wanted to open the discussion to *all* the voices in the class, I decided to work on issues related to immigration, biculturalism, and their effects.

Our opening reading for the immigration unit was Yoshiko Uchida's story "Tears of Autumn," an excerpt from her novel, *Picture Bride.* In this excerpt, a young woman named Hana leaves Japan to meet the man she is contracted to marry in America. I assigned a piece of writing: "Pretend you are Hana. In a diary entry or letter, describe your feelings and experiences after arrival in America." I wanted my students to take on an immigrant's point of view, to consider the many reasons why people immigrate and what they gain and lose.

My student Carlos imagined Hana as experiencing the language taunts of children whereas Karmala envisioned her taking a class to learn English. Many students focused on Hana's difficulties in day-to-day operations such as grocery shopping or taking a bus, whereas others envisioned her with an immigrant's drive, finding a job or opening a business. The story and assignment stimulated an empathy for the character and her immigrant status as well as a discussion of arranged marriages. Many students discussed their own cultural customs and related conflicts living as "Americans." For example, Billy, who is Mien (an ethnic group with origins in China but now dispersed through parts of Southeast Asia), told about his cousin's arranged marriage, and Sopheap, a Cambodian, revealed her parents' attitudes about dating. Immediately apparent was the involvement of those students who had previously shied away from oral response during the race unit.

As a complement to "Tears of Autumn," I asked this journal question: "Why do people immigrate to this country? What do they gain; what do they lose? What is your general feeling toward immigrant people? Give examples." I noted from these journal responses that students felt that people immigrate for a "better life" (job, education, politics). Southeast Asian students provided a reason related to personal experience: war. Students seemed aware of America's magnetic presence as "the land of opportunity," but some questioned the reality. Janet, who is Vietnamese, wrote:

> Hoping to seek for a new life, my parents left the country when I was 14 months. They, like most other foreigners at the time, were told about the golden opportunities America held, but what they were not told was that golden opportunity rarely knocked at your door.

Of what is lost through immigration, students cited "family," "friends," "culture," and "respect." Ann, a Chinese student, stated, "Sometimes because you're an immigrant you're not treated with respect. People think you're ignorant."

Given the new voices in the discussion and the strength of opinion both oral and written, I judged that the topic of immigration was generating the inclusion I desired. It stimulated the previously quiet to share their expertise. Interestingly, the inclusion of more students led to a greater diversity of opinion; more voices meant more potential for controversy.

During discussion of this same journal topic, JoAnn, an African American student, reacted to immigration: "Immigrants take opportunities away from Black people."

I asked, "Are you saying that if no immigrants were arriving in this country, Blacks would have more opportunities?"

"Yes," she replied, "they're given more respect than Black people. An employer would hire an immigrant over a Black person."

Tamika, another African American student, responded, "That's not right. Just because they come and work hard to make it, they shouldn't be blamed if we don't make opportunities for ourselves."

JoAnn went on to strengthen her argument, "Look at what happened at Garfield School. It used to be all Black. Now it's all Asian and it's a better school. They made it better because Asian kids are going there instead of

Black kids. I'm Black and I want to learn, so why can't they make it better for us?"

JoAnn was not the only student who thought that immigration had negative impact on Americans. Lester, another African American, wrote in his journal: "I think the United States should curb immigration. We could live more simpler with one type of culture."

Likewise, Tyler, a White student, wrote: "I don't like it when people immigrate over here just because they might not get caught. I don't like the whole point of immigration in the first place. . . . we have enough people. Classes, stores and other things are too crowded."

Jesus, a Mexican American student, puts conditions on immigration: "I think that people should only immigrate if they got papers. Put policemen on every possible way they could come through, on the river on the hills, everywhere."

I viewed this divisiveness among Latino, Asian American, and Black students as interesting and important to explore. To the eye the divisions were racial, but in reality, they stemmed from cultural differences. As Lester stated, "We could live more simpler with just one type of culture." Judging from written and oral response, I found my African American students divided in opinion, many viewing immigration as negatively affecting society, others viewing it as a matter of personal freedom. Overwhelmingly, the Latino and Asian American students were in favor of immigration, many of them immigrants themselves or first-generation Americans.

Intending to mediate the controversy through discussion, I relied on strategies that I had set in place during the race unit. Because we would begin discussion as a response to text, verbal response was directed toward ideas rather than personalities. Ground rules for discussion evolved as a result of our experience in the discussion of race. For example, if discussion lapsed into the shouting of opinions, I would instruct my students to stop and write, directing strong thought to paper. I expected a range of emotion in such discussions, including anger, but I wanted my students to articulate the origin of emotion. I wanted critical thought, and my directives and probes evolved with this in mind.

What was particularly interesting about the immigration unit was the confrontational nature of the discussions. Though the race unit prompted strong response, students were more often in agreement, their criticism/attacks generally directed toward an abstract "they" (i.e., "White people," "racists," "society") rather than toward classroom members. Perhaps because of this abstract context, Tyler, my one White student, was never targeted. Knowing and liking Tyler, my students didn't subject him to criticism. However, with the immigration focus, confrontation was inevitable; students were directing comment to a concrete opposing side. Though they continued to express their opinions openly and honestly, I noted that they did so with more sensitivity and less verbal attack than before. Perhaps by this time certain ground rules had been internalized; I'd like to believe that a sensitivity to each others' feelings came into play. As we maneuvered through the "hard talk," I expected students to learn that differences in opinion do not necessitate division, and I anticipated that they would view the function of discussion as I intended. Tony sums up my position well: "This class should have more discussions because they will be effective for all of us. To speak and show what we think."

I wanted to facilitate strong opinion, even from the less vocal; thus, I made a point to read as anonymous the opinions of my students, particularly if a point of view had not been addressed in discussion. I wanted to provide alternate avenues of expression for my quieter students as much as I wanted to present good models of critical response. Finaith, a Laotian student, quiet during discussion, wrote the following as a response both to an article we read in class as well as to JoAnn's remark, "Immigrants take away opportunities from Black people":

WHAT I NEED TO TELL BLACKS AND WHITES

So far what I heard about what other people had been talking about Asian people is wrong. The only reason why we came here in the first place was not to take anyone's job. We're not here to get on anybody's case. All we were here for was to get our education and find a better life. First of all, the White people was the one who wanted us to come to the US. . . . Now after we are here and they find out how hard we try to make a difference from where we lived, they start saying that we try to take there jobs or take over there lifestyle. But its not only the White people complain about us but the Black too. Well if they want what we got then they should try hard too. Cause if they only sit there and complain about us, there not going to get too far. So all I got to say is, "if you want a good job and want to be smart, just don't sit there and complain about other race, and get to work." I'm not saying all the White people and Black people say that to us, I'm just saying this to the people that think of us like.

Finaith's title, written in huge letters taking up half a page, seemed an invitation for me to read her piece aloud. I read her text, among others, as anonymous, inviting students to respond orally. In the short discussion that followed, no comments were directed toward Finaith's text, but her opinion was "heard," and in this way validated (her smile communicated this much to me). Equally important, through hearing the opinions of the less vocal, students were exposed to viewpoints of those they may not have encountered otherwise. In this way everyone was included; every opinion counted.

There were times when student opinion directed my selection of text and assignments. At these times my students' voices were a focal point in my day-to-day direction of curriculum. One example came early in the immigration unit. A student complained about foreign language use around English speakers: "I feel like they're talking about me. It's rude. Why don't they just speak English?" Others agreed, asserting: "If you live here you should be speaking English only! Otherwise go back where you came from!" The next day I brought in an excerpt from Sandra Cisneros' *The House on Mango Street,* "No Speak English." The main character, Mamasita, a newly arrived immigrant, is homesick and reluctant to learn the language of a country she wants to leave. The story ends with her cry of distress as her toddler son sings the jingle to a Pepsi commercial.

"Why does Mamasita refuse to speak English?" was one question I posed as an in-class essay question. The responses revealed students' empathy; they sympathized with her homesickness, her insecurity, her fear of a strange, new life.

I asked, "Why do people who know more than one language choose to speak the non-English language?" Again, my students knew the answers: "Because it feels more comfortable," "It's the language you use with family and friends," or "It's a way of keeping the culture."

Although the issue of language seemed divisive initially, my students were in agreement in their understanding of why someone would choose to use a language other than English. Because of the political nature of my research question, I asked political questions. That day I wrote on the board: "Should use of a non-English language be prohibited in certain places like work or school? Should we eliminate translations in use of certain forms, such as medical and voting forms?" The overwhelming majority of my students responded in favor of using non-English translations. Surprisingly, the same students who felt annoyed at speakers of languages other than English now felt that it was a matter of freedom to use the language of one's choice. What happened? I wondered. Hadn't I heard the voice of discontent the previous day? I hadn't anticipated a complete change of opinion; I merely wanted students to think more critically. Still, my text material and questions proved to be strong influences in directing students toward some understanding of immigrants' lives and languages. Reciprocally, the students' voices proved strong influences in directing my choice of curriculum.

I continued my immigration unit with an excerpt from *Pocho,* a novel set in the 1950s by José Antonio Villarreal. I chose a segment that takes a hard look at the topic of assimilation. I asked students to focus on the main character, Richard, as a victim of discrimination—he was beaten by the police because he was Mexican—but also as a person of dual culture in the process of discovering his marginal status in society. I asked questions focusing on Richard's discovery. Citing a passage from the story, "Richard feels discriminated against for the first time," I asked, "Why doesn't Richard think about the discrimination against other Mexicans until it happens to him?" I also asked, "Why does Richard say, 'Let my people take care of themselves'? Does he want to dissociate himself from other Mexicans—why or why not?" I asked questions that required personal analysis: "Do you see yourself more as an individual or part of an ethnic/racial group? Explain." I had my students tackle the notion of assimilation: "Richard is a 'Pocho'—in taking on American culture he rejects some of his Mexican culture. How would this affect his relationship with his parents and other immigrants who are more 'Mexican?'"

We wrote and then discussed our responses to the excerpt. Some felt that Richard was a "sellout," a "wanna-be." Maria wrote, "I can see that he doesn't hang around with Mexicans and someone that hangs around with people who are not their own kind (in my point of view) is because he doesn't like his own kind."

Others saw him as a person who didn't want any negative stereotypes applied to him. Sharon wrote, "He doesn't want to be part of a racial group because he doesn't want people to think bad things of him."

I noticed that the students identified more as an "individual" or more as "part of a group," depending on their personal understanding of what I had asked. For example, Margarita, who is Mexican, embraced the idea of group identity: "I don't think of myself as an individual. I want to work and to help my people. I want all people to be important and to take a role in this life. I want to change the statistics about my people."

Others asserted individuality in defying group expectations. Eric, who is Hawaiian, wrote, "I see myself as an individual because I don't try to act like others just as myself." The division of opinion on Richard's character seemed related to the dual roles he played as a "Pocho," both Mexican and American. I believe that my students considered their own experiences in reacting to Richard.

To continue on the topic of biculturalism, I next tried an excerpt from *No-No Boy* by John Okada, a story set in a World War II internment camp with a Japanese American main character. Again, issues of dual identity surface in the story. The main character, Ichiro, is dealing with his decision *not* to fight for his birth country, the United States, a decision prompted in part by his parents and their ties to their mother country, Japan. He concludes that he could be neither Japanese nor American because he could commit himself to neither.

I posed the question, "Would you go to war against the country of your parents/ancestors?" The vast majority of my students identified with Ichiro and said emphatically, "No." I asked my students what identifying name they gave themselves: "Do you call yourself an 'American,' a(n) '_____ American,' or another name? Why do you use one over another?"

It was during discussion of *No-No Boy* that the concept of dual identity became clear for some of my students; I asked them to identify aspects of their cultural identity as being either "mainstream American" or a product of another culture. Using chopsticks as opposed to using a fork was a simple response, as were responses connected with food, celebrations, parental attitudes, and expectations. However, Sharonna, an African American student, pursued the idea of "selling out"—denying background, community, and home culture in favor of a mainstream "acceptable" way to be. Despite the unit title, the issue at hand was more than one of immigration. It became an issue of acculturation, which everyone experiences in a variety of ways, and thus included all my students, native born or otherwise.

In judging from various written and oral responses, I noted not only that my students were acknowledging their marginality to mainstream America, but also that some were aligning themselves with other ethnic groups. José, a Mexican American student, wrote:

> I think the so called "Americans" took advantage of all the people that were here before them such as the Mexicans and Indians and using the Blacks as slaves. Now the Mexicans, Indians, and other races now need to be a citizen or need green cards . . . when this country used to be theirs.

Valerie, an African American student, aligns herself with immigrants against antiimmigrant sentiment: "If this is the land of opportunity then we should live up to our name. . . . Picture you in their (immigrant) shoes how would you react? Would you like it if you got shipped back to your country?"

A close focus of the issues pushed students to think more critically than emotionally in reaching an opinion, but the questions I posed and the discussions that followed also directed their thoughts toward understanding that "_____ Americans" are marginal groups within this country. Not fully participating in mainstream culture, they are defined as much by mainstream viewpoints as by their own perceptions of themselves. Like Ichiro, who was "both" and who was "neither," it could be destructive for them to choose.

At the culmination of the immigration unit, I posed "the" key question to my students, one born out of the dual-status dilemma, student writing and discussion, and class readings: "What is a 'real' American? Are you a 'real' American?" I did not realize I would end my unit with this question, this concern. I hadn't seen the forest for the trees, so to speak, but I suppose my personal quest led me toward this question as much as student discussion or the implicit theme of a story. In posing this question I heard what I thought to be divergent viewpoints.

Javier wrote, "I consider myself a real American because I was born here."

Finaith claimed, "A real American has white skin, hazel eyes and blond hair. They act stuck-up. No, I don't see myself as a real American cause the only connection I have with America is that I speak American."

Margarita, (Mexican) asserted, "I don't think nobody is a 'real American.' Why, because everybody has a past and in that past you are from another culture."

When I announced to my class that I was a "real American," Elvia immediately responded, "Ahh, Ms. Juarez . . . sellout!"

"Why am I a 'sellout,' Elvia?" I asked.

"Because you're Mexican," she said, "It doesn't matter if you were born here." Elvia admitted that she was American born, but said that it didn't make her American.

Julia defended Elvia's statement, responding: "*We* never gave ourselves that name, Ms. Juarez, that's why *they're* American and we're not." Her implicit understanding of marginality, especially the significance of the power of others to name one, caught me off guard.

Most of my African American students claimed to be "real Americans," like Teya, who wrote, "I call myself an African American because that's what I was taught I am." However, a handful, like James, claimed, "I'm not an American. I'm an African living in America."

On this topic, there was no consensus, no friendly agreement on what an American was, or whether any or all of us can classify ourselves as "real Americans." When I took time to reflect, I noticed something that had not been clear to me initially. Many students were responding from the viewpoint of someone on the outside, looking in. Theirs was a reaction of both pride and defensiveness. If Lester, who is African American, said he was a "real American," it was because "A real American looks just like everybody else, HUMAN!" If Alicia, a Mexican American, denied her American roots, it came out of a perception of not fitting in or being accepted:

> Real Americans are white colored eyes freckles blond or red hair. Like if they are good and follow all the rules. Most of them know that I do not act like them or look like them so I do not consider myself one.

When Vivianna, a Chicana, claimed to be American it was because "Americans can look like anything they want to look like, they don't have to be a certain color. A real American has its own type of behavior."

"American" or not, my students recognized their marginality. They asserted themselves in reference to their nonmainstream status. They addressed mainstream America in saying either "Yes, I am an American" or "No, I'm not," I saw their responses as influenced by their own beliefs about how the mainstream perceived them. Maybe I wouldn't have been able to understand their reactions if I hadn't understood my own reaction to the question. As I explained to my class, when I assert that I'm a "real American," it is because I don't fit the European norm that Finaith and Alicia accepted. My assertion is a response to any or all who define me with their eyes. Again pride and defensiveness.

Despite disagreement among my students on the issues of immigration, I found that many of them came to some understanding of shared marginality, "being in the same boat." I didn't expect this to happen when I began my unit on immigration. The understanding of shared marginality happened as a natural consequence of many things, I suppose: the literature, oral exchange, directed questions, heightened consciousness, and my personal knowledge of an America that does not promote multiculturalism. Perhaps no two pieces of my data exemplify this point better than the papers of two students in separate classes. Both responded to William Wong's (1993) article, "The Complex Issue of Immigration," in the *Oakland Tribune,* which discussed the potential deportation of 180 Chinese refugees picked up by the Coast Guard, as well as American perceptions of immigration. When asked to respond to any aspect of the article, Sharonna, an African American student, wrote:

> In my opinion Columbus took away land and a common culture from "real" Americans, who are of course the real native Americans.
>
> Whites are hypocrites. They came over her from Europe and just invaded America. They messed it up forever. Now they want to condemn others for coming over here for political reasons such as freedom of speech and freedom of religion. Oh how soon they forget that they came over here only a few hundred years ago for the same reasons.
>
> I think we (Americans) are just looking for a bad guy, someone to blame for all the problems we have. These so called culprits are usually gays minorities, immigrants etc. etc. etc.

Janet, a Vietnamese student, responded similarly, but with a different emphasis. She specifically reacted to a quote from the article:

> "Many love to say this is a 'nation of immigrants', a 'melting pot'. Others believe America is being overrun by 'foreigners' who are taking away jobs and a common culture from '*real*' Americans".

What the hell is a real American anyway. We know it's not the Europeans.

So what European character is America loosing? If Mr. [Pat] Buchanan and Mr. [David] Duke are referring to the character in which the Europeans stole this land, then America still hasn't lost that yet. People are still stealing, robbing and killing like the Europeans did years ago.

I can't really say what's best for America 'cause I don't know. Maybe deporting these 180 immigrants is best or maybe it is not. There are good things about having foreigners here because with a land with many different races, you're able to be more educated about these cultures.

You can't always assume that just because a person is a foreigner that they're on government support. Lots of foreigners bust their butts to get a measly couple of bucks a day. And haven't people ever realized that with the foreigners opening businesses like 7–11's will mean more jobs for people. No one ever looks at the good things about having foreigners in America. Why? Because too many ignorant people are to busy blaming foreigners for all the bad things in America.

Just remember that if you took away *all* the foreigners in America, then it wouldn't be the land of the brave anymore, rather the land of the cowards.

On the surface, Janet and Sharonna are coming from two points of view. Janet is herself an immigrant and refugee, the subject of the William Wong article, whereas Sharonna is someone who identifies herself as an American. Despite these differences, the two girls occupy the same space of thought, their experiences more closely tied than is initially apparent. Both girls deny that Europeans are the "real" Americans. Janet stated, "We know it's not the Europeans," and Sharonna remarked that "Columbus took away land and a common culture from 'real' Americans . . . native Americans." Whereas Sharonna said that Europeans "invaded America," Janet said that "they stole this land." Both believe, as Sharonna asserted, that "it is messed up forever." Janet elaborated, "People are still stealing, robbing, and killing like the Europeans did years ago." Though Sharonna includes herself in saying, "*We* Americans are just looking for a bad guy, someone to blame," she agreed with Janet, who said, "Ignorant people are too busy blaming foreigners for all the bad things in America." I didn't quite understand what Janet meant when she wrote, "If you took away all the foreigners in America then it wouldn't be the land of the brave anymore, rather the *land of cowards*," until I read Sharonna's concluding statement: "America is OK, but generally *we are afraid* of anything that strays from the very straight and very narrow."

The implications stand out clearly for these two students, as well as others, whose defensive positions reflect an understanding of a shared experience of marginality and a questioning of a belief system which favors some individuals over others.

In the end, I can't claim that Tyler or Lester changed their position against immigration, or that Janet or Sharonna would not have recognized their common marginality without my curriculum. However, of some things I am sure: For my culturally diverse students, I provided an arena where they could safely express their thoughts and opinions on issues that affect their lives. Within this arena, their thoughts were challenged by the thoughts of others: authors and fellow students whose experiences and points of view they might not have known otherwise. In the process of such exchange, my students were expected to think critically. Most important, my eighth-grade students demonstrated their ability to act out tolerance, acceptance, and respect. Perhaps the primary achievement of the research was not this chapter, not the findings, but the classroom dialogue that was created because of the process.

My research came to a close at the semester's end. The loss of a teacher in our school, and the resulting reassignment of most of my students to other classes in an effort to even out enrollment, disrupted both my new focus on class issues and my day-to-day momentum. Resigned to this change, I packed my data away—bags of student work, my personal journal—to be sorted through at another time. I felt relieved that my mad quest for curriculum was over. At the same time, I felt disappointed that I could not witness the culmination of what we had built together, leaps in thought that seemed to be just around the corner. What more could my students have learned? What more could I have learned? Still, I am convinced that a curriculum focused on race, culture, and class provides a means of developing social communication and consciousness among individuals. I know that for us as Americans, it is as much a part of our cultural makeup to speak to such issues as it is to believe that "all men are created equal." Moreover, in such discussions, I found that junior high students of ethnically diverse backgrounds can interact in a mature manner with one another, despite differences of opinion. For teachers who believe in multicultural education, it is our task to create a disciplined setting where we can practice it. If my experience is any indication, teachers may have to create such a curriculum in order to present it.

I also ended my research with a finding particular to my minority-majority class: a sense of marginality among ethnically diverse students to mainstream America. Was it part of my "plan" that my students focus on their marginal status? Directed questions such as "Are you a 'real' American?" would indicate that the answer is yes. Admittedly, it was my intent to invite student reality into the class, to affirm it, and to learn from it. "Separatist" viewpoints are a cultural reality, worthy of discussion, and cannot be neutralized with a curriculum that highlights only what we have in common. As a teacher and individual, I began with the belief that a discussion of our differences is itself a validation and would not further divide us; rather, it would allow us to accept that which we have in common. It became the backdrop against which we could better view our similarities.

Even so, as a teacher, I didn't want to end my research with a focus on a shared sense of marginality among my students; I believe the multicultural perspective goes well beyond this point. The "voices" I want my students to "hear" are not limited to the voices in the classroom but include all Americans, particularly those not represented in my class. The very ethnic composition of my school, which is 98% students of color, demonstrates America's separatist reality. It speaks to the need for an open and ongoing discussion among us, one in which critical thought reigns over emotional response. For my part, I attempted to move my students toward this end. Empowering students meant providing opportunities for them to intellectualize and articulate their concerns. We in this country have the task of dealing with these issues that are often perceived as threatening; however, the greater threat is denial. More than being ineffective, denial is debilitating, building walls rather than breaking them. Either we deal with issues of race, culture, and class or the issues will deal with us.

I conclude feeling some sense of accomplishment. Through the use of multicultural literature, I provided alternate views of American thought and validated the cultural experiences of my students. I tackled potentially charged issues, requiring from my students critical thought in response. I developed a curriculum the hard way—through absolute necessity, feeling at times overwhelmed, unsure of what I was doing and of its effect. However, in retrospect I believe that the research was worth the effort and the anxiety of treading new ground. In the process of trying to build self-esteem from within for my students, I gained esteem for myself. In trying to empower my students, I empowered myself as a teacher.

I still see a long road ahead for us as educators, we who must come to terms with the very political nature of our profession. We will reinforce the status of race, culture, and class divisions through a traditional course of denial, or we will play an active role in the discussion of our diverse American culture. For myself, I see a commitment that goes beyond this year of research as I continue to develop a curriculum that invites a critical discussion of race, culture, and class. In any case, I expect my research question to remain with me throughout my teaching career, just as the life lessons of a father remain intrinsic to who I am.

CHAPTER 7

"Yes, Girl, You Understand": History Logs and the Building of Multicultural Empathy

Karen Alford

IT'S 1956, and my mother is calling. "Karen, come in. Dinner's ready." But I am not ready to go back into my suburban ranch house. I am living with the Ingalls family in 1876, and there is a blizzard, and I am really worried about Pa getting home. That's how it has always been with me and history. I might find myself fighting alongside Lancelot on a misty plain in southern England, or I could be running with Kunte Kinte, trying to escape the slave master, or I am hiding with Anne Frank, or—well, you get the picture. I've never just read history; I've lived it. History transformed me. Studying Egypt in the seventh grade, I may not have been able to put all the dynasties in order on a pop quiz, but I was thinking, "Wow, wouldn't it be neat to have all that art around you and to have those pyramids and to look at the mummies and think of the Pharaoh and the Nile."

I have never understood people who think history is boring, although the subject is often mentioned on students' least-favorite-subject list. I believe that the problem is not the past, which, after all, carries with it all the drama of hundreds of years of miniseries, but with the way in which history is often taught, as little more than an ongoing barrage of laws, doctrines, and provisos, the provisions of which must be memorized for Friday's exam. When I took my current position as a seventh- and eighth-grade history and language arts teacher at the Audubon Montessori School in New Orleans, I was determined to help my students feel the same passionate connection to the past that I have felt. I don't want my class to be presented with "Well, George Washington was elected, then John Adams; now let's talk about Thomas Jefferson. Oh, look, it's the War of 1812. Next stop—the Civil War." Rather than this historical gallop, I wanted my students to learn some of the rudiments of thinking like historians, in particular to prepare to learn about historical analysis and interpretation by developing empathy for those who lived in the past. I wanted them to start a conversation across time. Put us there. How did it happen? How did it feel? Manipulate the time, feel the texture, smell the foods, listen for different sounds.

126

In many ways, Audubon Montessori is an ideal place in which to teach. Although this K–8 public school follows Montessori methods in only the first six grades, the entire school is informed by the Montessori philosophy. At every level, Audubon stresses active, collaborative, project-oriented learning. I knew this was the environment students would need if, for them, history was to become an activity of heart and mind rather than a rote-memory exercise.

Audubon is a culturally diverse magnet school open to all students in the city limits of New Orleans. Each year, on registration day, parents line up at the school to register their children. Our enrollment is on a first-come, first-served basis, although we aim for a class balanced by race and gender. Most of the students who enroll in kindergarten are still at the school as eighth graders, making for a bonding among students and between students and teachers not found at most schools. Since most New Orleans public schools are all African American, Audubon Montessori is uniquely situated to help students learn to work together in a multicultural setting. My classes have about the same number of boys as girls, and like the school, they are composed of about 55% African Americans, 40% Whites, and 5% Asian Americans and Latinos.

Because our school is small, I am both the language arts and the social studies teacher. I work with all the seventh and eighth graders in two mixed-age classes. Half of the seventh and eighth graders (about 27 students) meet with me for social studies and then return later in the day for language arts. Although other teachers have expressed surprise at how I manage to teach two grades at once, I find that this arrangement works well. Rather than teaching Louisiana history to the seventh graders and American history to the eighth graders every year, I teach American history and Louisiana history in alternate years to both classes. I find that teaching a combination seventh-eighth grade has important advantages for the class. Because I teach these students two periods a day, one for social studies and one for language arts, over 2 years I get to know them well, and they bond with one another as a class. These classroom bonds and my familiarity with students' abilities play an important role in my instruction.

I structure language arts as a writing workshop. When I first began teaching this way, I found that it took the first school year for my seventh graders, despite their Montessori elementary experience, to really understand how to participate in the workshop effectively. When the students came to my class as eighth graders the next year, however, I saw the fruits of our labors. The eighth graders not only were working steadily and writing increasingly sophisticated pieces but they also were modeling the process of participating in the workshop for the seventh graders.

In addition to the scheduling arrangements, the physical environment at

Audubon is itself supportive of the building of community. The middle-school wing is in a house. My classroom is on the second floor in what used to be three small bedrooms and a bathroom. There is an upstairs porch with a couch. There's even a kitchen sink. It's good that we generally get along, because in this setting we are crowded. This cozy, if unorthodox, environment is just right for the teaching-and-learning atmosphere I want to create.

As I thought about my research, I began to wonder what I would have to do as a teacher to help students create characters who would live in their memories, just as Laura Ingalls, Lancelot, Kunta Kinte, Anne Frank, and the other historical characters lived in my memory. What would happen, I wondered, if I asked my students to imagine they were a person in another place and time? What if I asked them to write something from the point of view of that person? This idea of looking at history from the viewpoints of people in the past was based on a book I had read, *The Story in History* by Margot Fortunato Galt. Galt presents a number of activities that use imaginative writing to help students understand history. She writes:

> Imaginative writing in history . . . helps us get inside the points of view of others, no matter how different they may be from us. In the shrinking world, such an ability may prove not only useful, but crucial. (p. 4)

From this thinking, my M-CLASS research question emerged: In my social studies class, when my multicultural students assume the voices of historical figures and include their personal voices in their writing, what do they learn about history?

I thought I could get my students to take different perspectives on American history by using learning log prompts after they read a section of their textbook, *America, the People and the Dream* (Divine, 1992). In the prompts I would ask them to consider how the events that they were reading about might be observed by a person living in that time. The purpose of these role-playing learning logs would be to help students become more empathetic with those who had been here and were gone and also to apply what they were learning about the past to the issues they face in today's world. After writing, they would then share their logs with their classmates by reading their entries aloud to the whole class and then discussing their ideas with the group. This routine of reading one's writing aloud to share it and to stimulate discussion was comfortable and even enjoyable for my students. Across their years at Audubon, they had experienced the pride of reading their writing to the whole class in language arts where students had learned to respond respectfully and thoughtfully and to recognize one another's strengths. It also seemed important that the students had been in classes together for many years and knew that they could trust one another.

I explained to the students that I wanted them each night to consider the people behind the generally peopleless words in their textbook, to become these imagined characters, and to write in voices of the characters they created. In the analysis of my teacher-research data, which includes students' role-playing logs across the year and my notes about their whole-class discussions, during which students read these logs aloud, I show the students' tentative movement away from reproducing the textbook toward log entries that became increasingly unfettered, imaginative, creative, risky, and empathetic. This is not to suggest that students moved in lockstep toward more sophisticated log entries. Instead, they all moved at different paces and in different ways, toward writing entries that demonstrated a growing connection to the past. As I tracked my students' different paths, I also began to understand more clearly the common journey that we had traveled together as a class. Working to develop historical empathy through role-playing was particularly important, I saw, when studying the sensitive topic of slavery.

In the beginning, many students used the log entries only as a way of reformulating the information in the textbook. Jon's log provides a typical example:

> Dear Richard: I have decided to become a Federalist. I am very excited about this whole thing. The Federalists believe in the strong central government, the United States should not support the French Revolution and (should) support policies favorable to business.
>
> I am writing to you to try to convince you to become a Federalist. I think that you would make a great Federalist. Also some of the things you and I have discussed together sound like you would be a Federalist.

Even these early, relatively unimaginative entries demonstrate that students were prodded to feel some involvement with the material. The logs made it necessary for them at least to think enough about what they had read to put the ideas in their own words.

Increasingly, as students pulled facts mostly from the textbook, they created characters who were allowed to feel, who were living, breathing, albeit imagined historical personages. For example, Darlene, taking a male persona, wrote to a pretend wife:

> I've been assigned to a privateer, that's a ship that somebody owned but the military's using it. We had a battle. The British wanted us to surrender, but my commander yelled, "I have not yet begun to fight!" His name is John Paul Jones and I'm proud to fight beside him.

Students also began to put themselves back in time. Rachel, inspired by a couple of sentences in the textbook about the New England whaling industry, wrote:

> We all sit around the hearth. Papa's cheeks glowing from the days hard work in the fields. Mama squinting to sew by the dim light of the fire. Uncle George with his bad arm in his lap, silently complaining to himself about the whales. One of his fellow workers missed the whale and hit Uncle George's arm. Patty, my sister, asleep on my lap with her knitting in her hands. Me, wide awake, trying to remember all that father had taught me.

As students began to feel more comfortable assuming historical roles, they increasingly allowed their imaginations to roam, giving expression to their own language and personality. The diary entry by Jordan from "King George III" illustrates this tendency well:

> It's 5:03 PM and 12 seconds. I just heard about the Boston Tea incident. Really I'm not mad, I'm really just disgusted. I feel like a father to a town of children, they whine about the stamp act and this and that. And then they do something like this. I'm very disgusted. I need to send everyone to their rooms for a month.

As students created increasingly vivid characters, they became close to their creations, empathetically projecting themselves into the characters. In the following entry, after reading a few sentences about the colonial "dame" schools, Mary Catherine transported herself back to one of these schools and considered how the students (or as is more likely *she*) might have felt in such a school. She drafted the following petition:

> We, the boys and girls of the dame school in Pennsylvania would like more education, not just to know about our ancestors, and our families or how to plant, grow and sell crops; we would like to know more about what is going on over the world. We would like to have some different teachers, and we would like to read different kinds of books, not just the Bible!!

Thinking about what I had learned and how I would present the findings of my research, my initial plan was to end about here, after demonstrating that history learning logs had given my students a chance to evolve as more involved and empathetic students of the past. But by examining more of the students' logs and through reflecting in my teacher-research group about issues of race and ethnicity, a new and potentially more important finding jumped out at me. The process of writing these logs and the discussions they stimulated were allowing the history class to become a forum where my students and I could explore together what is perhaps the key issue of our times: race.

The issue of race lurked behind a facade of unity at Audubon Montessori. A visitor to the school might be impressed by the seeming interracial harmony. Yes, students tended to divide into racial groups at lunch, a fact some students explained away as a division not along racial lines, but rather according to musical preferences. Black and White kids could also be seen walking our hallways arm in arm. What the visitor might not see are some of the subtle signs of tension. For example, when one of the African American girls was told her shorts were too short for school wear, she charged, "It's because I'm Black." In another incident, two Black girls running for student council pressured White students not to vote for Whites because the "Black students want a Black student council." In a city with a majority-Black teaching force, Black teachers were not adequately represented on the faculty. For seventh and eighth graders, only the computer teacher and the PE teacher were Black. No Black teachers taught required academic subjects. The African American students particularly noticed their absence.

In my classroom, my students and I generally get along well. But I have also recognized signs of tension. During Black History Month, LaDonna told me she only likes Black history and hasn't learned much history in my class. Nelson supported her, but others felt more ambivalent.

Further, I probably expect a quieter environment than do some other teachers, and I think some of the African American students, in particular, prefer more talk than I as a White teacher who values more quiet than most can tolerate. Once when I was explaining to the students that I required an orderly, subdued environment, Tamika, who is African American, blurted out, "Yeah, you got that right." The African American students will say to me, "You sure are quiet, Miss Karen." I don't think of myself as quiet, but I seem quiet to them, and that has consequences.

In the most personally devastating example of these tensions, Briana, who is Black, wrote in her journal: "That bitch [meaning me] told me to shut up." I found this writing on the floor. Briana said she had written it and then thrown it away. I had not told Briana to shut up; I would never say shut up to any of my students. I asked her why she was so angry with me. She said I had told her to be quiet, but not the White girls. I realized that when I merely stare at the White students, they pick up on my message to stop talking. In retrospect, I think what happened with Briana was that I didn't see that she didn't understand that nonverbal sign nor did I see that she was not in tune with my lack of tolerance for noise, and so she felt discriminated against when I made my request for quietness more explicit for her.

When I went back to the logs and thought back about our in-class discussions, I found that most of the issues around race arose when students were writing about and trying to come to grips with the meaning of slavery. Slavery has always been one of the most difficult topics for me to teach, especially as a White teacher in this integrated, largely Black-and-White school in the deep South. This time, I decided not to teach slavery as a discrete unit, encountered just before the Civil War. I wanted my students to see slavery as a story embedded in America's story. Slavery is not a "one shot" event. Slavery has woven its way through every aspect of American life, as an economic issue, a political issue, and a social issue. It is not possible to remove the legacy of this institution from the story of America. I hoped that if we embedded the study of slavery in the context of American history rather than treating it as a separate "unit," my students would better understand its tragic consequences.

In the log assignments, four prompts, spread across 4 months, addressed the issue of slavery directly, and others allowed students to choose to write about slavery. By rereading and reflecting on these log entries, I found that my students looked at slavery from their varied cultural and personal perspectives and that depending on their perspectives, they came to different understandings of slavery's meanings and significance. However, these differences did not prevent constructive dialogue. Producing a large quantity of log writing about what they were learning and regularly sharing their logs with the class established a base for serious discussions of controversial and sometimes flammable issues. The sharing of this writing and the accompanying class discussions helped build a community and ultimately led the students to a greater appreciation of one another's points of view. I now recognize that by playing out the roles of characters in this most divisive American drama, students in my multicultural classroom paradoxically had an opportunity to come closer together. How did this coming together unfold?

The first slavery-related log-writing prompt came early in November. The students had read about the Southern British colonies and some of the problems of the people living there. These problems included but were not limited to slavery. I asked the students to write about one of the problems as someone living in these colonies. I did not specify what problem to address. I wanted to see what characters the students would create and what difficulties the people would face. About 75% spontaneously included something about slavery in their entries. Through their written reflections and our subsequent discussions, the class began to learn how slavery became a part of American history and to think about some of the probable emotional effects on the slaves. In these early entries most of the students were choosing roles that were easy for them to identify with.

In her log, Rachel chose a character who reflected her Southern White heritage. She wrote as the daughter of a plantation owner, imagining how she would react if faced with owning slaves:

> I see these poor people treated like they are worth nothing and it makes me very upset. Father has bought a dozen of these slaves and is being just as unkind to them as the rest of the slave owners. Father will be angry because I have been helping the slave children and adults [learn] how to read and write. The thing that would make him angriest though is that I helped one slave, who was only a young child, to escape. She has found a ship to go back to Africa.

When Rachel read her entry aloud to the class, it sparked a discussion about slave owners. None of the students were willing to consider writing as slave owners yet, but in this class that was over 50% African American, Rachel took a step in writing as the daughter of one. Rachel wrote about how she wished events had unfolded rather than how they did unfold historically. The class wondered about the reality of a child doing something so opposed to her parents' "wishes." Framing the past from the perspective of the present, Rachel said she thought that someone her age could really rebel that way. In discussion, we also addressed the geographical impact of bringing slaves across an ocean and talked about the reality of finding a way for a slave to get on a ship to go back to Africa. It seemed like an impossibility. Rachel had included accurate historical information about slavery as well: slave owners, like the father, were cruel; slaves were not allowed to be educated.

William, an African American born in Africa, chose to write from his cultural perspective, much as Rachel did. He put himself in the place of a new slave in this new land, writing to someone back in Africa:

> Dear Neera
> I hope your allright. If you are, I can not say so much for myself. I have been brought to a plantation where I work day and night. Anyone who won't work will be whipped. Our masters give us enough to eat though. I'm planing to escape soon.
>
> Yours
> Lasina

Like Rachel, William wrote about how he wished that events could have unfolded rather than about how they did unfold. He understood that his entry was an impossibility. A new slave from Africa would not be able to write to his family to explain what had happened. William said he was really reflecting the inner wishes of the slave to return to Africa and see his family. The beginning of the tragedy of slavery was just that—taking people from their homeland and from their families.

My students knew something about slavery, but I understood that we had a journey ahead. At this point the students were creating characters who could somehow change slavery. I didn't want my students to come up with a romanticized version of slavery—one in which slaves could write back to Africa or even escape.

The complexity of slavery became more apparent as the class began to search for why the Southern colonists decided to institute slavery and why the Northern colonists were relatively apathetic for as long as they were. It was, as William put it, about work. The plantations needed lots of workers; slavery was the quickest way to get them.

Meanwhile, our study of the writing of the Constitution and in particular Article I, Section 2, made it apparent that Northerners needed concessions from the South on other articles and so were willing to compromise on slavery; Southerners wanted to keep slavery, but they also wanted the slaves to count in their population. The result was the Three-Fifths Compromise, which denied voting rights to slaves but had them each count as three fifths of a person to determine the number of electoral votes a Southern state would get.

For their log writing on the Three-Fifths Compromise, I wanted to move the students beyond their romantic views by requiring at least some of them to take potentially unpopular stances. I asked each student to create a character who was a delegate to the Constitutional Convention. The students were assigned states at random and were instructed to present the viewpoint of their delegates. Given the framing of this assignment, those students who were writing as representatives of Southern states had to favor slavery and take risks in the context of our class. When these students realized their position, some complained that they did not want to argue for slavery. I assured them that I would explain their discomfort about their stance to the class before they had to read their log entries aloud. Their risk taking became fodder for our class discussions, forcing the group to deal with this uncomfortable side of slavery.

In this second slavery-related log writing, Dwayne and Peter both were assigned to write as Southern delegates, opposing the North's ideas about voting rights for Blacks. Dwayne, an African American, wrote:

Dear diary,
I appose the ideas of the North because they object to slavery. It is cheaper to own slaves then to pay people to work for you. I hope this affair will disapere quickly.

Yours Peter

Peter, who is White, wrote:

> On the ishyou [issue] of slaves I must vote for them. They are what
> make our farms and plantains run. They must be alowed to stay at
> thier curent positions. I however am willing in comprismise on how
> much of a vote they are given. A half is not enfuf. I beleave three
> fouths would be more sixyse [successful] now that whe [we] have resovd
> this isiyou [issue] we will contyiou [continue].

Peter incorrectly called this population count a vote. We discussed the fact
that no slaves were being given the right to vote, but that even though slave
owners considered slaves to be property, they wanted slaves to count as part
of their states' population. The other students seemed to understand that
both Dwayne and Peter and other "Southern delegates" had written in support of slavery because of the nature of the assignment.

I used the framing of this second log assignment to push students to
move out of the safe zone of the first logs. In these no student had taken a
proslavery response. Hearing someone, even a made-up character, defend
slavery did not seem comfortable to my students. Being the creator of such a
character might even be more uncomfortable. For this assignment, besides
the fact that everyone knew the task, I worked during discussions to help
ease tense feelings. For example, with Peter and Dwayne's entries, I pointed
out that both of them came to the conclusion that slavery was an economic
issue, opening the way for a discussion of one of the bases of slavery. At
this point James countered, "But that doesn't give someone the right to own
another person."

"Well," Peter argued, "there weren't other workers around. And they
didn't have a lot of money."

I could tell that Peter felt strange trying to explain what someone in the
past might have felt. I put myself in his place, a White student trying to argue
for slavery to his fellow African American classmates. Although I did not see
signs that the African American students were feeling anger toward Peter, I
still decided to step in. "All of us agree with James, but at some point in the
past there were people who did not agree with him. It's important to explore
the way they might have thought." The nods from students made me think
that they were beginning to see the value of writing about these people whose
views were different from theirs. The students, moreover, were seeing another
way that slavery was becoming embedded in American society, not just as an
economic issue but also as a political issue.

Several weeks went by before the students wrote about slavery again. By
this time we were studying the antebellum period (1815–1860). I realized that
no prompts had yet asked all the students to take on the voice of a slave. I had
begun to see that many of my African American students had a connection to

slavery that I hadn't noticed in White students. I wondered if White students, who often tended to deny this part of their past, could face their identity with slavery too.

After reading about the Underground Railroad, we talked in class about why some slaves tried to run away and others didn't. Leanne, a White girl, wrote this entry:

> SLAVE 1: So have you decided to come with me tonight and leave this wretched place we now call home.
> SLAVE 2: I don't yet know, I mean I was lucky enough to be sold with my son.
> SLAVE 1: He can come to,—
> SLAVE 2: If we go and get caught, things will get worse. And Master Jacobs is not as mean as the others describe their master.
> SLAVE 1: But don't you hate being someone else's property.
> SLAVE 2: Slavery is all I've know all my mother has known and all her mother has known. And at least we get weekend passes off season to visit our friends.
> SLAVE 1: Week-end passes! Ha! I hear that there are people of color in the Northern lands that don't need passes—ever.
> SLAVE 2: And how do you plan on gettin there?
> OVERSEER: Enough chit-chat, back to work.
> SLAVE 1: I don't know.

The details of Leanne's dialogue showed many of the tragedies of slavery—beating, separating of families, and especially, the institution of it— "all I've known, all my mother has known, and all her mother has known." But Leanne's writing also prompted LaDonna to tell the class that her grandmother had told her a family story about a slave ancestor who had thought her master was nice.

A few days later we read our textbook's description of the daily routine on a plantation. I gave the students a prompt: "Write a journal entry from the owner of a plantation." Gloria, who is African American, read her entry:

> Dear Journal,
> I had to put a slave in line today. This big black monkey want to try to runaway and I got. I beat his butt to his black self was red. But back to my crop My sugar cane crop is doing really well. We are delivery wey up north from the Mississippi river. We charge it by the pound from the granulating machine.
>
> Bye,
> Lee Sanders

The class was quiet after Gloria read. The tension was palpable as the students listened to the power that Gloria's persona, Lee Sanders, emanated in his hatred of his slaves. The Black students looked at one another and White students looked at the floor, everyone knowing that Lee Sanders could have been an ancestor of some of the White students in the class. Gloria's fellow students, although uncomfortable, were impressed by the painful vividness of what she read to them. I knew that our writing community was growing in trust as we used the anger of the slave owner, mixed with the pride he had in his business, to reflect in class on not just the economic and political aspects of slavery but also the deeply personal and to us socially repugnant parts of the institution of slavery in the South.

As a community of writers we were learning about the deeply rooted tragedies of slavery as it became a true institution. From discussions of economic and political issues, our class had now moved to discussions of the personal and social impact of slavery. Leanne, a White student, had given us insight into the slave's life; Gloria, an African American student, had given us insight into a slave owner's life. Slavery was a social institution that led a woman to say that slavery was all she had known. It was a social institution that allowed a slave owner to beat his slave and to think of a man as no more than an animal.

As I looked over the learning logs and studied the entries about slavery, I realized that my students had shown feelings of connection to people from the past. By accessing worlds where there were slave owners who wanted profitable plantations and slaves who were beaten, who faced running away, who were separated from their families, my students had lived for a while in the past. Not only had we learned about slavery, we had had many opportunities to discuss the lives of their characters as the students shared their writing. The students had grown as writers too, becoming more and more able to think and write from points of view other than their own.

Despite these examples, I wondered if this history-based empathy and learning had any carryover into the here and now. An interchange between Rose and Angela gave me the beginnings of an answer. It was in language arts class, not history class, that Rose wrote the following poem, though it was obviously inspired by our study of slavery in social studies:

TO BE A SLAVE

The ancestry of a black American,
    To be something that
    will be known as nothing
    but a nigger cause the
    color of your skin,

withholding all of your
thoughts and feelings
cause of the white man
threats,
To be a slave.
If you want the negro history,
You will have to get it
From somebody who wore
the shoe,
And by and by from one
to the other the white
man tore you apart,
To be a slave.
Together the slave a vivid picture of how
slaves felt about slavery tore the
inside of them to pieces,
To get blood, family taken
away from you,
Your own black baby crying
in your arms, pulled right out,
with you just standing silent
hardly can't breathe will
not say anything for some
demon is staring at you,
You swallow desparately
wanting to beat the hell
out of him, will turn
around and just walk away,
To be a slave.
To see the white man for the
first time appeared to be the ugliest
creatures in the world,
The same person who
brought you down the
river,
Don't gives a damn
about how you feel,
Just receives the payment
don't even look back
at you just minds his
own business like

nothing ever happened
To be a slave.
The End!

As a way of sharing and providing guidance for revision during language arts, I asked each student to read a draft by another student and to respond in writing. I distributed the drafts randomly, asking the recipient to respond to a series of questions and instructions intended to aid in revision: What is the best part of the piece? Retell the story. What was the strongest image? What would you change if you were the writer? (Bishop, 1990, pp. 178–179). Angela, who is White, responded to Rose's poem:

The best part of her/your poem, is when you talk about babies being stolen from thier mothers. I can understand how they (the slave women) could feel about this. I would never be crazy about my child being stolen from me. On the other hand, I can't really understand how they feel. I mean, it didn't happen to me, not to you either, but I guess you think more about this subject. I appreciate that, though.

If I were to retell the poem/story, it would be interpreted exactly how it is written. It is expressing Rose Washington's point of view on the subject of slavery. She is expressing how evil the white men were to do such a wicked thing. To use another HUMAN BEING as his slave, is evil.

The strongest image you passed was when you wrote the verse of "Don't gives a damn . . . like nothing ever happened. To be a Slave." She/you/Rose is saying what slavery was all about. The white men NEVER gave a damn. They just got paid & that was good enough for them.

The lead . . . well . . . there wasn't really a lead. It's just like . . . there. The poem starts hard, and finishes hard, she never lets up on the subjects. She doesn't gradually get into it, it's just: HERE, throwing the meaning into full forse.

If this were my paper, first of all, it wouldn't be, because I could never express such feeling as strongly as Rose has in this piece. But, if this were my poem, I would be very proud of it, I wouldn't change a thing.

Bravoa!

When I returned the responses to the authors, I heard Rose exclaim to Angela, "Yes girl, you understand." Rose was practically cheering. Angela looked surprised at first. Then she gave Rose a big smile. Rose walked over to her and gave her a high five. Rose and Angela both showed an understanding of slavery and why it was such a terrible tragedy in American history. They understood the culture of it, the economics of it, the geography, the sense of history. Both acknowledged the meaning of it, but each one brought something of her own heritage to her understanding of slavery. Rose wrote: "If you want the Negro history / You will have to get it / From somebody who wore / the shoe."

As an African American, she could identify with the feelings of the slave who was beaten, who lost a baby, who viewed White people as ugly creatures. Angela acknowledged the power of Rose's writing. "The poem starts hard, and finishes hard." She also understood Rose's ability to identify with the slave: "I mean it didn't happen to me, not to you, either, but I guess you think more about this subject." And when Rose expressed her joy at Angela's understanding, I saw a lesson they learned about understanding across racial divides and that I hoped others in the class had learned as well.

Maybe the biggest point of my study was not what my students learned about history by exploring these characters. Oh, they learned all right, and I do think we found a good way to explore history. In the end, the log writing showed increasingly sophisticated thinking about slavery. The students took on different voices from the past in their writing and "lived" different points of view; they began to take increased risks with the kinds of roles they were willing to assume, and they deepened their involvement in those roles. The students learned that all Americans share the past culture of slave, slave owner, and abolitionist, just as we share the past of the others in our history—revolutionary, soldier, explorer, suffragette. They also learned the depth of the tragedy of the lives of America's earliest immigrants from Africa and the tragedies of the generations of their descendants.

But there was a bigger lesson. When it seemed like my students weren't looking at things the same way as one another, I initially felt upset. When James said, "Well, Ms. Karen, if you all hadn't brought us over from Africa, we wouldn't have had all that trouble (meaning the Civil War)," I felt defensive, not only for myself but for the White students in the class. Maybe James sensed this when he added, "Well, I don't mean you and me. I'm just thinking like I lived in that other time."

On reflection, I think he did mean "you and me." The idea that Rose had—she can tell us the story—and the idea that Angela acknowledged— "You think more about the subject"—showed that there is more than one way to hear a story, to read about history. My students seemed to understand that.

I did a lot of soul searching and came to a new realization of the importance of nurturing my students' diverse views. Lisa Delpit (1988) writes about a silenced dialogue, caused when Blacks feel that they are being silenced when they interact with Whites. I think a multicultural classroom must provide an opportunity for communication—written and spoken, loudly and in many voices. Rose and Angela (and in retrospect other students) taught me that their feelings don't always require as much protection as I thought they did. Rose and Angela rejoiced in learning from each other.

Even though my students and I found it hard, I finally came to understand that conflict was necessary to help us grow. Sonia Nieto (1992) quotes Mary Kalantzis and Bill Cope:

> Multicultural education, to be effective, needs to be more active. It needs to consider, not just the pleasure of diversity but more fundamental issues that arise as different groups negotiate community and the basic issues of material life in the same space—a process that equally might generate conflict and pain. (p. 277)

Conflict and pain are an inextricable part of America's history of slaveholding and, through our discussions about the characters my students created, these factors necessarily became part of learning about slavery in my class.

Diversifying Curriculum in Multicultural Classrooms: "You Can't Be What You Can't See"

Elizabeth Radin Simons, with Kathy Daniels, Junia Yearwood, and Darcelle Walker

THE M-CLASS TEACHERS agreed that the curriculum should include authors who reflected the faces in their classrooms. They also wanted it to address the questions about race and ethnicity that were on their minds and on those of their students. In this chapter, diversifying or broadening the curriculum refers to expanding the literature, making it more multicultural and refocusing classroom goals to address issues of race and ethnicity.

Although M-CLASS teachers agreed on the need for diversification of curriculum, they differed in their reasons. Many teachers of color spoke with a special urgency about broadening the curriculum. Roberta Logan, who was both a teacher and one of the site coordinators in Boston, and who is African American, explained:

> You can look at something from many points of view and sort of dismiss multiculturalism. But I'm not in that position. I'm not in the position to do that because I'm always looking with a double lens. The lens of the outsider, the lens of the person of color. So that when I look [for example] at a textbook, I say, "What topics are we covering and how are we covering them?" I'm always keenly aware. (Local meeting, Boston, January 7, 1993)

At the same meeting Junia Yearwood, who is also African American, wondered how people could question diversification of the curriculum. Yearwood considers diversification critical not only for her students but for the survival of American democracy.

> [It] validates your existence. [It says,] "I'm important too. Look at me, I'm here!" To me it seems simple. To the academic world, it's a big issue. They're talking about how it factionalizes, it brings down cohesiveness. But what good is cohesiveness if it's built on lies, if it's built on ex-

clusion of other people. I don't see how inclusion could weaken
society. (Local meeting, Boston, January 7, 1993)

At another meeting later in the year, Yearwood talked of the dangers of a
mainstream America that is ignorant of minorities. Changing the curriculum
is about "survival," Yearwood said, ". . . because this society is structured
[with] the dominant group teaching and ignorant of what the minority group
is fussing about all the time, [so] you have problems!" Darcelle Walker,
another African American, agreed with Yearwood and added, "You have a
minority group who's not learning about themselves either!" (site meeting,
Boston, May 23, 1993). These teachers see two benefits of broadening the
curriculum: "The dominant group" will learn about people other than themselves, and people of color will see themselves represented and studied in the
classroom.

Susanna Merrimee, a Chinese American teacher in San Francisco, interpreted the tension over curriculum, to which Yearwood was referring, as a
struggle for power. "When I come across the word [*multiculturalism* in the
curriculum]," she wrote, "I see different kinds of ethnic groups struggling for
power. I see tension. I see the winners, and I see those who are defeated. How
do we ensure the silent ones can have a voice?" (site meeting, San Francisco,
June 12, 1993). African American teachers in separate cities, James Williams
and Brenda Landau McFarland, like Merrimee, focused on sharing power.
Williams wrote that multiculturalism in the curriculum was "the willingness
of people of different cultures to share with others who are different" (site
meeting, Boston, October 31, 1992). Landau McFarland added that it is "the
actual ability to accept other cultures without feeling threatened" (site meeting, Chicago, October 18, 1992).

School curriculum is often prescribed by the state and the city and reflects the political power structure. The teachers of color just quoted here
look at America through the lens of a person of color. They have experienced
racism and argue for a multicultural curriculum, to validate racial and ethnic
groups and, at the same time, to educate American students about racial and
ethnic groups. In this way, it is hoped, students will learn not to be threatened
by difference and to share political power.

It is important to stress that the White teachers do not disagree with
these points made by teachers of color. But White teachers, as well as some
teachers of color, in their arguments for a diversified curriculum, emphasized
the richness found in diversity, the importance of honoring diversity, and the
commonalties we share across ethnic groups. Kathy Daniels, a White teacher
in Chicago, wrote that multicultural education "means recognizing and celebrating the diversity in the country. Recognizing and celebrating the richness
that can *come* from that diversity. And finally recognizing and celebrating

those things that we have in common" (site meeting, Chicago, October 18, 1992). Nancy O'Malley, a White teacher from Boston said, "It's a real respect for the equality and the individuality" of the students (site meeting, Boston, May 23, 1993). Verda Delp, a White teacher from San Francisco, described multicultural curriculum "as honoring individual cultural diversity" (site meeting, San Francisco, October 22, 1992).

These reasons for using multicultural curriculum did not preclude political issues. Delp continued, "I do believe that teachers need to empower kids and give them the skills of literacy, and in order to do that you have to give them the powers that make them succeed in the White world. But does that assume that therefore I think that's the power structure that *should* be, is that a racist thing?" (site meeting, San Francisco, October 22, 1992). Delp's question led to discussion about the importance of teaching literacy skills, what it means to question the power structure, and what it means to assimilate.

In "The Silenced Dialogue: Power and Pedagogy in Educating Other People's Children," one of the first articles the M-CLASS teachers read, Lisa Delpit (1988) writes about the "different lenses" of White and Black teachers. She recommends:

> We must learn to be vulnerable enough to allow our world to turn upside down in order to allow the realities of others to edge themselves into our consciousness. In other words, we must become ethnographers in the true sense. (p. 297)

In teacher-research projects such as M-CLASS, inner-city teachers of color and White inner-city teachers can come together as "ethnographers," open up to each other's realities and further the dialogue on multicultural education.

The M-CLASS ethnographers found that two types of models were fundamental to their students' success. The first was the teachers themselves; the second was found in the portraits in multicultural texts of people like and unlike themselves. Through both of these models, students can stretch their cultural knowledge and find both heroes and warning tales. At a meeting in Chicago, Stephanie Davenport quoted her minister, who in talking about the dilemma of many young people today, said, "You can't be what you can't see." Students need models of what they can be.

No matter what their argument for diversifying curriculum, teachers agreed on two ideas that underlie a successfully diversified curriculum. First, it must be ethnically and racially inclusive and explicitly address issues of race, ethnicity, and prejudice. Second, in order to successfully deliver this curriculum, teachers must have empathy and concern for the students for whom they will be acting as models and guiding through some volatile issues. This second theme was labeled "caring" at the last Boston site meeting when the teachers were reviewing the 24 papers written by members of the M-CLASS project. Roberta Logan observed:

> There's an ethos of caring throughout the papers, you . . . care for your subject [and] . . . you care for children, and they blend together, but there's a definite ethos of caring and responsibility. (Site meeting, Boston, May 23, 1993)

The "ethos of caring" as defined by Logan encompasses students and subject matter. Caring takes multiple forms, beginning with the more obvious, to like and *enjoy* the students and to believe in their potential. Less obvious forms of caring are revealed in the responsibilities implicit in caring (some of these overlap the first theme): the responsibility to design a multicultural curriculum in which students can see reflections of themselves and models of whom they might become; to create curriculum through which they can engage reluctant students; to risk addressing the volatile questions; and to teach the necessary literacy skills.

This chapter presents the work of three teachers, Kathy Daniels, of Chicago, and Junia Yearwood and Darcelle Walker, both from Boston, whose research addressed the broadening of curriculum. The complex variables surrounding the two themes of diversification and caring are demonstrated through the research of three inner-city teachers teaching different multiethnic populations in different settings. Daniels works with students who are unskilled and disengaged; Yearwood's case study student is skilled but disengaged; and Walker's students are both skilled and engaged.

Daniels's challenge is to interest her students in school and develop their reading and writing skills. Yearwood focuses on students' self-image and how reading can influence self-image and have an impact on learning. She has a theory about how to motivate students based on her adolescent experience of self-discovery through reading about other Blacks such as herself. Walker's research question, like Yearwood's, comes from an adolescent experience of extreme ethnic discomfort over a text read in class. Walker investigates students' comfort level reading literature depicting racism.

DEVELOPING INTEREST IN READING: KATHY DANIELS

Faced with the challenge of teaching high school freshmen 3 to 4 years below grade level, Kathy Daniels set about changing her curriculum, pedagogy, and class size. The previous year, with a colleague, she had proposed a restructuring effort at her school, using both ESEA (Elementary and Secondary Education Act) and Chapter I funds, to create small classes for low-skilled students. Their proposal was adopted by the Chicago Board of Education as an "innovative organizational approach," and they were able to create two classes of 10 students and order a new set of teenage fiction with multicultural themes. It was in one of these classrooms that Daniels did her research. The introduction from her M-CLASS research report establishes the context for her work.

> I have been teaching English at Farragut High School for more than 16 years, and three things have remained pretty constant during that time. First, the reading scores of 75% of our entering freshmen are below grade level. Second, gangs and racial tension have been serious issues in the community. Only the complexion of the school has changed. When I arrived, 85% of the students were African American, and 15% were Latino. Today, the school is almost 90% Latino (mostly Mexican) and a little more than 10% African American. Gangs are formed along racial lines and gang activity has escalated in the past 4 or 5 years. When a fight breaks out in school, even if it begins with two individuals, it quickly explodes out of control. When something gang related happens in the community we can expect to see its effects— either continuation or retaliation—in school the next day.
>
> The third constant is that the great majority of our students have always been good kids who respond to kindness, sensitivity, and respect—kids who want to do better, who want a life without violence, who still have some hope for the future, and who are willing to keep trying. It is for them that I keep trying too.
>
> Against the backdrop of violence, I'm still looking for answers. What do we do about kids who come to high school reading 3 or 4 years below level? Actually, in all my years at Farragut, I have only known a handful of students who truly *couldn't* read, in other words, decode, but too many of them *didn't* read and didn't care about reading. . . . I have had a "gut feeling" that the only approach that would work was one that was centered in real reading and writing. This belief was based partly on my experiences with journals at another school in the late 1960s. . . . When I rather timidly suggested this idea, some of my colleagues at Farragut reminded me that my previous school was all White and middle class, and they assured me that it wouldn't work with "our kids" because "our kids" just couldn't read!

Despite the almost desperate conditions of this environment, Daniels recognized that the students wanted to learn. Moreover, for 16 years she had been observing these students and saw what her colleagues overlooked—that despite low test scores, the students arrived with reading and writing skills that she could build on. Daniels hypothesized that her students would be better served by a structured workshop approach to reading than by the decontextualized skills pedagogy advocated by some of her colleagues.

Daniels, who radiates warmth and humor, is a magnet for students. They flock to her with questions about both school and life as she walks down the corridors and when she sits at her desk in the teachers' lounge. Her classroom is decorated with photos she takes of each student in the first weeks of school. These accompany write-ups of interviews her students have done of each other. She begins the year asking the students to tell her about the high and low points of their lives. She gets to know them from the start, and they get to know her. As Delpit (1988) suggests, she offers the students her world, taking the risk of sharing personal stories, even silly ones, to edge her life into their reality.

> I try to set the tone of community in our classroom the first day by telling them about myself—my life at Farragut and my life outside of school—and then inviting them to tell me about themselves and their reactions to Farragut in their first journal entry. I told them about my cat Fluffy and how goony she was. I told them that I had two children. . . . I also told them that I don't have many rules in my classroom, but the major one is that we respect each other and work together to help one another, that no matter what goes on outside, it doesn't come into the class.
>
> I hoped that they would recognize my respect for them and feel safe enough to be honest even in those early entries, and they were. The first journal entries showed the concerns one might expect from freshmen, as well as some others. Elena wrote about the difficulty of finding the classrooms, but she also said, "I wish I could get a education because right now I'm nobody just a freshman. Wen I graduate from H.S Im going to be somebody because for now Im nobody." I responded, "Even freshmen are somebody!" Later in the same entry, I assured her that it would get better. Melissa wrote that she thought she would be scared and get lost, but she added, "This is my second day here at Farragut and I almost know how to be in the halls and how to go to my classes." Eduardo told about his family and his interest in football, but also wrote, "Most of my friends were dropouts. But I am going to stay in school." My response was, "I hope you *do* stay in school!"

Even in their first journals, Daniels's students were candid, offering her their reality. She wrote back assuaging their fears, such as Elena's concern that she was "nobody." Daniels encouraged them academically, not didactically telling them what to do, but expressing her personal hope for them, as when she wrote to Eduardo, "I hope you *do* stay in school."

The journal writing, one piece of Daniels's writing curriculum, served multiple purposes: Students were learning how to communicate through writing and they were getting personal attention from Daniels. At the same time, Daniels was laying the groundwork for the reading workshop, where students would also keep a journal. The early journals were informal and unstructured. Their reading-workshop journals, although retaining the informality, would be built around specific questions designed to teach skills of summary and analysis. Now, in the beginning of the year, caring and curriculum intertwined; teacher and students were getting to know one another through their informal correspondence while students practiced their writing and reading skills.

In the first few months of the school year Daniels talked with her teacher-research group about incidents in her class, incidents that demonstrate her continual care in building community for her students and that show how she was slowly and deliberately connecting the students to school and thus to learning. In mid-October several students were considering transferring to another school and were discussing the move *sotto voce* during class. Because of the small class size, Daniels overheard the conversation and told the class, "Well y'know if any one of you transfer, it will really affect all of us. I mean that would really be *sad*." The students were jolted and said, "You mean you really would mind, you mean you really would miss us?" and made her repeat her statement. As Daniels observed, "That's kind of neat so early in the year, and it wouldn't happen in a bigger class" (site meeting, Chicago, October 18, 1992).

Also in October, Daniels mentioned to a Mexican American boy that her family liked a salad she made with *nopales*. The incredulous student blurted out, "You like Mexican food?" Daniels had risked the corniest of connections, the one often dismissed as patronizing and as avoiding the hard issues; she shared her love of a part of the culture of her students. Daniels explains, "That's a kind of a recognition for them. Here's this Anglo teacher and she knows some of this. So, I think that's a real teeny teeny part of it" (site meeting, Chicago, October 18, 1992). Sharing a love of food is not false deference or condescension as long as it is part of a larger picture of concern, teaching strategies, and expanded curriculum.

Daniels had planned to start the reading workshop in the fall. By February, impatient with district snafus that delayed the arrival of the multicultural books she had ordered, she made do with what she could buy and find at school, teenage fiction written by White authors. By now Daniels and her students knew each other well. The students did not yet find pleasure in reading, but they trusted her promise that together they would find books they would want to read. To set up her reading workshop, over and over again Daniels modeled through her enjoyment of reading the importance of the activity. She also stressed finding books of genuine interest to each student. To foster individual taste in reading, Daniels told her students to reject any book they didn't like. "This particular aspect of choice must be a new one for them," she wrote, "they all tested it out frequently!" Daniels's description of the first weeks of readers' workshop reveals the patience, effort, and time she put into finding the exact book to match each student's interest.

Two of the girls, Tuana and Sandra, had a difficult time finding a book that they liked well enough to read all the way through. They started several, read 20 or 30 pages, and then switched to something else. Finally, I found an old set of books in the English book room titled *Gang Girl.* Both girls finally settled down. Tuana finished the book in a week and wrote in her response journal, "This book is about a girl that was 14 and she had a friend that was in a gang and she felt lonly and she joined in and she never thout she was going to be the leader. She had an exsedent and she regret what she had done. Its a great book its like real life and I would like to read another book like that."

The next day, after I read Tuana's journal, I questioned her about what she meant by "real life." She decided that she meant that she could identify with the main character, who was a girl faced with many of the same problems that she and her friends had to face, such as the decision to join a gang. Now my job was to find "another book like that."

When Juan was reading *Durango Street,* he wrote, "Im reading a book called Durango street. Each day I read it, it gets better and better. I'm going to read this book untill I finish reading it." Eduardo chose a book called *The Perfect Crime* and wrote in his response journal, "The book is getting pretty exciting and I met keep the book after all." The day that Melissa finished reading *The Divorce Express* by Paula Danziger, she wrote, "I just finished reading 'The Divorce Express.' It's a nice book about two parents of two girls who are divorced and they become good friends. Rosies mom and Phoebes father are going out so now they are like sisters. I recomend it to girls."

After several false starts, I offered Manuel (who told me he hates to read) a book called *Chico,* mostly because it's short and easy. It turns out that the teenage hero has some of the same problems Manuel himself faced, and he eagerly picked up the book each time we had a reading-workshop period and read with a concentration and intensity that he had not shown previously. He moved to the back of the room where no one would disturb him. The other students were aware of what was happening.

Daniels's students connected to these books in multiple ways. Often the link was situational, as in *Gang Girl* and *Divorce Express*. But Daniels noticed another interesting connection: students read ethnicity into texts that were not ethnic but that depicted their lives; this happened with *Gang Girl*. Sometimes the connection was ethnic, as in Manuel's reading of *Chico*. In fact, Daniels thought Manuel connected to this book on several levels, since both Chico and Manuel had alcoholic fathers.

The daily response journals show the value of Daniels's experiment with the reading workshop with her underskilled, disengaged freshmen. The students were beginning to enjoy reading. Tuana liked her book about "real life" so much that she was willing to try another. Juan was learning that a book can hook him and get better and better. Melissa was recommending a book. Manuel liked reading for the first time because he saw himself on the page. Students were learning some basic literacy skills as they summarized and gave broad critiques of books. They were learning to select books of interest, rejecting ones they did not like after 20 or so pages, and they were recommending books to one another.

Research from the educational establishment that questions the importance of smaller class size in learning goes against the grain for teachers. Daniels's study offers some useful insights into why class size can make a difference, especially for students who do not trust school, and for teachers and students of different ethnicities trying to make personal connections. They need time to get to know and trust one another, which is easier in a small class. In a small class Daniels could more readily personalize the curriculum, have one-on-one talks and regular writing exchanges with each student. She could respond immediately to the reading journals, as she did with Tuana, and have the time to find "another book like that." Because the class was a small supportive community, there could be, early into the reading workshop, a moment like the class response when Juan called out, "Manuel finished *Chico*!" and everyone cheered. In a small class, Daniels could tell a student he would be missed—in a large class, in October a student might barely be known, let alone missed. Moreover, because of the quick buildup of trust, students could accept as sincere Daniels's concern about the loss of one of them and what it would mean to the group.

Out-of-school bragging about a class in inner-city schools is extremely rare. Daniels's students grew proud of the class and told their friends, who began to appear in class. Daniels wrote, "Kids who had study or lunch or whose teacher was absent that day, sometimes they came in and did their homework. Sometimes they selected a book and read along with us."

Daniels's students experienced the creation of a strong classroom community by a caring teacher. In the small class, reading young adult fiction, they made a 180-degree turn in their attitude toward school and began to enjoy reading. Daniels regretted that she would not be their teacher the following year. In this first year she had succeeded in getting them reading, even enjoying it. A 2nd year could have solidified their change, improved their reading and writing skills, and allowed time for more-challenging literature.

KNOWING ONE'S HISTORY AND SCHOOL SUCCESS: JUNIA YEARWOOD

Departures from the status quo in school—departures necessary for capturing the attention of disinterested, inner-city students—require structural changes in the school. Such changes are enormously time consuming and difficult to accomplish, especially for teachers who often don't have the leverage to make change. Yet just as Daniels created a new small class, Yearwood, in an attempt to turn around failing students, made two changes: She created a multicultural library for her school and designed a new freshmen course called Personal Growth. Yearwood, an English teacher, agreed to develop and teach Personal Growth, a one-semester social-living course, in order to address what she saw as a major cause of her students' failure, their lack of knowledge of the history of their race or ethnicity and a lack of positive ethnic role models. Yearwood's belief is rooted in a life-changing moment in her adolescence:

> As a Black woman of African and West Indian descent . . . upon learning my history, I acquired a strong sense of who I was and developed a sense of pride, importance, and purpose. This occurred . . . in my early teens [in Barbados], when I first learned about the history of my African ancestors in class, the horrors of slavery, and the strength and resilience of my people. . . . I became extremely motivated to find out as much as I could about my heritage.

The history curriculum in Yearwood's own school in Barbados did not include West Indian history, only that of Britain and Europe. As an adolescent, on her own she went to the library and learned about the "strength and resilience of [her] people." After emigrating to Boston, she continued to read widely in ethnic literature, which reinforced her convictions about the value of knowing one's roots. Reading Malcolm X's sentence, "Just as a tree without roots is dead, *a people without history or cultural roots also becomes a dead people* [emphasis added]" (p. 25), Yearwood reflected on its meaning for her students:

> "Dead" students have no desire to learn. Dead students do not understand the importance of learning. Dead students cannot learn from the mistakes of the past. Dead students have no sense of their history and, therefore, do not value the present, and have no goals for the future! To educators, dead students are a liability; dead students are not successful and thereby prove us to be failures.

Yearwood offered a remedy for "dead" students:

> When you see yourself in a history book, when your people are referred to in the history book doing . . . positive things, then it does something to your desire to learn. It does something to your self-worth, to your pride, to your self-esteem. (Local meeting, Boston, January 7, 1993)

In her research, Yearwood wanted to see if the epiphany she had experienced in discovering her history in Barbados was relevant to her students in Boston in the 1990s.

Anyone walking into Yearwood's classroom of African American, Latino, White, Asian, Middle Eastern, Cape Verdean, African, and West Indian students knows immediately that she cares about these students. English High School in Boston, where she teaches, looks and feels like a locked-down prison. But when the door opens to Yearwood's room, one sees sunlight coming through high-set windows that run the length of the far wall. Below these a shelf overflows with flourishing plants. The other three walls are covered with inspirational sayings mounted on colored paper, looking like fields of multicolored flowers. Many students, however, do not arrive eager to learn, so Yearwood tries different curricular approaches to catch their attention. Before she can teach them literacy skills, they need to have a stake in school. The ultimate goal of her Personal Growth course, which includes her multicultural library, is to help students learn the value of education. At the San Francisco conference that began the M-CLASS project, Yearwood listened to a discussion about teen culture. Realizing its pivotal role in her students' self-image and attitude toward school, she added it to Personal Growth. Her students' reflections on their teen culture produced some disturbing writing. One journal read:

Teens feel that school isn't that important in our life. . . . We don't understand why we need to learn so many different things. The youth culture make[s] me not want to learn. That's the effect it has. In school you have to watch your back . . . sometimes you don't even want to come to school, other teens make fun of you. (Site meeting, Boston, October 31, 1992)

Yearwood envisioned her Personal Growth class as an opportunity to combat the negative power of youth culture and the racial and ethnic self-deprecation she saw in many of her students. Personal Growth directly addressed the aspects of her students' lives that Yearwood believed severely interfered with school, such as lack of self-esteem, confusion about self-identity, puberty, peer pressure, friendship, drugs, gangs, violence, anger, racism, and prejudice. While studying these topics, students would learn critical thinking skills in decision making, goal setting, and career choices. Since self-esteem and self-image are linchpins of academic success, Yearwood opened with a 2-week introductory unit on identity where she introduced race and ethnicity, themes maintained throughout the semester.

During this first unit, Yearwood introduced the students to the multicultural library, which she physically brought into the room, on a large rolling cart. The library, the informational backbone of Personal Growth, was also a vehicle for teaching literacy skills. The library contained biography and autobiography by writers from many races and ethnicities, professions and walks of life, the famous and the ordinary. Yearwood had contributed many of her own books to the library, which covered a wide range of reading levels and interests. It included works by Toni Morrison and Alice Walker as well as recent popular books about athletes, television personalities, and movie stars. Like Daniels, Yearwood attempted to catch the interest of all her students.

In Yearwood's experience, her male students were less likely to be readers. Therefore on the day that she dramatically rolled in her library cart, she kept her eye on the males. She instructed the students to browse and choose a book. "All of my male students eagerly chose a book," Yearwood wrote, "and there was utter silence for the next 35 minutes as they read. With rare exceptions, students chose books that reflected their ethnicity and culture." Most, she noticed, chose the books by their covers, scanning them for faces like their own. Throughout the semester, while studying the Personal Growth topics in class, students continued to read independently from Yearwood's library.

For her research, Yearwood followed one student, Robert, and his use of the multicultural library. Robert was born in Cape Verde of Portuguese and African parents and came to the United States at the age of 4. He self-identified as Black. Yearwood interviewed Robert throughout the semester and continued to do so for several years after. Early on, he told her, "I always saw White people as being heroes and Blacks as inferior, low-life druggies." Yearwood was not surprised; she has seen vestiges of this attitude in her own family:

> This quote from my student, Robert, reinforces what I've known for most of my life: . . . the lack of knowledge of one's heritage contributes to one's lack of positive self-esteem, which in turn fosters self-hatred. . . . Robert's perceptions of Whites and Blacks are no different from those of my acquaintances, friends, family members, and even my own mother, from whom I've heard similar statements of self-deprecation.

In class, Robert was a leader, and others listened to him, but he was the kind of leader who orchestrated trouble and got suspended. His junior high school cumulative record was a roller coaster of semesters with straight Fs followed by semesters of As and Bs. He was capable, alternately attentive and disruptive. While taking Personal Growth, his grades went up in most subjects. His English teacher reported improvement in his writing, which Robert attributed to the extensive reading he was doing in Personal Growth.

Yearwood was interested in monitoring Robert's attitude toward Blacks. He told her that he knew where he had learned that Blacks were inferior; it's "because of what I saw on TV and what I was taught in elementary school . . . that Whites were better than Blacks." Yearwood then asked him, "Did your elementary teachers actually say this?" Robert explained:

> No, but the only thing they ever taught me was about slavery. They never explained why Blacks became slaves. Nothing else, just the fact that Blacks were slaves. I had a very negative opinion of Blacks.

Robert's school experience in the United States wasn't much different from Yearwood's in Barbados. In Personal Growth, Robert became a voracious reader. He preferred biographies of famous African Americans—Malcolm X, Dick Gregory, and Dr. Martin Luther King, Jr. Reading these books, he realized, perhaps for the first time, that in America there were Black heroes. He began to notice African American heroes in popular culture; viewing television with a new perspective, he saw Arsenio Hall, Montel Williams, Oprah, and Bill Cosby as role models. After a semester of immersing himself in Yearwood's multicultural library, Robert saw some practical value in what he was reading. He told Yearwood, "Students of all races should learn their culture in American schools so that they wouldn't feel inferior to Americans, and they should learn it and be proud so they wouldn't get put down."

One way to measure Robert's change in racial identity is with Tatum's (1992) model of racial identity development for Blacks. In the first stage, Tatum posits that Blacks internalize the idea that "White is right." Robert began there. During the semester he moved toward a later stage where he had a more secure sense of his own racial identity. As he told Yearwood, the information he learned made him proud and gave him the knowledge to defend himself against "put-downs." Furthermore, he was able to get beyond self-interest to suggest that all students could benefit from similar experiences.

Like most M-CLASS teachers, Yearwood describes herself as strict—no hats in class, no bad language, only respectful behavior. At the end of the semester Robert reported some changes in his own behavior to Yearwood, "I don't call people names and stuff. . . . I don't call females 'bitches' and I'm not rude. . . . I also try to teach my friends things because some of my friends are real ignorant." It's probably not far-fetched to say that Robert, seeing a caring teacher modeled in Yearwood, has in a small way taken the teacher role on himself.

At the end of the year, with a laugh, Yearwood admitted to her teacher-research group that Robert's response to Personal Growth and the multicultural library was something of a best-case scenario. He read voraciously, even right through the night on occasion. Not all students became avid readers, but the great majority evaluated the unit with thanks to Yearwood for giving them the opportunity to learn about themselves and to be proud of their heritage.

Yearwood and Personal Growth, however, did not immediately change the course of Robert's life. The following year, he was dismissed from the school. Along with others, Yearwood helped to find him a good alternative school where he could study drama, a field he liked; but he dropped out. Lost for a while, he kept in touch with Yearwood, visiting her at school, borrowing and returning books from her library. When last heard from, he had completed his GED and was hopeful about starting junior college.

Students sitting in Yearwood's class have an inspirational model. They see an African Caribbean woman who believes that her students want to learn—even when they arrive saying that they don't—and who has a well-developed idea about how to help them. They see a teacher who acts on her beliefs, designing and teaching a new course in an effort to turn her students around academically. They see a teacher who furnishes the school with ethnic literature that it had lacked and that she deems critical for her students. She includes books from her own library, an intimate, personal offering to the students through which she models liking books enough to buy them, and that shows that she is a reader and that she reads literature of interest to them. Presenting the students with a library of choices, she honors their individual ethnicity and interests. For her students, Yearwood is a living embodiment of the intimate connection of caring and curriculum. Through her actions, her teaching, and the literature, she models what they "can be."

ETHNIC LITERATURE AND THE COMFORT LEVEL OF STUDENTS: DARCELLE WALKER

Darcelle Walker, like Daniels and Yearwood, is committed to multicultural literature as an important way of helping students "learn about themselves." Whereas Daniels focused on helping students to become readers and Yearwood on building self-esteem through literature, Walker, whose students are more engaged and skilled, takes on a thorny aspect of multicultural literature: the comfort/discomfort level for students when race and ethnicity are depicted in ways that students experience as insulting or painful.

Walker's interest in the comfort level of literature originated in her adolescence. Early in the year she read her written description of the memory to her fellow teacher researchers at a Boston meeting.

> Several years ago I paused from my teaching, and I noticed one lone Asian face that looked more pathetic and more uncomfortable than any face I had ever seen before. I realized that this student was internalizing and feeling very vulnerable about a story I was teaching, "Confessions of a Soldier," by Iris Rosofsky. This story is about an American alcoholic who is describing the roots of his addiction to a group of people at an AA [Alcoholics Anonymous] meeting. He admits shooting down three young, unarmed, Vietnamese men. He describes the hurt, fear, and pain that the Vietnamese men experienced before he killed all of them. He describes the subsequent guilt he faced after this incident and how he had never told anyone about it before AA.
>
> As a teacher, I had taught and discussed this story many times before. . . . But this time the story was different for me, because I now felt uncomfortable for my Asian American student, who was obviously very uncomfortable. It dawned on me that this was the first time I had had an Asian American student in my class.
>
> The only face that had ever been more pathetic, uncomfortable, and vulnerable than that was my own. That is why I could empathize with this student so much. When I was in high school, I was a member of a program called ABC, or A Better Chance. This program recruited talented minority students to send to private schools or to public high

schools with a wealthy student population. Usually the students were sent too far away for them to live at home, as was the case for me. During my high school career, I was often the one and only Black student in an all-White classroom, and whenever the literature had a negative depiction of a Black person, it had a profound effect on me.

Walker paused and told the group, "This is hard to read," and continued:

I felt the teachers had no empathy for my comfort level and I also developed a hatred for certain types of literature, like *Huckleberry Finn*. (Site meeting, Boston, March 27, 1993)

It had been many years since Walker's experience, but the memory was fresh enough to bring tears to her eyes and to those of her listeners. Walker explained how she experienced *Huckleberry Finn:*

All I saw was this clever, wise White boy, Huck Finn, who was so much smarter than the Black boy, Jim. Jim had to be taught everything. And he was often called *nigger* more than his God-given name. I noticed that my White classmates and teacher were very comfortable with this kind of literature, and it was obvious to me why that was. I felt then, and not just in retrospect, that my classmates were comfortable discussing and analyzing this literature because their own race wasn't being demeaned.

Walker has taught for many years at Boston's McCormack Middle School, which she describes as the "most academically successful middle school in the city." The students, who come from low-income sections of Boston, are African American; White; Puerto Rican; Asian American, mostly Vietnamese; Cape Verdean; and mixed Indian and African American.

From the first day of school, Walker, like Daniels and Yearwood, worked at creating a socially, emotionally, and intellectually safe classroom for her students:

I try to establish a classroom of trust and respect for one anothers' cultures at the very beginning of the year. I do that in many different ways, . . . [for example] I . . . tell bilingual students how jealous I am that they can speak more than one language fluently. I tell them that I studied Spanish for 10 years and still can't speak it as well or as easily as I like. [I do this] after I've overheard students in the classroom complaining about or mocking the Hispanic or Asian American students for speaking their native language.

Walker established trust by sharing her vulnerabilities and by modeling over and over again how she would like students to behave in the class through her personal stories. She is a riveting storyteller and very funny. A lasting impression for the visitor to Walker's classes is that the students never start to pack up before the bell rings—almost unheard of in most high school classrooms.

In her research Walker looked at the comfort levels of her multiethnic students through the reading of two short stories, "Confessions of a Soldier," by Iris Rosofsky, and "The Ethics of Living Jim Crow: An Autobiographical Sketch," by Richard Wright. Walker, who is not fearful of controversy in the classroom, chose the two stories "because they were not subtle in their racism," and because they contained unsettling portraits of three of the ethnic groups in the class.

Setting the intellectual and emotional climate for her study, Walker prepared her students by first sharing her own story about *Huckleberry Finn.* She considered this "the most important discussion I had . . . sharing some of my own classroom experiences with them." Then students talked of similar moments in their lives. Walker risked sharing her adolescent distress with her students. When they, through trust in her, were willing to share similar experiences, Walker had created a prereading activity that set the stage for honest reaction to the curriculum to come.

The first assignment was to read "Confessions of a Soldier" and to fill out a response survey. Walker wrote that she was unprepared for the reaction of her five Asian students:

> The first thing I want to mention is that all five of my Asian American students delayed both reading "Confessions of a Soldier" and answering the survey. I panicked and wondered what I had done wrong in preparing them for this study. I felt I would get my best, most personal responses from them—since this story was about Vietnamese soldiers. Each one of them came to me at different times asking if they could finish other lessons before starting "Confessions." I have to admit that this was a first. Never before had all of them required more time than was given the rest of the class. Eventually, though, almost 2 weeks after everyone else had finished, my Asian American students turned in thoughtful, detailed responses. Each response seemed carefully thought out, and I could tell that they discussed certain responses together.

Walker concluded that the Asian American students delayed their reading and writing from fear of the text. However, they dealt with their fears by collaborating, creating a study group and talking through their reactions. They sought comfort in numbers.

Walker's finding seems very useful—the importance of "safety in numbers" when reading literature in which one's own ethnicity or race is mistreated or demeaned. She shared some thoughts with the class at the beginning of the year that might have precipitated the Asian American students' study group. She told her students that:

> most people are more comfortable with their own race. To me, that is a natural feeling. But I also let them know that this doesn't mean that they should feel superior or inferior to any other race and subsequently engage in racist, discriminatory behavior. I tell them to learn to respect, admire, learn, and share with other cultures, but to maintain a sense of pride in their own culture.

In an anonymous-response survey to the readings, students identified themselves by race or ethnicity. Besides asking specific questions on the readings, Walker asked, "If you were not influenced by a teacher, parent, and so on, what ethnic literature would you most prefer to read? Why?" Overwhelmingly, students who identified as White answered that they didn't care what they read. A typical response was "It doesn't matter what literature. All cultures are good, none are more interesting than another." Of the students who identified as Black or African American, almost all said they would choose Black literature, adding such comments as "I would learn more about mine [Black] [*word missing*] because I would like to know what people went though to get the opportunity we have today." The other ethnic groups were split between not caring and wanting to read about their own culture.

Walker showed her concern for her students by stretching them intellectually and making them confront their discomfort when reading texts such as the Rosofsky and Wright short stories. She carefully prepared them for their task. Before reading the short stories, which she knew would cause discomfort among her students, Walker created both a socially and intellectually safe environment. She shared her own vulnerability with her junior high school students, telling them in advance that she was researching the question of comfort level and made them collaborators in her research. By choosing her research topic, she modeled her conviction that ethnic literature is important, even while admitting that it can be disturbing or painful to read when it demeans or presents unbearable historical behavior of one's ethnicity, either intentionally or not. Most important, she modeled, through a personal story, her discomfort when reading about racism in literature. At the end of the year Walker evaluated her teacher research:

One thing that worked for me was that my students felt validated. They were interested in sharing their intimate feelings because first of all they knew it was helping me in my study, but more important, it wasn't ending up in the trash somewhere.

SUMMARY: "YOU CAN BE WHAT YOU CAN SEE"

The work of Daniels, Yearwood, and Walker supports the M-CLASS theme that effective multicultural curriculum is based on "an ethos of caring for children and subject matter." In common, the three teachers began the year creating visually attractive and psychologically and socially safe environments for their students. Early on, in moving toward creating that environment, they shared their lives, edging themselves into their students' consciousness, while allowing and encouraging their students' realities into theirs (Delpit 1988). The environments set the stage for the major "caring tool" of a multicultural curriculum. The context, the teacher and her students, determined the questions each teacher asked and the literature they used. Daniels chose easy-to-read young-adult literature of high immediate interest to her students. Yearwood focused on literature emphasizing ethnic models to help the students see "who they could be." Walker, as well as Juarez (Chapter 6), focused on literature to help students face the tough realities of a racist society whereas Alford (Chapter 7) used social studies to achieve the same ends.

Constructing an Empowering Curriculum: Achieving High Standards

As HACKNEYED AS the concept of student empowerment may be in educational rhetoric, in practice, the concept is as vital as ever. At the opening M-CLASS conference, it quickly became clear that teaching in ways that help their students gain power in the wider society is a cornerstone of the M-CLASS teachers' goals for their work. Although they share a sense of purpose, they do not necessarily agree on what it means to empower a student, nor do they have a single formula for how a teacher should support a student in gaining power. The teachers whose research forms the focus of Part IV offer their visions of empowerment and of how their teaching serves their students' development.

Empowerment is often equated with teachers' giving students "control" or "choice." This equation has a particular history that has had significant implications for teaching and learning. Process writing and reader response, for instance, which arose in part from a critique of "drill and kill" literacy teaching, emphasize the importance of students learning to read and write, not from direct instruction, but by reading and writing. Influential teachers such as Donald Graves, Ken and Yetta Goodman, Nancie Atwell, Lucy Calkins, and Peter Elbow set out compelling examples of how students could learn by doing—how, through the process of acting on their individual choices about reading and writing, students grew in their knowledge about, control over, and love of literacy. Process-based teaching acts on the theory that to empower students teachers must give them voice by giving them choice.

Another pedagogical approach emphasizes that to empower students, teachers in multicultural settings must explicitly teach their students skills and strategies that other teachers may assume their students will acquire naturally—about reading and writing, but also about possibilities for acting in the world. Lisa Delpit's (1986, 1988) critiques of progressive teaching approaches, such as process writing, attack the premise that these approaches are, in themselves, empowering. Delpit argues that when teachers rely solely on process approaches, they may neglect to identify and teach critically important knowledge about literacy and power. According to Delpit, more middle-class White students have been exposed to this knowledge than have students of other classes and cultures. If all students are to have equal learning opportunities, Delpit concludes, teachers must offer explicit instruction in literacy skills.

Research in critical thinking, reading strategies, and genre instruction have added an important dimension to the literature on process-based and explicit pedadogies. Teachers have drawn from this literature to extend their definition of skills and to expand their understanding of how explicit instruction might empower learners. Carol Lee's (1993, 1995) work on developing African American students' abilities to interpret literature by building on their culturally specific oral language knowledge provides an illustration of a pedagogy in which explicit instruction is embedded in process methodology. Lee (1995) shows how teachers can define skills, not as decontextualized rules for students to memorize, but rather as complex thinking strategies for them to act upon. She sets out a clear example of how a teacher can analyze the ways of thinking that an expert might engage in when approaching a complex task—in this particular case literary interpretation. From this analysis, Lee builds a curriculum that aims to make these ways of thinking explicit and accessible to her African American students by showing them how they can use what they already know and can do to extend their knowledge and abilities. Though Lee's model was developed in a setting where most of the students shared a common language heritage, her work has significant implications for all teachers.

The M-CLASS teachers' research presented in Part IV illustrates how they have developed teaching approaches that integrate process-based and explicit instruction suited to multicultural settings. These teachers have found ways to successfully respond to heterogeneity, so that their diverse groups of students can achieve the high standards that they hold for them. The upcoming three chapters provide different models of pedagogy as the teacher researchers explore many aspects of empowering students through literacy teaching in both language arts and social studies.

San Francisco M-CLASS teacher researcher Ann Lew finds that a purely process-oriented approach to writing does not serve her diverse students, many of whom are second-language learners. Lew believes: "The process approach holds students accountable for things they haven't been taught" (site meeting, San Francisco, October 24, 1992). For that reason, she argues, she must take a greater role in structuring her student's writing experiences. In Chapter 9, through a case study of a student she taught both as a freshman and as a senior, Lew looks in depth at the implications of intensive correction of student writing—what she calls the "red pen" approach to writing instruction. Lew evaluates the benefits and the limitations of her approach to correcting student writing.

In Chapter 10 Verda Delp outlines her theories about explicitly teaching literary interpretation in a detracked middle school. She describes how she engages her students in structured activities that present skills recursively and that carefully balance student choice and teacher direction. In particular, Delp discusses how daily log writing and vocabulary study enable students to gain competence in literary analysis. In her chapter, she traces three students who follow distinct developmental paths in her classroom.

In Chapter 11, the concept of student empowerment is reexamined through the work of three teachers, Elena Valenti, Nancy O'Malley, and Stephanie Davenport. Focusing on geography, creative writing, and freshman English, respectively, the three teachers each define what it means to empower students in a particular way, and thus shape their curriculum and pedagogy differently as they work to empower their students to achieve in the classroom and in the world beyond.

The chapters in Part IV illustrate that there are no simple approaches for teaching literacy in ways that will empower students. Responding to students' coexisting needs for structure and freedom is highly complex. The teachers integrate process-based and more explicit, teacher-directed instruction in unique ways that are suited to their subject matter, their teaching goals, and their classroom contexts.

—Julie Shalhope Kalnin

CHAPTER 9

Writing Correctness and the
Second-Language Student

Ann Lew

I SIT AT my wooden desk every night and look at my students' papers by the
light of a small porcelain Chinese lamp. I read every word they write. I see
what they learn from literature. I learn how they think, and I learn about
their lives. Above all, I learn about their varied attempts to communicate in
written English. One student writes, "By now most people live in big cities.
The worked in big factory. They don't care about the nature. They dump the
nature alway." A second student writes, "My father have to worked two jobs
to support us. He didn't likes us to have no money." These stories express a
range of emotions and experiences. Many are rich in human drama. But the
voices of these students will not be heard or be given much credibility in
today's high-tech world, beyond the walls of my classroom, unless they are
expressed in more-standard English.

Such are the challenges I face daily teaching English in the urban classroom. I teach in a public high school in San Francisco that serves students
from all over the city. Those who want to attend our school fill out applications and then are selected for admission through a lottery system. There is
no exam or grade requirement in the selection process. My classes are filled
with students from many backgrounds, both native born and immigrant, and
who exhibit a wide range of skills in their use of standard English. In trying
to meet the literacy needs of this diverse student population over the past 15
years, I have come to some conclusions about the teaching of writing and
about how to address problems of expression as well as correctness.

First, recognizing that writing must be conducted in the context of a
language-rich environment, I require students to read books of their choice,
on their own, during the school year, and talk or write about them. The
books could be about sports, romance, mystery, movie stars, anything they
want to read. My aim with this "outside reading" is to promote enjoyment
of the printed word. In class, I assign readings from our textbook—short
stories, plays, novels, poems—about which there is much discussion and writing. We have large- and small-group discussions. We talk to clarify plot, to

analyze characters, to note literary elements, to explore ideas. We talk about what motivates the characters in literature, and how they are different from, or similar to, us.

The students also write. They write personal responses in reading logs and creative responses to stories or poems. Sometimes they write critically about a piece of literature. I make wide use of prewriting and drafting. I find prewriting activities (mapping, clustering, brainstorming) invaluable in getting students' ideas flowing, in helping them explore the range of writing possibilities on a given topic, and in assuring them that they have important things to say. Sometimes we talk and write for 20 minutes, other times for a whole hour. I read student samples. We swap stories from our lives. We talk until almost all the students know what they are going to write about.

Then they write their papers. The first draft is sometimes sparse, or long and rambling, with little attention to grammatical correctness. It contains the basics of the topic at hand. "I don't know what else to say," is a frequent comment. I encourage students to consult their classmates and suggest to one another where details, dialogue, or both might be used. I circulate around the room and try to pull ideas out of them. The students write a second draft and, if they choose, a third, each more refined and developed than the previous. They respond to one another's drafts on reader-response sheets. They tell the writer what they like about the piece and ask clarifying questions or make suggestions for development. I read all the drafts, making comments and corrections. Drafting is key to how I help my students develop their writing skills. It allows them to take risks, try out new ideas, experiment with language, and make mistakes. It allows for creativity and free expression. With drafting, writing becomes indeed a process, dynamic and fluid, with room for growth and development.

There are a couple of ways I have departed from activities that are often advocated for teaching writing. For one, I do not require students to work in teacher-assigned response groups. Instead, I ask them to exchange papers with others with whom they feel comfortable and to respond to one another's papers, using reader-response sheets. Sometimes groups emerge naturally; other times, there are students who prefer not to share their papers with anyone, and that's fine. A high school classroom is sometimes fraught with tension. I have no problem assigning students to work in groups on other tasks, but I am uncomfortable requiring them to have their peers read papers that are often highly personal. For one, this may discourage students from writing what they really want for fear of adverse reactions. In addition, the reader, for fear of antagonizing the writer and of facing unpleasant consequences in or out of the classroom, *may* refrain from making comments that could be interpreted as criticisms, thereby sticking to bland, safe responses. Since I do not assign groups, students will often form groups with peers of the same racial or ethnic backgrounds. To encourage more mixing, I give students "diversity points" for forming groups with others whose backgrounds differ from theirs. "Your ancestors must have originated on different continents," I tell them.

Nor do I require students to work in editing groups. I am uncomfortable allowing the issues of correctness and language use to be addressed in editing groups. I think peer editing is workable in a class where students have internalized standard English, but those who have not internalized standard English have difficulty helping one another with their papers. Having them do so sometimes leads to additional errors, reinforcement of bad habits, and time wasted. Immigrant youngsters, as well as others who do not speak standard English, feel insecure about the conventions of formal written language. They also have little confidence that their friends can help them with grammar or usage. It seems a disservice to allow them to write without my close supervision. I decided, after a period of trying to make editing groups work, that I had to impart my knowledge more directly to them. The students now turn in their two drafts and reader-response sheets to me, and then I read, correct (often in red pen), and grade the papers. Then they write a third draft. Throughout the entire process, I speak to the students individually and frequently about the content of their papers as well as about their language use.

Since the red-pen approach to correctness is often thought to stifle creativity, intimidate students, even damage their self-esteem, I decided, 4 years ago in a teacher-research group with the Bay Area Writing Project, to ask 60 eleventh graders what they thought about my approach. In that earlier study, I asked students how they felt about my heavy-handed treatment of their writing errors, about my red pen bloodying their papers with comments and corrections. In anonymous questionnaires given over several months, they told me that they did not mind my approach, and furthermore, that they felt uncomfortable when I did not correct their work. Though the corrections made them nervous, they liked knowing what their errors were so that they could improve. My students, most of whom were African American, Asian American, Pacific Islander, and Latino—native born and immigrant—were well aware that they needed to improve their writing. As for any deleterious effects on their psyches, some of them have survived extreme experiences of violence, war, starvation, and family trauma. I doubted that a few red marks on their papers would damage them as long as they knew that I cared. One certain way to foster self-esteem is to have high expectations and then help students reach them.

I felt satisfied with what some might call an old-fashioned approach to teaching writing; I wanted to tackle a troublesome point that has continued to plague me. The same students who told me that they appreciated my correcting their papers often persisted in making the same errors. For 9 months, I circled the phrase "he walk" on their papers. Each time, they dutifully rewrote, "he walks," only to revert to "he walk" on their next paper. Though their papers would show increased fluency and complexity over time, I continued to be bothered by the persistence of errors in grammar and usage.

And so the questions for me this time are: "What is the role of writing correctness in the overall development of the writing of students who do not speak standard English? What is the most appropriate role for the teacher of writing in teaching the conventions of writing? And, more generally, how is standard English internalized?" I use the term *correctness* loosely to mean anything from spelling to punctuation to phrasing of ideas. I think that all are learned through proper training in the language arts. Therefore, this time, I decided to look at the more developmental features of writing and standard English acquisition, and the teacher's role in the teaching of the conventions.

An overriding reason for the concern I have about students being able to communicate in standard English is that whether they end up in colleges or jobs after high school, they will face a world that requires a high level of literacy for success. They will, I'm afraid, be judged as much by the way they package themselves via the medium of language as they will by the message itself. My job is to help my students express themselves in such a way that their voices will be heard in the wider society. Issues of literacy are ultimately related to those of power—economic, social, and political.

As I focused on the matter of writing correctness as a developmental process and wondered how I could study the acquisition of standard English, I found the perfect candidate for a longitudinal case study in my writing class one warm November day in 1992, sitting near the window, putting on her lipstick. I had had Linda as a freshman in my study-skills and composition classes from 1989 to 1990. Here it was, more than 2 years later, and she was in my creative writing class, as a senior. In both ninth and twelfth grade, Linda was taking my classes in addition to her regular English classes. I had been in the habit of keeping papers that students left behind at the end of each semester. If I could find her ninth-grade papers, I could look at her writing across time.

A little about the young lady with the red lipstick. Linda immigrated to the United States from Hong Kong when she was 6 years old. She lives with her mother and four older siblings; her father died when she was in elementary school. She speaks Cantonese to everyone in her family except her brother, with whom she speaks English. Linda feels that she acquired English faster than some of her friends, who came to the United States at about the same time as she did, because she went to elementary and middle schools where there weren't many Chinese students, and she was forced to communicate in English. Her father encouraged her to meet children of other races and to learn English. She told me in an interview that in the seventh grade she blurted out a phrase in Cantonese and surprised her friends, who had not known that she spoke their language. Now she says that she speaks mostly English with her friends, except in class when she doesn't want the teacher to know what she is saying.

Linda, by her own admission, is not a model student. She says that teachers see her as "this type of student who's not willing to learn . . . cuz I cause them pretty much trouble sometime . . . because I talk and don't listen to them." She feels that she has had bad relationships with some teachers, and as a result, they write her off. Although she often thinks she doesn't care about what they think of her, she also realizes that the teacher's attitude can cause her "to give up and do a bad job."

Unlike youngsters who are caught in between cultures and who are criticized for trying to be either "too American" or "too Chinese," Linda reports that she has experienced little conflict between her home language and the language of the dominant culture, perhaps partly because of the strength of her personality and partly because of the independence and latitude she is allowed as the youngest in a busy family of five children. It is important to know the language of your culture, she says, but learning English is more important, for jobs. She is planning to major in business and is well aware of the role of English in international trade.

When Linda was in my ninth-grade study skills and composition class, I taught time-management skills, Greek and Latin roots, map reading, dictionary skills, vocabulary, and writing. For writing, I was mostly concerned with fluency and development, so I assigned lots of journals—both free and structured. I wrote comments in response to their ideas in the journals but did not correct mechanical errors. Students also wrote "show-not-tells" that received credit and comments, and longer narrative pieces that were reviewed in response groups and corrected by me.

When Linda appeared in the fall of 1992 in creative writing, a little more than 2 years had elapsed since the end of the ninth-grade class, and Linda wrote more easily and thoughtfully, but she still had language errors in her papers: run-on sentences, fragments, errors in subject-verb agreement, and awkwardness in expression. Some errors, such as run-ons and fragments, are common to high school students, but the errors in subject-verb agreement and certain awkwardness in expression are peculiar to immigrant youngsters. Even with the mistakes, I noticed that Linda's language and thinking had become more sophisticated. In the 12th-grade class, I read every word she wrote, circled mistakes I thought she might be able to correct, and rewrote passages that I thought she might not be able to correct herself. I wrote comments and questions in the margins and at the ends of her papers, about content as well as form. As much as possible, I tried to say something positive. However, if I found a piece of writing unacceptable, I told her so, keeping in mind that she was less than a year away from college and deserved my honest appraisal. I refused to send her or anyone else out into the world without warning them of how colleges or employers might view their ability to communicate in English. Having thus red-inked her paper, I would give it a grade and allow her to rewrite it for a revised grade.

The fact that I treated Linda's 12th-grade papers differently from the way I had approached her ninth-grade papers reflected changes in my thinking. I had been slowly making the transition from using the process approach as I learned it, to modifying it as I saw the need. When Linda was in the ninth grade, I assigned lots of free writing to encourage fluency and development and to help students overcome their fear of writing. I corrected only formal essays that had been revised through a couple of drafts. When she was in the 12th grade, I gave fewer free-writing assignments and corrected a greater percentage of the papers to prepare students for the demands of jobs or colleges after high school.

In December 1992, I asked Linda if she would be willing to be the subject of my study. After she agreed, I looked through several closetfuls of papers from previous years, tied in small bundles. In the one marked "1989," I found Linda's ninth-grade paper written to the prompt "Tell about a memorable moment from the past year." Thinking that two papers written 3 years apart to the same prompt might provide interesting data for a longitudinal study, I asked Linda to write a paper about a memorable moment from the past year. These papers and interviews with Linda became the primary data for my research. Here are the two papers, as she wrote them:

THE MOST MEMORIABLE (SIC) MOMENTS FROM THIS YEAR (12/12/89)

My most memoriable moment was in my eighth grade year. I had a lot of fun in that year. Since everyone is going to another school we were nice to each other and I met a couple new friends. I always went out with my best friend to the beach and just look at the waves. At that year I felt important 'cause I was an eight grader and I could just look down at six and 7th graders. It makes me think, was I like that when I was a 6th or 7th grader? I went to many field trips. They were really fun field trips. The best trips were from the advance band. We always or mostly have fun. We went to Great America, Davies Sinphony Hall, City Hall, Lafette Hotel, and many, many more. I use to just love band 'coz it was so fun. In my school, it seems like band is the only great highlight of that school. In my eighth grade year I started to help volunteer and it was fun. I ran for student body and most of the things I did was great. I just love that year in some ways.

MEMORIABLE MOMENT (2/17/93)

It was a cold and dark moring, when I forced myself to wake up and get ready for school. It's such a drag to be awake when I'm half asleep, but on that day it was one of those important days, again in school (my report for physics was due). Realizing that I didnt complete my work, I tried my best to finish it, but certainly there wasn't enough time. I left home feeling bad and full of worries, but I knew I had to attend school due to my poor attendance record.

In school I tried to ask my friend to let me copy her work, unfortunately her data was totally different from mine. I can't face getting a lower grade in Physic, so I finally made a decision to go home and return to school before 6th period. Time was very precious, so I couldn't afford to loose a second. The only thing I could do was to ask a friend to cut school with me and give me a ride home, luckily he helped me out. When we got back to my house, I invited him in and asked if he would wait till I finish my work and then we both can go back to school.

Time passed quickly and still I couldn't figure out the answers to my research, I then decided to go to Exploratorium and reexamine my project. Again I had to ask for his help and again he did me a big favor. Questions started roaming around my mind, why was he so nice to me? It was strange to see a person doing whatever I wanted him to do. Thoughts of school faded because now I'm more concerned about my friend. We were friends since the 7th grade and the first time I met him he was very kind to me. I always had good feelings for him but it never occurred to me that I would have feelings for him. I aways knew I that I liked him, but there were many barriers.

At the Exploratorium, he finally showed his true feelings for me. He actually held my hand throughout the whole tour. My heart was beating so fast that it felt like it was vibrating continuiously. That day was filled with excitement and there is nothing that can express my feelings at that moment. I'm glad I had to go home, if I hadn't cut, none of this would have happened.

The most striking differences between the two papers are those of focus and complexity. In her ninth-grade paper, Linda answers the prompt by talking about the fun she had had in the eighth grade, and in effect, not focusing on a moment at all. Instead, she lists the activities that were memorable, giving a sequential reporting of events. Her writing is bland and simple (everything was "fun" or "great"), and she keeps her readers at a distance, never letting them enter her thoughts.

By contrast, her 12th-grade paper focuses on a day, on a 3- or 4-hour span, which includes a very important moment. She writes directly to the topic, allowing the reader to enter her thoughts and feelings. With voice and confidence, she discloses herself, conveying mixed feelings and the questionable things she was doing. She not only reports what happened but evaluates it, questions herself about it—"why was he being so nice to me?"—and discovers the answer through her writing. Clearly, the two pieces reflect a person at different stages of maturity.

The two papers are also different in form, in the organization of Linda's thoughts, and in her manner of expression. Her ninth-grade paper is one paragraph, with 16 sentences, 20 T-units,[1] and 199 words. Her 9.95 words per T-unit makes her sentences seem choppy, with little transition from one to another; the average native-speaking eighth grader writes 11.5 words per T-unit, whereas fourth graders write 8.6 words per T-unit (Hunt, 1965, p. 43). Syntactically, Linda's writing is closer to a fourth graders' than to a ninth graders'. Half of her sentences are simple, with the basic subject-and-verb structure; the other half include combinations of prepositional phrases and dependent clauses.

Linda's 12th-grade paper, on the other hand, is longer and somewhat more complex. It has four paragraphs, 410 words, with 22 sentences, six of them run-ons, and 40 T-units. She has 10.3 words per T-unit, more than in her ninth-grade piece but still not what Hunt found to be grade level for native speakers. Although she included a number of compound sentences, many of her sentences are marked by varying combinations of clauses, phrases, and questions, making for an interesting flow. Linda also uses dependent clauses and prepositional and participial phrases to begin her sentences, adding variety to her style.

There are problems with shifting verb tenses throughout both papers, but noticeably fewer in her 12th-grade paper. In the ninth-grade paper, Linda switches from past to present six times in 199 words, whereas in the later paper, she switches only six times in 410 words. Keeping verbs consistent is a problem not only for immigrant students but for native speakers as well.

One big problem that surfaces in the 12th-grade paper but not the ninth-grade paper is run-on sentences. The five run-ons may have surfaced because of the somewhat greater complexity of the later paper.

Also worthy of mention is Linda's handling of the verb "can" and "could" in her later paper. The two words appear six times. Four are correct;

two are not, perhaps indicating a partial internalizing of the correct form. Also noticeable is the fact that the past perfect tense should be used three times in this paper, and she does not get it right until the third one.

About a month after she had written the second paper, I asked Linda to reflect on the two pieces and tell me something of her writing background. She was critical of her ninth-grade paper, commenting that the sentences were short and not as descriptive as ones on the later paper. She said she tried to tell about the whole year in one paragraph; she should have used "show-not-tell." She was bothered by the phrase "At that year I felt important." I asked how the phrase should read. She said that it should read, "During that year." Ah-ha, I thought, she has learned the correct use of this preposition, often a troublesome point for second-language students. She said that in the ninth grade she began the paper with "My most memorable moment" because she was trying to answer the question, but that it was "bad" to start off a paper that way. For the 12th-grade paper, she thought of the topic, and then figured out the beginning, middle, and end, whereas in the ninth-grade paper, there was no beginning, middle, and end. She thought it was better to begin with a showing sentence such as "It was a cold and dark morning." She explains:

> I used to write off the top of my head, without much thought to structure. I would answer the question and then go into detail. Now, I go more into detail, indirectly answering the question. It's better than just answering the question. . . . Now, I go around the question and try to give examples. . . . In the past, my writing was like a sentence-to-sentence kind of thing. It's not fully developed. Right now, I would try to extend my sentences fully and try to make it paragraph.

Clearly, Linda internalized many of the conventions of writing as well as developed a sense of rhetorical style over the three-year period. The later paper has a stylized, albeit a clichéd, opening line—"It was a cold and dark morning." Linda does, however, consciously try to tell her story, to convey the full flavor of the moment, as opposed to merely answering a question. Her new skills also include answering questions indirectly, developing an idea through examples, extending a thought into paragraphs, and creating a beginning, middle, and end to her story.

I asked Linda to explain the role of reading in her writing growth. She responded, "Last year, we read a lot in my English class. I learned a lot about stories, but it did not help me in writing." She said that reading is beneficial because it builds vocabulary. On the other hand, reading a book that is too easy or too hard is a waste of time:

You don't learn anything from reading an easy book, and if a book is too hard, you're not going to look up every other word in the dictionary, so you just give up. It's difficult to find a book at the right reading level, easy enough to understand, but difficult enough to be challenging.

Every year I have one or two students who read voraciously and write well. Invariably, when I ask them where they learned to write so well, they just shrug their shoulders and say they don't know. Youngsters don't readily make a connection between wide reading and good writing, but when I asked Linda later how she would know if her writing contained errors in usage or expression, she responded, "Through what I've learned in the past . . . and reading." The influence of reading on language development seems subtle yet potentially powerful.

Linda makes two other significant points in the interview. First, she said that acquiring a second language requires access to rich, whole-language experiences—reading, writing, talking, and living the language:

If you speak English with friends, eventually you'll get the stuff in your head and when you write, it'll go down on paper. But if you speak a lot of foreign language with friends, the English will never stick to you. . . . [The] English language has so many structures. . . . That's the hard thing for people to learn. . . . So they don't know what's right and wrong, unless they speak a lot.

To become proficient at handling the complexities of a language, Linda reported, she needed ample opportunities to engage in conversation with native speakers, something she could not get by just sticking with other foreign-language speakers.

At points in the learning process, immersion in a new language with native speakers of that language is extremely useful. But in some schools, such immersion is not possible because for one, there are not enough students who speak English to form a pool in which to immerse the non-English speakers. Whose language should be the language of the classroom has been a topic of discussion among educators for many years (e.g., see Crawford, 1995; Heath, 1981). I agree that students' home languages should be honored, encouraged, and retained. But whereas others in the community argue about the issues of hegemony inherent in this debate, I have practical reasons for requesting that all my students speak English in the classroom. First, I am teaching English, and students need practice to become proficient. Second, interacting with one another via a common language is a crucial first step to students overcoming their prejudices and breaking down stereotypes. I have found it instructive to address this problem openly in the classroom, giving my reasons for requesting that they speak English, and allowing them to air their views and listen to one another. Some students say that they feel excluded when their classmates speak another language. Others say that they are talking about unimportant things with their friends, and ask why they can't use the language that is more comfortable for them. This kind of exchange increases their understanding of their peers and of the complexity of the issue. Confronting the issue helps to "clear the air" for a more sensitive classroom community. Like Linda, I would like everyone speaking English in class, and for a variety of reasons.

The second point that Linda makes pertains specifically to the development of written language:

> Newcomers have a hard time trying to learn the grammar structures . . . the only thing the teacher could do is constantly remind them and correct them and try to be more strict at it. Grades are important to some students. Mark it and lower their grade. They might realize to watch out for grammar mistakes. . . . People that just came have a disadvantage because they have to learn what everyone else is learning. . . . These teachers expect you to know it already. . . . They're not about to spend an hour or two teaching you. Maybe afterschool hours would be good for those who need help.

Here, Linda puts forth a theory of written-language learning that entails traditional forms of instruction—grammar lessons, corrections, and strict grading—for students to learn standard forms.

Linda says that she discovers writing errors by going back to her papers a couple of days later. "It's like you read your mistakes and realize that that's not what you wanted to write. You proofread and find your mistakes." How does she know they're mistakes? "Through what you've learned in the past. It doesn't sound right when you proofread it." She remarks that most students do not proofread unless they are writing an important paper, and they write their papers at the last minute because so many assignments are given by teachers at the last minute, with due dates of the following day. Linda adds that students are likely to put more effort into their work if they are given more time and if the teacher treats the paper as important.

Linda says that her ninth-grade regular English teacher "only yelled at us, told us that we were ninth graders and should know our grammars." I'm sure that many teachers in our schools, even in classrooms with immigrants, believe that ninth graders should know their grammar. The fact that some of them may have been in this country for only 2 or 3 years or may have spoken nonstandard English all their lives doesn't seem to make a difference. These teachers need to become aware of the linguistic backgrounds of their students, the fact that language acquisition takes some time, and that nonnative speakers may not ever write exactly as do native speakers. They then need to figure out how best to support students in their efforts to acquire standard written forms. Linda suggests after-school sessions on grammar and usage.

Since completing my research, I've thought a great deal about Linda's development as a writer and about my role as a teacher. Linda did become a better writer in the years in which I knew her. What Linda has clearly internalized is a sense of text, the structure and development of a story, a feel for what makes good writing, and how to develop and express her thoughts, skills unlikely to be related to my corrections. In fact, these improvements may well have come from her own growth and development from a child to a young adult; and to reading, listening to, and speaking English. Although her senior "Memorable Moment" piece is relatively free of mechanical errors, other papers from the same year have grievous mistakes in syntax, sentence boundaries, and subject-verb agreement. The latter seems to be most resistant to correction, at least among the Chinese-speaking students I have taught.

My intensive correcting of student papers does not eradicate all the writing errors. According to Linda, however, my scrutiny of her papers did cause her to look closely at her own work and helped her realize that I cared about her progress, but it did not lead her to fully internalize all the features of edited written English. Linda reports several times in her interview that she needs teachers to correct her work; otherwise, she hands in "just anything." My close correction of her papers seemed to play a role in her growth as a writer, but the exact role remains unclear.

The implications for me as a teacher of writing are that besides correcting surface errors, I have expanded my "outside reading" requirement. Now each student reads six books over the course of a school year, and writes, draws, or talks about them. A culture of reading has grown in my classroom. I hear students recommending books to one another, and we put the titles of good books on the bulletin board. Students enjoy discovering ideas, learning about symbolism, and seeing connections among characters and between characters and themselves. As for writing, I still must read and spend time correcting student errors so that students can see that I care about their work and so that these corrections can act as a resource.

In a good program of writing, helping students to develop their own voices is very important. Voice is what gives a paper its flavor; without it, the writing is bland and lifeless. For this reason, I have heard teachers caution against an emphasis on correctness, lest the student's voice be squelched. I agree, for the most part. On the other hand, when one is dealing with a student whose native language is not English and whose prose is barely comprehensible, it is the teacher's responsibility to help the student make him- or herself understandable. The students I quoted in the beginning of this chapter all have ideas and voices, but the world will not take them very seriously unless they express their ideas more conventionally. I think it is better to help them say what they want to say in clear English than to be overly considerate of their voices. I know from my personal experience as an immigrant child who went to school speaking only Japanese that I felt relieved when someone understood me enough to turn my awkwardness into comprehensible language. What have I learned from Linda? She has reinforced for me the importance of a variety of language experiences in the classroom. Beyond that, I think of how I must read everything students write, so that they don't turn in "just anything." Linda reinforced my belief that the role of the writing teacher is extremely active—there must be a good deal of facilitating and coaching. I do not correct and grade all their papers, but when I do make comments, I am most critical about coherence and development, and make comments and suggestions accordingly. Then I point out language errors and show students how to correct them. I try to treat their papers respectfully so that they will learn to respect the written word. I want students to view writing as a conscious, deliberate activity that is as worthy of their efforts as anything else that they might do consciously and deliberately—fixing their hair or dressing for a date, for instance.

Linda has reminded me that writing is a skill that is acquired in tandem with the development of the individual as a whole. Because writing is a complex activity that integrates thought, emotion, experience, and language, it is a manifestation of the person at a given stage in his or her life. Linda has also reminded me that teaching English in an urban setting requires that a teacher not make assumptions about what an average ninth or 10th grader should know. With the constant influx of immigrants into our cities, a good percentage of them do not have the facility with standard English that one would expect of native speakers. For them, close supervision of their language use, via the red-pen and other methods, in a caring, language-rich environment, is crucial in helping them achieve proficiency in English.

Where is Linda today? I imagine that she has graduated from college by now, probably in business or accounting. I've heard that she is still with the young man who took her to the Exploratorium that day.

Linda is very much with me in my teaching. I have used her two "memorable moment" papers to talk to students about what makes good writing. Invariably, they identify such features as focus, details, development, and the use of standard English as essential to good writing. I supervise students' papers closely so that they won't turn in "just anything." And I give grammar lessons, not after school as Linda suggested, but for 7 to 10 minutes every day.

Studying Linda's papers and her interview has informed my teaching and has reminded me, once again, of the importance of reflection in teaching and learning.

CHAPTER 10

We Soar Together: Studying Literature in a Heterogeneous Classroom

Verda Delp

> And there is a Catskill eagle in some souls that can alike dive down into the blackest gorges, and soar out of them again and become invisible in the sunny spaces. And even if he forever flies within the gorge, that gorge is in the mountains; so that even in his lowest swoop the mountain eagle is still higher than the other birds upon the plain, even though they soar.
>
> —Melville, *Moby Dick*

THE QUOTATION ABOVE, hand-lettered and framed, is displayed above my chalkboard and was given to me by a former student on the occasion of a visit to his old classroom. He said that he brought me this particular quotation because these words reminded him of our class.

I try to guide my teaching with this image, but it is difficult. My heterogeneous eighth-grade English classes at Willard Junior High in Berkeley, California, have California Test of Basic Skills (CTBS) Total Reading scores that range from a grade equivalency of approximately 3.5 to 11.9. Learning disabled, learners of English as a second language, and compensatory education students are a part of each classroom. The population reflects the racial, ethnic, socioeconomic, and academic composition of Willard and of the city of Berkeley. Willard's student body is 45% African American, 45% European American, and 10% Asian American and Latino/Chicano. It is located less than one mile from the University of California and about one mile from low-income housing. Children of professors are in the same classes as children of AFDC (Aid to Families With Dependent Children) recipients.

When I look at the faces of my students, I can literally see their academic heterogeneity: Tinesha, in her shy manner, with her eyes down, is quietly following along in the text and making notes. Next to her, Emily is sneaking ahead in the novel, holding her finger to mark the page the class is on. On the other side of the room, Antonio is whispering with his sidekicks while he tries to keep up with his notes. When I look at the faces of these students, when I honestly look at the differences that I must consider, I know that I will have to work hard to be sure that all of these young people have the opportunity to embrace the literature and the writing. With a vision of them soaring with me far above the plain to the mountaintops, I teach.

When I began teaching seventh- and eighth-grade English at Willard in 1980, the year we detracked our English classes and began teaching heterogeneously grouped students, I remember that there were brand-new dictionaries beneath each student's desk, and texts for each grade level that I was required to teach. But that was all. There was no literature or writing curriculum in place. Only about half of the students read the assignments; only the same two or three students participated in discussions about the literature; and most students wrote short, meaningless responses to what they were reading, if they wrote at all. In the spring of that first year, after months of anguish about what to do, I remember watching a particular student after I had asked the class to write about a piece of literature. She got up first to sharpen her pencil and then again to get a piece of paper. Then she opened her book and thumbed through the pages. She appeared to be looking for something, some answer or idea that would enable her to know what to write. I remember thinking that this girl did not have the resources she needed to do the assignment. I think it was then that I first began to understand that I had not been teaching the skills my students needed to interpret and write about literature.

As a result of that distinctive moment, I developed, and I continue to refine, a structure suited to teaching in a heterogeneous classroom. The structure supports me in teaching those interpretive skills that students need to respond to literature in a meaningful and substantive way. Drawing upon a set of interpretive strategies that I believe help them respond in an individual manner to the literature we study, I expect my students to create within themselves a resource of skills that provide them with the support they need to move forward within the structure of our literary journey. As part of the structure, students use note-making techniques to create individual resource maps that support and guide them to read for meaning and to write substantively. Daily, students write in response to the literature, practicing the interpretive skills that they have drawn from classroom instruction and discussion. Because I believe that we create meaning for ourselves when we bring our individual experiences, culture, and history to the literature we read, I expect each of my students to put forth into our classroom community their own distinctive voice and individual perspective. By sharing these individual perspectives through daily writing and discussion, we create a common knowledge that reflects our diversity.

As part of my research, I found that my beliefs about how students learn and my approaches to teaching reading and writing in an academically and culturally heterogeneous classroom, developed through reflecting on and refining my practice, are supported by Louise Rosenblatt's transactional theory of reading and writing.

In her theory, Rosenblatt defines reading as a transaction that involves both the student and the text. This means that students bring to the text their historical and cultural self. It is in the process of bringing that self to the text, of interacting with the text, that new meaning, or what Rosenblatt calls evocation, is created. Because each student is drawing on a unique "linguistic-experiential reservoir," which reflects the reader's cultural, social, and personal history (Rosenblatt, 1994, p. 1064), each reading creates a new internal text that redefines the self and the text. Rosenblatt's theory helps me better define and understand what it is that I attempt to have my students bring forth in my class.

For my research, I wanted to understand the effects of what I was teaching on my students' ability to think and write about literature. I set out to answer the following questions: How do varied students in my heterogeneous classroom use the interpretive strategies they learn in the classroom literature study? And how does their use of these strategies change across time?

THE YEAR-LONG LITERATURE STUDY: AN OVERVIEW

For literature to have meaning for my students, for them to care and have conviction behind their ideas, for them to write from their hearts, my students must develop within themselves a foundation of literary skills and knowledge. Interpretation must become a way of thinking, a way of looking at the world, a classroom perspective. Over and over again I ask my students, "What does this represent? Yes. And what else? What does this tell us about the character? Yes. And what else?"

To create this classroom filled with students of literature, I establish what I call our yearlong literature study. I explicitly teach skills of interpretation using an approach that I developed when I realized that many of my students needed more skills and a structure within which to use these skills. We analyze character, imagery, and symbolism, making notes on resource maps and recording our observations and reflections in daily logs. We identify and keep track of recurring themes, often revisiting and reshaping our perceptions, and thus constantly enhancing our perspectives. At the end of our study of each piece of literature, the students write and revise an essay on a topic of their choosing. They also create a pictorial representation, including both writing and drawing, often about the same topic. Through the creation of these representations, students synthesize their ideas to show their final interpretation of the literature.

To instill interpretive thinking strategies, I teach my students to find meaning in characters' behavior and to uncover the significance of the imagery and symbolism. When we read *The Autobiography of Miss Jane Pittman* (Gaines, 1971), we interpret Jane's behavior: I ask the students, "When she asks for a drink of water from the woman who screams at her, how does Jane respond?" They answer, "She is polite. She doesn't scream back." I question them again: "What does this say about Jane? What does this tell us about her?" In *Light in the Forest* (Richter, 1953), we contemplate the meaning of *light* in the title. "What does the light represent? Is it significant that the light is from the sun? What about the shadows? There have to be shadows beneath the trees in the forest. What does that mean?" When we read *April Morning* (Fast, 1961), we notice that light brings war and death and that darkness represents shelter and safety. I ask, "Isn't this the exact opposite of the imagery we have discussed? What does that mean?" Through this recursive process of analyzing the imagery and symbolism as a class, students see how intricate literary details come together and learn how to use this knowledge to create interpretations of the characters and their circumstances in the stories we read. I want the students, all of the students, to use interpretation as a way of thinking, a way of creating meaning for their own worlds.

To establish a common resource of interpretive language, I steep my students in vocabulary to help them think and write about literature. Thematic vocabulary helps them explain their ideas whereas structural vocabulary helps them see the literary forms that support these ideas. Thematic vocabulary represents the concepts and themes of the literature. The students learn that *resentment* and *despair* characterize Richard Wright's position in *Black Boy; naive* reveals Moses' perspective in *April Morning;* and *compassionate* describes Miss Jane Pittman in *The Autobiography of Miss Jane Pittman.* We literally wait and watch, as though on a hunt, for True Son's *vulnerability* to become apparent in *A Light in the Forest.*

Structural vocabulary, by contrast, sets the students' thinking in a literary context. When we read *April Morning,* the students learn that Adam's jacket is a *symbol* of his perspective about war, new and unworn at the beginning and covered with dust after the battle. In *A Lesson Before Dying,* when we discuss the description of the plantation, the students uncover the significance of the *setting* as a reflection of the theme of oppression.

Thematic and structural vocabulary serve and support each other. Early on, the students learn that *tragedy* is brought about by *vulnerability* within a character. In *A Light in the Forest,* they determine that True Son's *betrayal* of the Indians was driven by his *tragic flaw,* his *loyalty* to the Whites. Together, the two types of vocabulary create a resource within the students, a reserve of interpretive language that helps them represent their ideas. This vocabulary also becomes the vocabulary of the classroom, a resource that we share.

With an interpretive stance and a common resource of language with which to put forth our ideas, we move forward as a community. The students fly with me above the mountaintop. Some are at the front, and some are farther back. A few must work hard to keep up, and a little blue space divides them from the others. But they, too, soar, as they learn to use the interpretive strategies of the literature study.

MY RESEARCH

From among the activities that make up our yearlong literature study, I chose the students' logs as the main source of data for my research because their logs clearly reflect how and in what manner students first understand and interpret the literature and how they change the ways they think about literature as the year goes on. Log writing is first-draft writing, responded to for content only. It is writing-to-think, to work out ideas. I teach correctness as a part of the writing process with other types of writing we do in the classroom, but not with log writing. Besides being a good teaching activity in a heterogeneous classroom, log writing provides me with ongoing reflections of the student's developmental level.

When I first introduce the logs, I offer concepts and standards related to literary interpretation. I tell the students:

> Dignity, respect, and integrity are *very* important in this classroom.
> When you walk through the door, you are entering a classroom com-
> munity, where dignified and respectful behavior exist at all times. In
> the literature we read and write about throughout the year, we will be
> studying characters, many of whom you will learn to respect because
> of their dignified manner and their integrity. These are very important
> words for you to understand.

As I explain these ideas, I point to a sign above the chalkboard that says FROM THE HEART. The sign was made by a student years ago, and whenever I talk with the students about writing, I point to it. "'Writing from the heart' is a metaphor that I want you to think about. It represents truth, honesty and integrity. In our classroom, I want you to trust your ideas. I want you to care about what you think. I want you to write about your ideas with integrity." I point to this sign over and over throughout the year. I want the students' ideas to meander their way through their hearts to become strong, enriched perspectives.

Log writing is fundamentally appropriate for teaching a heterogeneous class. I can teach the entire class the high-level interpretive strategies that I want each student to use because I know that in their logs, all students can write from their individual developmental levels and all have a place where their voices can be heard.

Modeling student logs is a powerful way to help students see how to use sophisticated interpretive strategies in their writing. The student models become standard bearers. On the first day, I inform students that they will be a part of a community of learners and that their writing will be read and responded to by students and adults in the classroom each and every day. In their logs, students put forth their individual cultural perspectives. Through honoring the diversity of ideas, we create and constantly expand our class-room community and our shared knowledge.

As the students read each others' logs, I move around the room and read logs as well. As I read, I underline particularly skillful interpretations and what I consider to be excellent writing. Using this model, students learn to respond similarly to their classmates' logs. When I finish reading a log, I hand it to another student. Sometimes a log is just plain terrific, and I will say, "You guys. You have to read this log." I identify the approach the student has taken, perhaps read a section aloud, and then hand it to the student in the next seat. When I recognize an interpretation or strategy that I think a particular student would learn from, I make a point of passing the log to that person. When we are finished reading each others' logs, I quickly cir-culate through the class and sign the log entries that I haven't read to give students credit for their writing.

I want students to read as many logs as possible to expose individual students to different perspectives and interpretive strategies. I want them to take in as many approaches to responding to the literature as they can. Hav-ing students read each others' logs provides a daily reminder of the academic standards for log writing in the classroom.

STUDENTS INTERPRETING LITERATURE

To answer my research questions, I analyzed the logs of three of my students, Tinesha, Antonio, and Emily, who reflect the array of achievement levels in my classroom. I concentrated on two log entries for each student, one from relatively early in the year, and one from the end of the year. I examined how each of these students, across time, took hold of the literature study, moved forward, and engaged in writing in distinctively different ways.

Tinesha, a quietly respectful African American girl, was in my first-period class. It took me a very long time to understand that she was commit-ted to doing well in my class. Throughout the school year, she was tardy two or three times a week. When she arrived late, she would sit down in the front row, and without disturbing the class, get out her materials and begin to follow along. At some point during the period, she would beckon me to her desk. With her eyes down, which I interpreted as deference, she would hand me her log and say, "Ms. Delp, could you sign my log?" Although she was well behaved and showed concern about getting credit for her work, for a long time it didn't seem to me that Tinesha really *wanted* to do well or really *cared* about my class. Wouldn't she get herself to class on time if she did?

It was perhaps in March when I came to see that I had misinterpreted Tinesha's behavior. Unlike most late students, who usually choose to cut class entirely rather than receive the standard after-school detention, Tinesha persistently came to class and accepted the penalty. Her respectful behavior and concern about getting credit, despite her work being marked down, was, I think, her way of demonstrating her high regard for her schoolwork.

Tinesha was a smart but relatively unskilled reader and writer when the school year began. She initially wrote what I thought were "skinny logs," responses that remained at a concrete level of interpretation. I wanted Tinesha to move beyond concrete plot summaries and restatements of dictionary definitions. I hoped she would develop her own interpretations of character and theme, to connect her personal experiences to the literature. The yearlong literature study proved to be a propitious journey for Tinesha. She grew in her ability to create meaning from the literature and to express her ideas.

Antonio was not quiet like Tinesha. Rather, when I think about Antonio, I realize that I wanted him to face forward in the classroom, to turn away from his clandestine conversations with his sidekicks, to move away from his laissez-faire attitude about writing, to boldly confront the study of literature.

I taught Antonio's sister, Marianna, in both seventh and eighth grade, and I got to know his family well. They live in the South Berkeley flatlands, a racially integrated, working-class neighborhood. Antonio's mother is African American, and his father is Italian American. When I talked with Antonio about his perception of his family and his racial identity, he said, "I don't really think about it. When people ask me, I tell them I am Black and Italian."

Antonio's first logs fulfilled the assignments with somewhat formulaic writing. Like many of his peers, Antonio seemed content with simply relying on *his* grade-level competencies. I remember thinking that he most likely did not like following in the footsteps of his literary sister, and daily faced the pressure of his basketball teammates to be cool and to focus more on athletics than academics. Nonetheless, I hoped that he, along with all of my students, would take hold of the interpretive skills of the literature study and move forward together.

Initially, I thought that in order for Antonio to move forward, he had to become interested in what we were studying, that his acquisition of skills was dependent upon his engagement with the literature. However, I have learned from him that as he gained strategies for interpreting and writing about literature, he became more involved and grew as an interpreter of literature, continually increasing his ability to substantiate his position with meaningful ideas and to make personal connections to the text.

Living in the same South Berkeley neighborhood as Antonio, Emily came to my class as one of the most highly skilled readers and writers. Because she already had strong skills and felt connected to the literature, I had to be sure that she not rest on her laurels. In heterogeneous classrooms, sometimes students such as Emily are neglected and manage to move through the curriculum without acquiring new skills.

Six feet tall, Emily, who is European American, was the captain of the girls' basketball team. Whenever we talked before class, she sat on my stool while I stood so that we would be the same height. I had taught Emily's older brother David, who was also a basketball player and a good student. On the first day of class, Emily told me that she hoped that I would see her as an individual. She knew how much I liked David, and she did not want me to make comparisons. Emily's assertiveness so early in the year foreshadowed the self-confidence she would continue to demonstrate.

Throughout the year, Emily steadily deepened her ability to understand the literature, especially the characters' behavior and the circumstances that affected that behavior. She consistently used log writing to explore her thinking and to create new meaning for herself.

SHORT-STORY UNIT: FIRST LOGS OF THE YEAR

The short-story unit, which I introduced in early September, includes "Hunger" and "The Kitten," excerpts from *Black Boy* by Richard Wright. I teach these stories because students easily identify with the characters and the circumstances that surround them. This immediate connection to the literature is particularly important in the early stages of literature study.

As I began to teach interpretive strategies with these short stories, I focused on the characters' behavior, teaching the students to notice what variables affect their behavior, to see that behavior is influenced both by circumstance and by the character's psychological makeup, and to understand that there are numerous ways to interpret behavior.

At the same time, to help students see the qualities of behavior that are particularly significant in these stories, I taught them the thematic words *powerless, fear, anger, violence, resentment,* and *bitterness,* vocabulary that I thought they needed in order to understand the characters in these stories. I introduced the structural term *driving force,* to help them conceptualize behavior that propels a character. Additionally, they learned the structural words *circumstance* and *situation* to help them identify the factors that affect characters' behavior. I explicitly teach these words, and encourage students to generate their own, to help build a reservoir of language that provides them with labels for their ideas. With their new linguistic resources, students learn to move away from plot summary and to infer broader concepts that underlie the events of a story, to substantiate their opinions about these concepts with precise language and with reference to the text, and to elaborate their evolving interpretations.

By the end of our study of "Hunger," the students had written three logs. For their final reflection, I asked them to draw stick figures of the last scene, where Richard has been slapped and locked out of his house by his mother. I read from the text while they drew: "I had the choice of being beaten at home or away from home. . . . With blind fear, he swings his bat at the gang and their parents" (p. 20).

I paused and then asked questions to guide their thinking: "What do we know about Richard at this moment? What do we know about the gang? Their parents? What has just happened to Richard that might affect his behavior in this situation? Yes, and what else? Where is his father? What else do we know?" During these moments of reflection, some students answered orally, some made notes next to their drawings, some just listened. Their ways of responding reflected their ways of learning. Allowing for such difference is especially important in a heterogeneous classroom.

In her final Richard Wright log, Tinesha draws upon the classroom vocabulary to begin to interpret the characters' behavior:

> I think that they [Richard and his mother] were both feeling powerless, because first the mom didn't know how to handle a situation about the kids beating Richard up. She didn't know how to explain how to handle these kids so she slaped him and locked him out the house with a bat. Richard felt like his mom was locking him out of her life. He didn't understand why she lock him out with just a bat. But when he finally went down to go to the store all the anger of the words his mom said and all the anger towards the gang came out. And when the gang came after him all the anger came out and he started beating theme with a bat. And since then he had his pride and I think he learned why his mom did that to him. He is proud of himself. First of all he won the pride of the streets and of his mother. When he was fight he really didn't know what he was doing but when he finished he felt good about himself.

In the first part of her log, Tinesha uses thematic vocabulary, the word *powerless,* and structural vocabulary, the word *situation,* to analyze Richard's and his mother's behavior. Defining *powerlessness* as, in part, not knowing what to do, Tinesha describes the mother's sense of uncertainty and shows her understanding of the circumstances that surround her by referring to events in the story: "the mom didn't know how to handle a situation. . . . She didn't know how to explain how to handle these kids . . . so she slaped him and locked him out the house with a bat." Incorporating her own metaphor ("locking him out of her life"), Tinesha shows her understanding of Richard's position.

Having put forth, albeit briefly, her interpretation of both characters' behavior, Tinesha moves from analysis to plot summary. Using the thematic word *anger* and support from an earlier class discussion, Tinesha cites events in the story throughout the second half of her log. She interrupts her plot summary when she asserts her opinion regarding the outcome of the situation, "I think he learned why his mom did that to him." However, she does not substantiate this position.

Using literary vocabulary and plot summary to sustain her writing, Tinesha demonstrates that she has begun to take an interpretive approach to the literature; but she is unable to sustain it. As the year went on, I hoped Tinesha would continue to use the classroom vocabulary as a resource in her writing and that she would acquire greater skill as an interpreter of literature.

With his Richard Wright log, Antonio writes tentatively and with a distant tone, but like Tinesha, he too begins to use the classroom vocabulary to focus his ideas:

> "I had won the right to the streets of Memphis." Richard had over-come his fears and anger towards the gang and won their "respect," and put fear into their hearts. Richard had also stood up for himself. Considering the circumstances he was in he made the right decision. Richard's mom was also under a lot of stress and pressure. She probably just didn't no what to do and by locking Richard out she knew that they could over-come that problem. Not that violence was the way out of ever situation, she had to do something, and do it fast. She was also probably letting some anger out because the father left and she had to get some steem off. And that probably why she slaped Richard.

Antonio uses structural vocabulary (*situation* and *circumstance*) and thematic vocabulary (*anger* and *violence*) as he analyzes the characters. He mentions the circumstances that surround Richard when he evaluates his behavior, "Considering the circumstances he was in he made the right decision." Further analyzing Richard's situation, Antonio creates a metaphor, albeit a cliché, to express his idea that Richard "put fear into their [the gang mem-bers'] hearts." The term *anger* guides his explanation of Richard's mother's behavior: "She was also probably letting some anger out because the father left and she had to get some steem off. And that['s] probably why she slaped Richard."

To substantiate his interpretations of the characters' behavior, Antonio puts forth ideas that seem peripheral—somewhere off to the side of the char-acter analysis. For example, when he explains Richard's mother's behavior, he makes assertions: "Richard's mom was also under a lot of stress and pres-sure. . . . Not that violence was the way out of ever situation, she had to do something, and do it fast." He does not include citations from the text. Also his repetitive use of the term *probably* produces a speculative quality: "She probably just didn't no what to do" and "She was also probably letting some anger out." "And that probably why she slaped Richard."

Although Antonio is tentative in the ways that he expresses his ideas, he is beginning to take an interpretive stance in this log. He approaches the literature as an observer who gathers information so that he can then reflect upon it. In the year ahead, I wanted Antonio to acquire additional interpre-tive skills and to become engaged with the literature so that he would be able to connect personally with it.

For her Richard Wright log, Emily uses the classroom vocabulary to create a more comprehensive analysis and evaluation of Richard's behavior than had Antonio or Tinesha at this point in the year:

> After reading "Hunger" once more most of my initial thoughts were re-instated. I still feel that without food, his resentment and bitterness are the driving force in his life. Much like how the hunger began as only a nibble but then grew so did his rage towards his father and absence. Just like sometimes there are certain necessary evils in life which you must overcome to lead normal happy lives. Although in Richard's situ-ation he seems to be hung up on the first hurdle. As far as the situation with the boys goes, I feel that in truth he probably had other options, but when those boys beat him up twice they lost the consideration nor-mally owed to any human being. Therefore I feel his reaction was fair but he overstepped the boundries when he disrespected the adults.

Defining precisely the qualities of Richard's character, Emily shows her understanding of the thematic vocabulary, using *resentment* and *bitterness,* and substitutes her own intensified word *rage* for *anger.* Unlike Tinesha and Antonio, throughout her log Emily discusses Richard's behavior in relation to the circumstances that surround it. She also establishes a psychological perspective by using the structural-vocabulary word *driving force* to analyze

Richard's actions: "his resentment and bitterness are the driving force in his life."

Unlike most of the other students, Emily probes the meaning of the "hunger" metaphor. She equates increasing hunger with Richard's increasing anger: "Much like how the hunger began as only a nibble but then grew so did his rage towards his father and absence." She then moves beyond this analogy to interpret the situation philosophically: "Just like sometimes there are certain necessary evils in life which you must overcome to lead normal happy lives." She extends her analysis of the characters' behavior to something universal and clarifies her own sense of how to live in an imperfect world.

Having analyzed Richard's behavior, Emily takes yet another step that the others do not. She evaluates his behavior by her own standards. She finds reason to excuse his first act of violence because "when those boys beat him up twice they lost the consideration normally owed to any human being." She then condemns his behavior with the gang members' parents: "He overstepped the boundries when he disrespected the adults." Throughout this evaluative section, Emily's voice of judgment is strong. She assumes the role of arbiter and in passing judgment articulates her standards and orders the lives of the characters in line with these standards. In the coming months, I wanted Emily to acquire more skill as an observer and interpreter of literature, most especially to see how characters are influenced by the circumstances they encounter, so that she would enhance and refine her ability to understand and to write about the complexity of the human condition.

Upon completion of this 2-week short-story unit, Tinesha, Antonio, and Emily all use classroom vocabulary to support their analyses. Tinesha shows the beginning stages of character analysis and demonstrates an initial ability to use the literary vocabulary to sustain her writing, although she does not explicitly connect the characters' actions to the circumstances that govern that behavior. Antonio has approached his log somewhat tentatively and awkwardly, but he discusses the characters' behavior and the contributing circumstances as he too incorporates some of the interpretive vocabulary of the literature study. Emily has written a character analysis that includes interpretive vocabulary and her first attempts at interpreting an extended textual metaphor, evaluating the characters' motives, and offering a philosophical interpretation of the situation.

A LESSON BEFORE DYING: LAST LOGS OF THE YEAR

I taught the book that is the focus for the last logs, *A Lesson Before Dying*, by Ernest Gaines, in the late spring. Set in rural Louisiana in the late 1940s, this novel is about two young African American men who must struggle to find their dignity in the face of unrelenting racism and oppression. Twenty-year-old Jefferson, makes a tragic choice to go into a liquor store with his friend, where he witnesses a robbery attempt going astray and three men die. He then faces death by electrocution for the murder of the White shopkeeper. Although bitter and cynical both about the intolerable racism and oppression that exist in the community and about the hopelessness of Jefferson's situation, Grant Wiggins, the teacher in what he and other Blacks still refer to as the "quarters," submits to his elders' request and agrees to try to help Jefferson find his dignity before he dies.

As with all of the literature we study during the year, we focus on character, symbolism, and imagery. For this novel, calling upon structural vocabulary to guide our study, I emphasize how the *circumstances* (the *setting* and the *time period*) affect the characters and their choices and how the author uses the *setting* and *imagery* to reflect the theme of *dignity* in the face of *oppression*. Some of the thematic vocabulary I teach for this book includes words that we revisit from our earlier units, such as *dignity, compassion, oppression, racism, literacy,* and *heroism.*

At the end of the novel, when the teacher, Grant Wiggins, awaits word of Jefferson's execution, he leaves his classroom, walks alone through the slave quarters on the plantation, and reflects. To prepare the students to write a log entry, I read a section aloud:

> Several feet away from where I sat under the tree was a hill of bull grass. . . . I probably would not have noticed it at all had a butterfly, a yellow one with dark specks like ink dots on its wing, not lit there. What had brought it there? There was no odor that you could detect to have attracted it . . . so why did it light on a hill of bull grass that offered it nothing? I watched it closely, the way it opened its wings and closed them, the way it opened its wings again, fluttered, closed its wings for a second or two then opened them again and flew away. I watched it fly over the ditch and down into the quarter, I watched it until I could not see it anymore. (Gaines, 1993, pp. 251–252)

After I read, I asked the students to copy the quotation as a preface to their logs. While they wrote, I asked questions: "Why did Mr. Gaines put this butterfly scene in the book? What does he want us to think about? Yes. And what else? Why bull grass? What about the ink spots? What do you think? Yes. And what else?"

In her "Butterfly in the Bull Grass" log, Tinesha maintains an interpretive stance throughout. She no longer relies on plot summary to develop her writing. In addition, she offers an extensive analysis of the metaphors in the passage and sustains her analysis in a manner that reflects her new abilities to use the interpretive skills of the classroom:

> I think the spots on the butterfly that looked liked ink spots represented the writing on the diary of Jefferson. The butterfly represents Jefferson how he could have just went on about his business but yet he went on in the door with Bear. Just like the butterfly he had all good things like flowers and weeds to choose from but yet he chooses the one thing that offers it nothing. When the butterfly fluttered and struggle to fly that represented Jefferson struggle to become a man.

By discussing how the butterfly in the bull grass replicates the tragic choice Jefferson made to go with Bear instead of going "on about his business," Tinesha demonstrates her understanding of how, in tragedy, a character's life is changed forever by one seemingly insignificant choice. Extending her analysis of Jefferson's behavior, and reflecting her growing ability to use language models, Tinesha takes a phrase from the text ("that offers it nothing") and uses it as part of her analogy to show the options that Jefferson tragically overlooked, "Just like the butterfly he had all good things like flowers and weeds to choose from but yet he chooses the one thing that offers it [him] nothing."

Marking her interpretive stance with the structural-vocabulary word *represents,* Tinesha shows how the butterfly imagery acts as a symbol for Jefferson. Although the elements of her interpretation are not fully developed or integrated with one another, they reflect Tinesha's growing proficiency as an interpreter of literature. She attributes the *ink spots* on the butterfly to the writing in Jefferson's diary, "the spots on the butterfly that looked liked ink spots represented the writing on the diary of Jefferson." She shows her understanding, albeit cursory, of the theme of *literacy* and its power in the face of intolerable *oppression.* She also portrays her understanding of the characters' *struggle* against *racism* when she analyzes the ink spots and the butterfly's "struggle to fly." She conveys her awareness of the relationship between the writing in Jefferson's diary, his struggles against racism, and his struggle to become a man.

Through her understanding of the character's tragic position, and by uncovering the significance of the imagery, Tinesha makes progress in her ability to approach literature with an interpretive perspective. She also progresses in writing about her ideas, and making meaning for herself.

For his "Butterfly in the Bull Grass" log, Antonio, like Tinesha, presents a substantive interpretation of the scene's imagery, integrating his interpretation with his own perspective. In the process, he discovers its relevance and makes new meaning for himself:

> This yellow butterfly represents Jefferson. The butterfly landed on the bull grass surrounded by weeds and a fence, just as Jefferson being put

in the jail behind a barred fence. The tree and the flowers represents the outside world, the better things untouchable to Jefferson. The pecan tree, the tree representing the children working as hard as they could picking pecans just to donate them to Jefferson. Then the butterfly flutters its wing as Jefferson did as he rose above his hog image. A second flutter representing Jefferson becoming dignified, becoming a man, becoming a true hero. And a third flutter, lifting off the ground going up off the bullgrass to forever be a true hero among his people, being known as the *man* to break the cycle of oppression. The third flutter of it's wing represents Jefferson going to the chair a man, and a hero taking his last flap of his wings to places beyond, to be rememeberd forever.

Far from the tentative and indirect approach in his first log, Antonio writes about the scene's imagery with a sense of confidence: "This yellow butterfly represents Jefferson." He sustains his analysis of the imagery by systematically setting down a series of analogies that portray his interpretation. Using his own terminology *just as* to introduce his analogy, in the first half of his log Antonio interprets the imagery that surrounds the butterfly to show the corresponding circumstances that surround Jefferson: "The butterfly landed on the bull grass surrounded by weeds and a fence, just as Jefferson being put in the jail behind a barred fence." Using the structural-vocabulary word *represents* (and *representing*) to guide his interpretation, Antonio expands his explication. He discusses how the tree and the flowers represent "the outside world." He also shows how the children from the quarters, by picking pecans to *donate* to Jefferson showed their devotion to him, ultimately helping him in his struggle to find his dignity.

For the second half of his analysis, Antonio continues to use the structural-vocabulary word *represents* and steadfastly interprets the *flutter* imagery with a litany of analogies that portray his understanding of each stage of Jefferson's struggle "to [become] a man." Antonio expresses how Jefferson overcame the self-hatred that tormented him throughout most of the book when he no longer accepted the white man's description of him as a hog: "Then the butterfly flutters its wing as Jefferson did as he rose above his hog image." Using thematic vocabulary (*dignified* and *hero*), Antonio describes the qualities that Jefferson finally attained before his execution when he was "becoming dignified, becoming a man, becoming a true hero." Antonio ties the third flutter of the butterfly's wing and the theme of oppression to his personal perspective about manhood. Jefferson, Antonio asserts, will "forever be a true hero among his people" and will be known as "the *man* to break the cycle of oppression."

By combining remnants of the author's repetitive, rhythmic style with his interpretive skills, and, with a compelling sense of urgency, Antonio puts forth a thorough and substantive analysis of the scene that reflects his connection to the ideas he writes about.

Presenting a more sophisticated level of response than do Antonio and Tinesha, Emily considers not just one interpretation in her "Butterfly in the Bull Grass" log, but two distinctly different ones:

> The butterfly means many things. In one way, the butterfly is Jefferson, a touch of beauty, who lands on the lives of the people in the quarters with their sorrow filled lives. With his landing, he spreads his knowledge and his example to everyone who's never seen a black man stand and lead. Grant is the bullgrass this way. The one who will never leave, who continually teaches without caring. But this way does not explain everything I want it to. The way that does makes Jefferson the bullgrass, the uneducated, unappealing one who doesn't offer the most of everyone, but still attracts the educated butterfly, (Grant) with the ink spots of his intelligence. It attracts this butterfly even through the hardships of the fence, racism. They are attracted to each other by a force more powerful than either of them. They need each other. They need each other to grow and know everything.

After first presenting an interpretation of the imagery that explores the idea of Jefferson as the butterfly, Emily speaks directly to her audience to change direction, "But this way does not explain everything I want it to." She then puts forth her alternate interpretation of the scene, with Grant as the butterfly. With the patience of a scholar, Emily places herself on the hill of bull grass and watches Grant and the butterfly and thinks about Jefferson. It is as if Emily is anticipating the questions that I ask the students repeatedly throughout the literature study, "What does this tell us? Yes. And what else?" Just as the classroom vocabulary study creates an ever increasing array of definitions, Emily's awareness of her role as an observer with interpretive options enables her to see the multiple facets of meaning possible in this scene.

In her last three lines, Emily unifies her explication by delineating the power of Jefferson and Grant's attraction and judging that "They need each other to grow and know everything." In the act of passing judgment, Emily creates a sense of order, enabling her to see for herself the augmented meaning that she has created with her dual interpretation.

With this log, Emily moves forward developmentally, from using interpretive skills to integrating these skills within an interpretive stance. For Emily, interpretation appears to have become a way of thinking, a way of looking at the world, a perspective. As Rosenblatt describes, Emily is no longer only reporting her internal text or evocation; she is now analyzing and explaining her evocation—treating it as "an object of thought" (Rosenblatt, 1994, p. 1070).

CONCLUSIONS

Tinesha, Antonio, Emily, and their classmates each embraced the yearlong literature study in distinctive ways, yet they also participated in the classroom community. They cared about the characters and they assumed strong positions, creating for themselves significant relationships with the literature. The skills that they acquired enabled them to look more deeply at the literature and to achieve higher levels of interpretation. With an interpretive position well established within each of them, they were able to generate an array of substantive and grounded interpretations, rather than putting forth superficial responses. As a result of these interactions, they brought forth personal connections to the literature and found meaning from their individual perspectives. With a foundation of interpretive skills and literary knowledge, the students read and wrote about the literature from their hearts.

Tinesha, Antonio, and Emily soared with me far above the mountain. I wonder how these three students would interpret the imagery of the scene they created and were a part of? Would Tinesha recognize the interpretive skills that she acquired and that enabled her to write about an African American man's struggle with oppression? Would Antonio understand that the literary skills he attained were one source of the conviction in his writing about the issue of manhood? Would Emily be able to see that in her attempt to create order in her world, the scholarly stance that she secured enabled her to envision an array of interpretations, and thus, an interpretive perspective? And how will these three students appear in the morning sky, when they fly away, on to their next journey?

As a teacher researcher looking at my students' work over the entire year, I have come to see how this study has affected me as a teacher. Despite the intensity that absorbs me while I teach, I am now better able to notice and identify student growth in the moment because of the insights I have gained from reflecting on Tinesha, Antonio, and Emily's development. In response to this awareness, I find myself making adjustments to my instructional program with individual students and with the entire class. I am more confident that teaching in the way that I do serves my students, and that they will, as Tinesha, Antonio, and Emily did, take hold of the literature over time.

I began this research with questions regarding the effects of what I was teaching on my students' abilities to think and write about literature. I was particularly interested in how varied students use interpretive strategies, and how their use of these strategies changed over time. My research has affirmed for me that teaching high-level interpretive skills to my students did affect the ways in which my focal students approached and thought about the literature and the ways that they wrote about their ideas. I feel, even more strongly than ever, that no matter what a student's competency as a writer and reader, each one deserves the opportunity to engage with and respond to the critical ideas that we encounter in literature. Access to high-level interpretive skills is essential for all of my students. Those with low skills in correctness and form should not be excluded from the opportunity to be exposed to and be expected to use high-level interpretive skills. Even the weakest students in our heterogeneous classrooms must be provided the opportunity to think about and write in response to quality literature so that they can learn to express their ideas with conviction built from a solid and well-developed set of interpretive skills. The strongest students, who are too often neglected because of their apparent competencies, must not be overlooked either. They too must be given consideration for their individual needs—whether it is access to a particular skill, a need for time to integrate skills, or a need for freedom within the structure.

When I began this research, I had no idea how difficult it would be for me to write this chapter. I remember distinctly how comfortable I felt discussing my ideas at our site meetings and with the early stages of data collection, but from the very beginning, I was concerned about the writing I was expected to do. Looking back, I see that in the first year I did not yet have a focus or a structure for my ideas nor the perspective or voice of a teacher researcher in my writing.

During the next 3 years, I drafted and redrafted—over and over again. These drafts were places for me to try to focus and refine my thinking, to begin to build a structure upon which to attach my ideas, and to slowly learn how to write about my findings.

Just as I was forced, in a sense, to gain skill in the teaching of literary interpretation and writing when I began teaching in the secondary schools, and in a parallel fashion, my students must acquire skills in order to write interpretively, I, too, had to secure the skills I needed to write about my research. For me, the struggle has been exhilarating. Through the writing I have done for this research, I have defined and redefined myself as a teacher. As with my own journey, I believe that my students also experience a sense of exhilaration as they work to take hold of the literature study and as they learn to define and redefine themselves as interpreters of literature.

CHAPTER 11

What Teacher Researchers Say About Creating Communities of Achievement: Empowerment in and Beyond the Classroom

Julie Shalhope Kalnin, with Elena Valenti, Nancy O'Malley, and Stephanie Davenport

AT THE OPENING conference for the M-CLASS Project, student empowerment was a major issue. Although the teachers agreed about the importance of empowering students, New Orleans teacher researcher Elena Valenti observed, "Everyone in the room wasn't talking about the same things when they used the word *empowerment*. We had different ideas about what that meant in the classroom" (opening conference, M-CLASS, September 11, 1992).

Through the year, as the M-CLASS teachers worked together, they continued their discussions of empowerment, and the range of meanings to which Valenti called attention became clearer. The term *empowerment* encompassed a spectrum of concerns—from classroom-based considerations about how and in what way teachers can involve students in classroom decisions to social and political questions about how students can situate themselves in the larger society. The teacher researchers described many kinds of changes as empowering to their students—acquiring knowledge; building skills; coming to see themselves as learners; developing the ability to make choices, gaining the confidence to offer contributions; and understanding people, texts, and their own abilities in new ways. The teacher researchers valued particular kinds of changes in varying degrees, but in general saw these ways of defining empowerment as compatible. In some instances, however, the features of the teachers' definitions were not as easily reconciled. For example, most of the teachers felt it was essential to foster their students' sense of their own cultural uniqueness in order to empower them. A few teachers of color, however, worried that too great an emphasis on cultural uniqueness could lead to ethnocentric ways of thinking that could have the unintended effect of disempowering, rather than empowering, students of color and divide the multicultural class of which they were a part.

Across all of these variations and even contradictions in how the teacher researchers defined empowerment ran one overarching goal that all of the teachers fully endorsed: helping their students gain power in the wider society. That the daily events of classroom life will accrue in a way that will prepare students to succeed in an uncertain future is, of course, the very purpose of teaching, the fundamental goal of every teacher in every classroom. What is worth noting in the experience of the M-CLASS teachers is the way in which each one focuses specifically on a set of resources that they believe their diverse students will need to negotiate in a society often inflexible and intolerant of difference.

The different ways that the teachers envisioned accomplishing this overarching goal does not dilute the potency of the concept of student empowerment. Rather, through their various interpretations, individual teacher researchers highlight specific elements of a fundamental educational concept that have personal meaning for them and that they judge to be of greatest importance for their students and their setting. For that reason, and as the authors of Chapters 9 and 10 have already shown, even when the teachers shared the belief that there must be strong connections between the classroom and the world outside, each acted upon this belief by shaping curriculum and pedagogy in different ways.

This chapter explores how three teachers, Elena Valenti, Nancy O'Malley, and Stephanie Davenport, structured academic communities in geography, creative writing, and English, respectively, to empower their students in and beyond the classroom. In each classroom, the teachers' definition of empowerment, background experiences, and different academic purposes yielded distinctly different relationships between the classroom and the world outside the school; and, consequently, each teacher led students along different routes to empowerment.

In her geography classroom in a suburb of New Orleans, Elena Valenti, who as a child came to the United States from Cuba, built a path to empowerment by increasing her students' knowledge about the world through written conversations with adults outside the school. Nancy O'Malley, drawing on her own experiences as a White single mother and freelance writer with working-class roots, structured a Boston exam-school classroom in which her tenth grade creative writing students moved toward empowerment through self-discovery. The principles of Kwanzaa suffused the pedagogy of African American activist Stephanie Davenport; she guided her freshman English students to empower themselves through action as they worked interdependently to accomplish both real-world and school-based tasks in her Chicago high school.

These three teacher researchers, by investigating their own teaching practices, convey the difficulty, and the necessity, of accepting students as they are, to foster their own self-acceptance. At the same time, their work illustrates the importance of teachers structuring learning experiences that simultaneously support and challenge students to fulfill their teachers' high expectations and that increase students' abilities to think critically and act effectively both in school and in society.

EMPOWERMENT THROUGH WORLD KNOWLEDGE: ELENA VALENTI

A social studies teacher in a mostly White and mostly working-class high school on the outskirts of New Orleans, Elena Valenti's persistent attempts to initiate classroom discussion in her geography class met with silent resistance. She came to her research with a fundamental question—how to increase class participation among her students, who ranged in grade level from sophomores to seniors. Valenti believed that if she made her classroom less teacher centered and gave students more control over its functioning, their increased ownership would lead to more class participation. Valenti discovered through her research that sharing classroom control was important in increasing student participation in learning about geography. Even more important, though, was creating a structure in the class curriculum that connected her students to broader conversations with adults who were actively engaged in what the students were studying. These outside connections gave her students access to additional information about the world and new perspective on their lives and personal goals.

SOMETHING REAL

By Elena Valenti

"If you want to know what works best in your classroom, ask the students." I had heard this advice many times, but after the opening M-CLASS conference in San Francisco, I decided to act upon it. For my research, I wanted to find out how to increase student participation in my classroom, so on the flight home to New Orleans, I wrote a letter to my students asking them to evaluate our classroom activities. The subsequent responses were varied and enlightening. They knew that my letter to them came from a real desire to understand their opinions, and they responded in an open and honest manner.

While I was pleased that I had found a productive way to communicate through writing with my students, I wanted to know more about how to integrate their writing into our geography class. How could I extend their interest to the essential text materials? Remembering a successful project in which my students had written to celebrities asking about their reading experiences, I responded to Abigail Van Buren's "Dear Abby" newspaper appeal for "Operation Merry Christmas" participants, a program to write to service people aboard navy ships. My students were eager. Luck was with me: The soldiers wrote back that they were visiting port cities in Africa, Italy, France, and Greece, just the countries we were covering in class. We learned about the soldiers' families, what it was like to sleep in a tent on the ground in Somalia, and what the soldiers did to make friends with the children of the regions in which they were working.

Soon thereafter, John (a student who routinely stays up half the night listening to the radio instead of doing his homework) told the class something he'd heard on the radio the night before about a truckers' organization that wanted to get involved in education by matching individual truckers with students. I agreed to enroll the class. Our trucker, Buddy, who travels throughout the United States delivering those goods we talk about exchanging when we study geographic regions, wrote to us the very next week. We followed his routes on a map mounted to the wall in the back of the classroom; he sent us material and information from historical sites across the country.

To help with our observance of Black History Month, Buddy sent us audio tapes of songs sung by African American soldiers during the Civil War. Along one of his routes, he stopped at the birthplace of Andrew Jackson, for whom our school is named, and mailed us pamphlets, a book, and some pictures from the historical site. As my classes followed Buddy's travels, we discussed the Pennsylvania Dutch country and the poor areas of Appalachia. The students researched and wrote about population distribution and trends as they relate to natural resources.

Buddy's great interest and many letters to the class forced me to think about how to handle postcards and letters from this man who wrote my students that he had graduated from high school with the ability to read only 10 of 25 words; his letter-writing skills reflected that struggle. One of my students commented, "I find it amazing that someone can make so much money, yet cannot read or write a complete sentence."

One of Buddy's early responses to students' letters helped explain: "My mom and dad didn't care if I made A's or F's. They didn't even come to any of my school programs. I started high school reading two words out of ever twenty-five. So it was a fight to graduate." My fellow teacher researchers helped me see the possibilities in the letters written by this man who, in every letter, encouraged my students to stay in school:

> I would like to say to anyone in the classes who is struggling, stick with it. There are many ways around your handicaps—for that's what it is—and graduate. You can see I'm proud of all of you who make A's and B's with your hard effort. At the same time those who are fighting to barely pass, I am very proud of you all since you are giving it your all. You can do it.
>
>   Your friend and buddy.

This letter was particularly significant to one student, a repeat sophomore struggling to become a junior. She wrote back to him:

> Buddy, I just want to let you know the letter Mrs. V read to us today meant a lot to me because I am kind of like that. . . . I was about to give up, but I guess I will keep trying for myself and for you because I know you have been through the same thing. If I pass everything this year and

go to summer school I will pass to be a senior next year. Pray for me. Please write back my new friend.

Buddy continually cheered my students on toward fulfilling their goals. Buddy wrote a paragraph especially for the seniors: "TO ALL OF YOU SENIORS: I would love to have a graduition anouncment. I am proud of each and every one of you. Keep your Dreams Alive and, go for it!" Fifteen out of the 22 seniors in my geography classes sent Buddy a graduation announcement, and he sent them each a five-dollar bill. One senior called me at home just 20 minutes before I was leaving to attend her graduation to tell me with great excitement, "I received my most beautiful graduation card from Buddy."

I discovered that writing makes a difference in students' attitudes and willingness to respond. And I rediscovered something that I had really always known: People respond to what interests them. Learning in conversation with ourselves and others is a part of literacy. Give the students something *real* to do and they will participate in the learning process.

After Valenti wrote to her students to ask how they wanted the class to be organized, she saw that student involvement was a necessary first step to student empowerment. She involved her students by sharing decision-making power with them. She listened to their replies to her initial letter and to their ongoing suggestions for the curriculum. In response to students' requests, Valenti designed more collaborative projects and reduced the amount of lecture and whole-class discussion, changes which were consonant with her purpose of increasing class participation. Valenti later noted that students had written more, and more enthusiastically, in response to her letter than they had to other assignments. She speculated that it was the authentic quality of their interchange—her sincere request for information and belief that students had worthy ideas to contribute—that had altered their willingness to communicate.

Remembering how enthusiastically her former students had participated a year earlier in writing a letter to a celebrity asking about their experiences with reading, Valenti decided to again capitalize on students' interest in letter writing. During the research year, she hoped to enliven the study of geography by aligning her students' letter writing with the subject matter. She involved the class in writing to sailors in the U.S. Navy for the holiday season. The resulting exchange of greetings accomplished both of Valenti's goals—students participated enthusiastically and they also gathered personal information from the sailors about the regions they were studying in class. Valenti believed that her students were motivated to write because they had ownership of their letters—one view of empowerment: "They say what they want to say in there and ask what they want to ask. And so they *really* enjoy those letters. They love getting them. They bring them. They bring the pictures and they want to read them in front of the class" (local meeting, New Orleans, December 22, 1992). Fellow New Orleans teacher researcher Karen Alford hypothesized that through this letter-writing exchange, students were beginning to "see writing as something to use that's for real, real life." Valenti immediately seconded the idea: "For real. Right" (local meeting, New Orleans, December 22, 1992). Involving her students in meaningful activities that brought the outside world into the classroom motivated Valenti's students to learn about geography and to build their own literacy skills. The message she had heard earlier in the Greater New Orleans Writing Project about the importance of students' writing for authentic purposes now resonated clearly.

Although Valenti's experiences reinforce the widely acknowledged importance of students writing for a real audience, her experience also shows the inverse—the significance of writing *from* a real writer. Buddy frankly admitted his struggle with reading and writing and sometimes chose to dictate his letters to his fiancée rather than write them himself. Valenti could have been deterred by Buddy's rudimentary writing skills, insisting that she should provide students with stronger writing models. Instead, she recognized the power of the resources he provided for students to enhance the concepts they were studying and of the values he communicated to students— the importance of faith, hard work, persistence, and academic achievement, especially for her struggling students.

Buddy's descriptions of the details of his routes and the products he transported, as well as the tangible artifacts he sent—tapes, brochures, and maps—grounded abstract geographical concepts such as mapping and exchanges of goods. Students also saw Buddy's intellectual curiosity. His letters showed that his interest in the history and geography of the United States was genuine and that his travels gave him pleasure as well as profit:

> Dear Buddies: Today Jeanne [Buddy's fiancée] and I are writing from Newark Ohio where we saw the earthworks constructed by Hopewell Indians over 2000 years ago! . . . Two weeks ago on a fall foliage run we headed for Monticello, Thomas Jefferson's principle home. The name Monticello means little mountain. We were very impressed with Jefferson's brilliance and his inventions.

Valenti commented that many of her students, though living in some of the most cosmopolitan areas in the United States, have a rather parochial view of the world. Few had opportunities to travel, even within New Orleans, and thus knew little beyond their own neighborhood. Through their interaction with Buddy and their vicarious participation in his work life, Valenti's students extended their knowledge about geography, and also gained insight into dimensions of life in unfamiliar parts of the nation.

Perhaps even more important, however, the students' connection to Buddy clarified the purpose of being in school. Although Buddy made a decent living without much education, his letters emphasized to students how hard he had worked to get his high school diploma and how much it meant to him. His clear message about the importance of staying in school, his insistence that learning was critical, and his faith that students could find the strength, as he had, to persist in the face of challenges, supported students in thinking about how the decisions they made in school were decisions they made about life.

In a multicultural setting where teachers cannot share similar cultural and social class backgrounds or life experiences with all of their students, Valenti's decision to take her student's suggestion and include Buddy's voice in the curriculum takes on added significance. Despite Valenti's positive relationships with her students, she could not connect with them all as deeply as she wished. For instance, she was less able than Buddy to provide inspiration to her student who had already failed sophomore year once and was facing the prospect of another failure, for this was an inspiration built from the shared experience of failure and the shared determination to succeed.

By including another adult voice in her classroom on an ongoing basis, Valenti opened opportunities for more students to establish positive relationships that could support their learning. Unlike the letter writing Valenti's students had participated in during previous years and even the exchanges with the sailors—which were enrichment activities that yielded positive but temporary results—Valenti facilitated an ongoing exchange with Buddy that continued through, and even beyond, that one school year. In the years since, Buddy has continued to exchange letters with Valenti's students and twice rearranged his itinerary so that he could visit the school. This evolving relationship allowed Valenti to restructure her curriculum to explicitly integrate Buddy's experiences in ways that made the students' learning of geographical concepts more concrete and rich. Through the students' dialogue with Buddy, the curriculum extended beyond the classroom.

Early in the research year, Valenti told her fellow teacher researchers that in the 8 years she had been teaching, she had been trying to understand how to develop students' literacy skills to prepare them to succeed in the world outside:

> I felt that it was extremely important for students to express themselves and use their knowledge and experience to their advantage in order to participate in the world, but how was I going to help them learn, to do it? (Site meeting, New Orleans, October 31, 1992)

Through her research, Valenti began to understand how. Rather than always focusing on preparing students for some nebulous future participation in the world, she discovered, by creating a framework in her classroom in which students could participate in the world today, she more successfully supported her students in preparing for tomorrow.

With her students and with the adults who participated through their writing, Valenti built a classroom community in which academic and personal issues were interwoven, where learning was a multivoiced conversation, where students were involved in the curriculum in ways that extended their understanding both of subject matter and of ways of being in the world. Developing connections to the world outside transformed life inside by making school tasks more real and by opening ways for students to see themselves in the larger society.

EMPOWERMENT THROUGH SELF-DISCOVERY: NANCY O'MALLEY

Working in one of Boston's more prestigious "exam" schools, where students must pass a test in order to be admitted, Nancy O'Malley taught a creative writing class, which was required of all sophomores. In this context, O'Malley taught her students to look inward so that they could reflect upon and express who they were and what their experiences meant. The foundation of O'Malley's vision of empowerment is built from individuals' journeys of self-discovery. Students become empowered as individuals when they learn to use writing to shape the stories of their lives and to draw upon the stories they craft to enrich their sense of identity.

For her research, O'Malley wanted to learn whether, and how, her creative-writing students developed a new sense of themselves as writers. She looked particularly at a group of five focal students who first met individually with her in her office, and later as a group without her outside of class to read and discuss their writing. O'Malley's vignette, focusing on her interviews with one of these students, illustrates the critical role of writing in achieving her vision of student empowerment. Larisa, an African American student on the periphery of the classroom and school community—often absent and openly critical when present—told about loss, and, in the process, began to understand the function writing could play in her life.

LARISA AND THE GIFT FROM HER MOTHER

By Nancy O'Malley

From the beginning of class in September until the day when she read her "ruby ring" poem, Larisa was a study in sadness. She sat at the edge of the class with downcast eyes, her sorrow separating her from the others. She complained a lot about the "stupid writing assignments," especially if they called for opening up about one's personal life.

Her attendance was spotty; she was failing most classes and during the winter would miss days at a stretch. I took a chance on her, inviting her to be one of five focal students for my research study of how students learn to see themselves as writers. The very first day I recorded an interview with Larisa, I knew that she was absolutely right for the project. She did not hold anything back on the tape and all of the sullen guardedness that she brought to the class—even her oversized coat—was gone. What remained was the voice and heart of a young woman struggling hard with a sorrow that could swallow her, except that her will and her writing were, and are, strong enough to keep her afloat.

With no prompting from me, she began talking into the tape recorder: "My mom passed away a little over a year ago which is something hard that I am trying to deal with. Because I realize that I have to be a role model for my brothers and sisters." Larisa worried that her young siblings' memories of their mother would fade.

I advised her to "write some of the good memories for them." In discussing the best way to do that, I suggested that she think about an object of her mother's of great value to her. Immediately she looked down at her long hands and the red ring on her fourth finger. "That's it." She was pleased, and so was I.

The next day, Larisa read an impromptu poem based on the ring. Her voice on the tape was barely more than a whisper. She began, "The most valuable thing that I possess, which my mother gave to me." Gradually her voice became stronger, edged with grief, but clear. Her eyes, long dimmed by sadness, looked up as she read, "Nothing else could brighten up my day but to see her smiling face." I watched the light of the smile on her woman-child's face gradually illuminate her eyes. Larisa finished her poem and smiled another radiant mother-blessed smile. I sat in the chair near my desk, crying a little for the beauty of the poem, for the hope that her mother heard this, and for the wonder of the gift of writing. Larisa, not at all embarrassed, looked at me comfortingly and said, "Writing this for her will help me to recover."

Shaping the stories of themselves and their families in writing gave Larisa and my other students an opportunity that society as a whole did not afford—the chance to emphasize, indeed celebrate, the strength of that family and by extension, of that young individual. Even when the story was one of loss, as was often the case, the shaping, the hewing out in strong and loving details, carefully remembered and recorded, gives to that individual an identity of a strong person, not of a victim. Listening to Larisa's poem, beholding the gift in this 15-year-old girl, helped me to recover also—to recover the awe of the beauty inside our students, the courage of their lives and their struggle to shape their individuality in a world that would see them as suspect—and sometimes intimidating—faces in a crowd. In the process, I recovered my own sense of worth as a teacher, privileged enough to witness great beauty and fortunate enough sometimes to help make it happen.

Larisa and Nancy O'Malley's interaction is a clear and moving example of what O'Malley describes as the redemptive power of writing. O'Malley believes that as a teacher of writing she can support students in reflecting on their histories and their identities in ways that empower them in and outside of school. This belief shapes her entire approach to teaching. "Society sees first what would generally be seen as deficits," she claims. Her goal is for her students to develop through the act of writing "an identity of a strong person, not of a victim." When she reflected on the pedagogy described in her own research journal, in her interviews with focal students, and in taped sessions when the focal students met as a response group, O'Malley gained new insight into how students began this development.

O'Malley had long been convinced that a writing-workshop structure would support her students in using writing about their families and their communities to strengthen their identities. At the same time, experience had taught her that engaging her multicultural students in a creative-writing workshop where their experiences formed the basis for their texts and for discussion could all too easily exacerbate feelings of powerlessness and defeatism. For years, she believed that having her students interview family members about their personal histories, write, and then share the family stories with the class would "invest them with a sense of the richness and triumph in so many of their families—most of whom were immigrants." Instead, however, O'Malley had discovered that:

> the resulting oral histories, read aloud to the class, were anything but a triumph. They were instead long litanies of failure: "I asked my dad if he had any dreams. Yes it was to go to school. He never finished. He had to quit at fifteen." "My grandmother came from Cape Verde with nothing and had to marry a stranger. She gave up her dream of being a teacher."

O'Malley decided to "refocus the lens"—to ask her students to attend to the specific rather than the global. She asked those students, as she later asked Larisa and her classmates, to bring in an object of great value to them, personally, or to their family:

> My students came with an array of interesting objects—a blue silk dress brought from Peru, a set of ivory earrings from Fogo, Cape Verde, a wide-brimmed sombrero from Mexico brought from its place of pride on the wall of a Dorchester apartment. When the stories of those objects were read, I knew we had something. Those objects, carefully treasured or even mysteriously saved from destruction, were invested with all the richness of the family history. And even when there

was loss, there was triumph in the passing down of the memory from generation to generation.

O'Malley found that refocusing her students' writing on positive particulars, in this instance a valued object, effectively moved them to write powerfully about their lives. Many of her students, O'Malley believes, too easily accepted the identity society gave them—of being suspect or intimidating. Writing about, and thereby reflecting on, their strengths offered them a "kind of salvation from anonymity"—a means through which they could empower themselves to oppose confining and potentially debilitating stereotypes. Her research affirmed her approach to creative writing. "When I write," Eric, one of O'Malley's focal students, stated, "I feel like I am in a holy world—a world of my own. I feel powerful because anything I want I can just write it down. It's in my head."

The five students in O'Malley's focal group all used their writing to discover something new about themselves and their families. Larisa wrote down her memories of her mother. Eric first shared orally, and then drafted and redrafted, the story of his family's life in and flight from Vietnam. Alban, who identifies himself as "East Indian, Puerto Rican, and White" wrote love poems and created stories about good and evil inspired by a family book of hymns. Carole, with the help of her sisters, began writing a series of children's stories from the oral tradition of their family in Barbados. Demetrios, a Greek American who told the group that his mother never said anything about herself, interviewed her and gathered the information to write "Love at First Sight," the story of how his mother at age 12 pined for a beautiful but unattainable dress, and how her brothers put off important purchases of their own to scrape together enough money to buy it for her in time for Easter. As all of O'Malley's students did, when these five writers were ready to take the "Author's Chair," they read their stories aloud to the class. The students' pieces later became part of an anthology, which this class chose to title "The Ruby Ring Anthology" out of respect for Larisa's bravery in sharing her grief.

The process of self-discovery through writing followed by public sharing allowed O'Malley's students to situate themselves, first within their families, then within the community of the classroom, and potentially, within the larger society. The students brought their personal, family, and community values into a new context through their writing. The dual emphasis in O'Malley's class on students' first writing their personal stories and then reading them out loud to their peers created a community in which students had the opportunity to listen to many stories that did not necessarily match the narrow vision of success or failure communicated in media portrayals of family and culture. After Eric read the story in which he told of his father's struggle to carry him from Vietnam to the safety of an Indonesian refugee camp, O'Malley commented on the impact his words had had on the class, "Nothing that we could have read about the Vietnamese struggle during the war could have been more vivid than that firsthand account, told by the infant who was saved, now a writer telling his own father's story." By having access to the stories of their classmates and by sharing stories of their own, the students created a new yardstick against which individual students could measure, and perhaps, positively reevaluate, their own experiences in the broader society.

To help her students develop this ever deepening sense of empowerment, O'Malley emphasized that asking students to write and share their writing was not in itself sufficient. Students needed to be explicitly taught skills so that they could articulate their ideas powerfully. O'Malley's research showed how deliberately she created a classroom in which students learned writing techniques as well as productive ways for interacting together as writers and readers, authors and audience.

O'Malley believed that students could develop these skills if they were taught to listen critically to language:

> The single most difficult thing to achieve in promoting the art of writing in a classroom is teaching the art of *listening*. In order to be convinced of the importance of words the students have to develop and practice the art of listening to words out loud. Listening with depth and understanding, to hear the words, is the key, the secret. It almost astounds me in its simplicity.

Explicitly teaching her students to attend carefully to language and to their classmates' ideas required the "breaking down of old classroom habits." O'Malley began this process on the first day of class. She distributed a handout with one rule: "There is absolute *respect* for every writer in the class (This includes the teacher). There is absolute attention when a writer is reading his/her work." She immediately put this rule to the test. Each student interviewed one other student briefly, wrote what he or she learned, and then introduced that student to the class. O'Malley asked her students to be prepared to ask questions based on what they had heard. This request not only reinforced her expectation that students would listen, but also, she observed, required "students in the circle (or square, or whatever configuration you can make) to look at each other, *not* just at the teacher." By immediately modeling that each student's voice in the class is important, O'Malley showed students that they were responsible to each other, as well as to her.

Later, when students were ready to share a piece of writing, O'Malley asked the class to identify particularly strong word choices as they listened to a classmate reading aloud:

> I asked the students to write about a place that felt like a refuge to them. Some wrote about their rooms. Tina wrote about her grandmother's kitchen in the projects. She described the hallway leading to her grandmother's apartment as a "foul crusty old place." When Tina read her piece I asked for good word choices. Jocelyn offered "crusty."

When O'Malley asked students to listen to text, whether it was written by a classmate or a professional author, she encouraged them to notice what makes a piece of writing effective, so that they, too, could manipulate these techniques as writers. "From the circling of specific words I then proceed to underlining whole sentences that are powerful or show 'writing mastery.'"

O'Malley further strengthened her students' abilities to evaluate their own and others' writing by modeling critiques of early drafts with the whole class. She led the class through the response process step by step, by reviewing a relatively strong piece of student writing, emphasizing the attributes of good writing, and seeking suggestions for revision. With each paper, she repeatedly emphasized careful attention to language:

> What I try to do, and it seems to work, is that you take a reasonably good paper and then everybody looks at that, and after you've . . . been real specific and very detailed on what works well, what's a good word choice—my classes get tired of the language that I'm constantly using . . . [*knocking on the table with each word*] circle a good word choice. What's a strong sentence, what, all of that. But they do do it. And then to say, "Is there anything we can tighten up here? Is there anything that makes this better?" (Site meeting, Boston, October 31, 1992)

The repetitive act of noticing language provided students a structure they could build upon, and helped them see the fine details of writing craft. With this structure O'Malley explicitly demonstrated to her students that writing is not only a creative art but also involves making choices and considering their potential effects upon readers. Through reading, listening to, and critiquing writing, students developed an ear for a strong turn of phrase and a well-crafted text. They honed their ability to judge writing and to reflect on how their own experiences could be interpreted through writing.

Over the year, O'Malley's students internalized the careful attention to language as well as the processes of interaction that she modeled so explicitly. O'Malley was surprised at how clearly students demonstrated their learning when she listened to a tape of her focal students' response group. Following Alban's reading of his poetry, the other students' questions reflected the academic skills and interpersonal interactions that O'Malley had stressed in class. First the students focused on the writing:

> They all listen to his voice reading his poems. They question him about details, word choices, and inspiration—all questions they practiced and learned from the creative writing class.

Then they questioned the writer about whether one poem was successful at wooing the young woman for whom it had been written. Alban responded that the poem had not worked the romantic magic he had hoped, "Course she didn't like me," but, even so, "It's a good poem. It's worth something." Alban drew this conclusion, not as a solitary writer, but as a member of a writing community. O'Malley came to understand that Alban's standards, and those of his classmates—grew out of listening to and responding to his own and others' texts, as well as out of his increasing experience in writing.

Reflecting on this discussion, O'Malley wrote that her students had begun to empower themselves through this process of self-discovery rooted in writing:

> Listening to their discussion, taking elements from the class, reinforcing the specifics, I am stunned by the way they have transformed themselves from 10th graders who reluctantly spoke up in class to speakers with loud, clear voices that, as they resonate for each other and singly, state that it [their writing] is "worth something."

O'Malley's students felt able to judge their work as "worth something," able to assert their identity in a world that, as O'Malley writes in her vignette, often sees them as nameless.

With her vision of students empowered, not just in her classroom but in their lives, O'Malley taught her students to acquire interpersonal skills—ways of listening and responding—and analytical skills—ways of interpreting and expressing experiences—that allowed them to grow as creators and assessors of writing. Through acting upon these skills, her students gained power to impose meaning on their experiences—to create a story, an identity—that celebrated, rather than diminished, their lives. O'Malley concluded: "They speak for themselves and for an American dream that will be better because they not only wish it, they speak it, write it, and shape it."

EMPOWERMENT THROUGH ACTION: STEPHANIE DAVENPORT

Chicago teacher researcher Stephanie Davenport offered a vision of empowerment that, in many ways, integrates ideas brought forward by Valenti and O'Malley. Like Valenti, Davenport intentionally opened her classroom to the world outside. She involved students in meaningful, real-world activities—hosting authors for school assemblies and participating in field trips. Like O'Malley, Davenport structured those activities to explicitly teach students both interpersonal and literacy skills.

Working in a large high school on the north side of Chicago with more than 80% students of color and a high percentage of students from conditions of poverty, Davenport imbued her pedagogy with values such as collective action, cooperative economics, and self-determination drawn from the principles of Kwanzaa. In a small but significant example, Davenport reserved one of her desk drawers for students' notebooks and works in progress as well as blank paper and a supply of pens for students who may need them during class. She demanded that students act respectfully and supportively:

> In the first days of school, at the teachable moment when some student had acted disrespectfully to another, I became enraged. "We are in this room to be able to learn and to be safe. All bets that endanger our learning or being a full human being in this classroom are off. The world is tough enough for everyone here without us contributing to it also."

She followed through on these words by asking students and their parents to sign a contract that sets out standards of respectful behavior in her class.

Within what she called the "safe zone" of her classroom, Davenport emphasized another precept, which she drew from Kwanzaa—the need for creative action in the face of a society that is resistant to change. Students must learn strategies they can apply to academic problems and real-life challenges. They must learn *how* to take risks, Davenport argued. "That's showing them how you step by step are able to empower yourself to do something in your life" (site meeting, Chicago, May 7, 1993). Davenport praised the model provided by a group of students from a nearby junior high who collectively operated a business marketing African fabrics. She said:

> They have the ability now to say, "Hey, if there isn't a job created for me, I can create one for myself because I can think. I can write. I can write memos. I can write letters for grants. . . . I can do these things."
> (Site meeting, Chicago, May 7, 1993)

For Davenport, teachers who empower students apprentice them in the social and academic skills that will help them gain power when they leave school. To achieve this goal, Davenport embraced teaching approaches that appear to be contradictory. At times, her curriculum was highly structured and teacher directed. At other times, it was open ended and directed by the students. At times, Davenport expected that students would work collectively and interdependently. At other times she encouraged students to work independently and in their own ways. These apparent contradictions, Davenport showed, may be just what is needed to empower students to act.

Davenport's research question focused on one specific skill—how students develop the ability to draw inferences from and make connections between their reading and their personal experience in their writing—but her study documented how she used every opportunity, even those as commonplace as a research assignment, a school assembly, and a field trip, to support her students in taking action in new ways and in making connections between the academic world and their own lives. In the vignette below, Davenport describes her ninth graders' first ever writing experience in her classroom. She shows how she creates a situation where students can link writing to their own experiences and how she supports them in taking new academic steps.

LESSON OF FAITH

By Stephanie Davenport

Instilling in students the belief that what they don't now possess —such as the confidence and validation of their own expression—will materialize is a lesson of faith. But it's a two-way street. The teacher must also believe that every child can learn and then insure that every child does learn.

On a warm September day, I noticed that many of the teenagers who were whizzing past me on their way to their next class wore brightly colored T-shirts and jeans with the Cross Colour logo. The then popular Cross Colours outfits were distinguished by their colors, red, green, and black—the colors of the African American liberation flag originally designed by Marcus Garvey. In the late 1980s, two African American sportswear designers began the Threads of Life Incorporation as part of the Stop the Violence campaign in Los Angeles. The slogan "Racism Hurts Everybody," printed on each piece of clothing, promotes the message that knowledge, self-respect, love, and peace will overcome barriers of hate and prejudice. When I reached my classroom door and saw my new freshmen waiting patiently, I realized that many of them, like the upper-grade students of whom they were as yet so in awe, were also wearing Cross Colours. Now was the time, I decided, for my freshmen to leave behind the world of awe and enter their own community of achievement.

"Our assignment is a research project," I explained. "Everyone believes that teenagers dress like everyone else. We will find out if teenagers blindly follow clothing fads or select their own style of dressing. Let's look to see who wears what. What's popular?" First, everyone paired off with someone else so that one could observe and the other keep a tally. Next, we selected locations in the school where we could observe students. Then, during the passing time between our double period, we fanned out across the building to collect our "data."

After the students came back with their figures, we determined that all ethnic groups and both genders wore Cross Colours and that Cross Colour jeans were the most often worn. We discussed the results, debating whether students chose to wear the clothes for their message or only for their appearance. At the end of our discussion, I asked students to write in their journals, "What is your personal comment about the message behind Cross Colours clothing?"

The next day I returned with a synopsis of what each group had observed and the conclusions that the class had come to from their discussion. First, we all did "brain dribblings"—writing on the topic of students' fashion choices for about 5 minutes without stopping. I displayed my own "dribblings" on the overhead projector and underlined repeated or significant words to show students how to select key words from what they had written. I also brought into class some of my "homework" writings so that they could see how an organized final draft could evolve from the messier first and second drafts.

After students underlined key words, we each wrote one sentence that summarized our main idea. We then discussed personal experiences that supported our main idea before going to the computer lab to write our first drafts. Being in the computer lab allows me to move among the students, advising, cajoling, and bolstering fragile writing spirits while they are still composing.

Before we began reading our first drafts to one another, I prepared students to listen actively by reminding them that our class is a "safe" zone. Each student read to a small group, and the others told the reader what they liked in what they heard. Then the reader read again. The others then told the reader what they thought the reader was trying to say. If it was not the same idea, then the reader wrote down the listeners' comments in order to close the gap between what was being heard and what was written.

After the students had written their essays, I displayed them on a bulletin board in the classroom. I had just finished stapling the last essay to the board when the students began to arrive. Five minutes later, one student came up to another and asked, "Well where is *my* essay?" Another student immediately responded, "Oh. Right there beside mine." I could see their pride in their writing and in what we had accomplished together. With faith in each other, we had begun to create a community of achievement.

Davenport created a classroom that is a direct conduit to the world outside. She offered her students both freedom to act and a structure in which to make their actions meaningful. For her freshmen students' first research project, Davenport took an active role and explicitly taught students the strategies they needed to do this new kind of writing. She chose a topic in which her students had both interest and expertise—an investigation of fashion trends in the school. She organized their research collaboratively, to give all students both access to her expertise as a more experienced writer and the support of their classmates. She structured their analysis of their findings to create a constant interplay between student input and teacher direction. In this initial academic experience in her classroom, Davenport guided students' actions carefully. From one standpoint, her decision to choose the topic of this research and to control the writing so carefully might be seen as disempowering because she was depriving students of choice. Davenport decided to take control of important pieces of the process because at this point, the goal for empowering students involved giving them the support they needed for acquiring new learning strategies and writing skills.

When Freedman visited Davenport's classroom in late September, soon after the students had completed the Cross Colours assignment, she witnessed a kind of interaction between Davenport and her students that gave additional evidence of the "community of achievement" that Davenport describes. During that class session, Davenport passed out the newly arrived issue of Scholastic's *Scope Magazine* and briefly described its contents, which included Gary Drevitch's dramatic adaptation of Robert Louis Stevenson's story *Dr. Jekyll and Mr. Hyde.* One of the girls suggested that some of the students act out the play. Other students volunteered to join her. The rest of the class gathered as the students who wanted to read divvied up the parts. Two of the students who had lobbied for, and gotten, the most lengthy parts, read haltingly, with numerous miscues and repeats. Freedman watched with some surprise as the students in the "audience" enjoyed the play and listened without any judgment of their classmates' hesitations. In her experience, students who struggle with reading aloud are usually reluctant to make their difficulties apparent to their classmates because of the ridicule that might accompany their efforts. Freedman noted that this classroom offered the students "an environment where they could practice their reading without feeling embarrassed but instead feeling proud of what they could do" (field notes, September 20, 1992).

As the students' spontaneous dramatic reading illustrates, Davenport built upon any available occasion to create situations in which students could gain the confidence to act by practicing something they had never done before. When a local bookstore approached her with the suggestion of having authors visit the school, she agreed, and suggested that her freshman class could serve as hosts for the first author, Yelena Khanga, a Black Russian American Jew. When Davenport presented the project to her class, she emphasized that working on committees was a part of life they needed to learn about. The class brainstormed together about dividing up the work. In committees, the students then organized different aspects of Khanga's visit. Each committee's responsibilities also included writing: developing an article about the speaker for the school newsletter, creating invitations, previewing the event for the attending classes, designing banners, preparing menus, organizing time schedules and seating charts, and generating questions for the discussion following the speaker's presentation. To further prepare for their tasks, the whole class read the first chapter of Khanga's book, *Soul to Soul: A Black Russian American Family 1865-1992* as well as a newspaper review of the book.

Davenport's structure provided models for action. First as a class, and then within committees, she and her students recursively acted out the following process: Consider all that needs to be done; decide who will fulfill major responsibilities; break each overall responsibility into manageable tasks; do each task well. She further asked students to complete written progress reports that allowed her, without taking ownership of the process, to check how well they were fulfilling their responsibility, thus ensuring that she could intervene if need be. Davenport gave a telling example of how she invited a student back into the activity when he had moved off-task for too long:

> During a committee meeting, Jimmy was doing more talking about a popular rap group, A Tribe Called Quest, than he was contributing to the ushering committee's work. . . . Instead of scolding Jimmy about not "being on task," I went over and privately told him that, perhaps, he could think of a name for our class as school hosts. Jimmy was pleased when the class agreed upon the name that he had proposed, "The Class Called Quest."

Jimmy's contribution was an important one. The students continued to refer to themselves with this name throughout the year.

By hosting the author, Davenport's students learned about planning an event and working interdependently; they provided an educational service to the school; and they read and wrote. After Khanga's visit, Lilianna explained that she appreciated the experience because "we got to learn how to treat a guest and we had to be responsible and organized." Hosting this event increased the students' sense of efficacy and contributed to their knowledge about how to get things done in the world. The students also saw that Davenport believed they were responsible, capable people who could make an important contribution to her class and to the school.

As her students' competence increased, Davenport provided them with less and less structure. After her class had taken a field trip to view Spike Lee's film *Malcolm X,* they asked to read the book. The autobiography was unavailable at her school, but to capitalize on the students' interest, Davenport used her own funds to purchase a copy for each student. While her other young students avidly read this difficult work during class one day, one group of three came to her desk to discuss the movie and the book. Davenport describes how they set out a project for themselves:

> Gene said, "Just like in the movie, my friend looked up the definitions of *white* and *black* in the dictionary. You should see what they have in there. But there's no mention of Hispanics or Native Americans."
>
> Jared reached for a dictionary. He read aloud the positive connotations for *white,* such as "purity" and the negative connotations for *black,* such as "evil."
>
> Charity asked, "Can we go to the school library and look up the definitions in a bigger dictionary?"
>
> Gene piped in, "Yes. Then can we work on a project where we could write our own definitions that are fair to all people."
>
> I agreed to them going to the library to consult unabridged dictionaries.

In this instance, Davenport allowed the students to act on their interests and explore their ideas freely. In fact, when she offered students assistance, they politely refused.

Deciding when to provide structure and judging how much structure to provide is a difficult call. Davenport explained that she does not always judge accurately. She created a writing assignment related to Malcolm X's autobiography, which failed. Davenport had asked students to describe the qualities of a personal hero and to illustrate these qualities with references to the autobiography. Most of the students did not complete the assignment. Davenport was reminded that students' interest and willingness are not sufficient for them to participate in a challenging task:

> I think that the times when things do not work is when I push them without support, without structure. 'Cause this thing with the Malcolm X vignette, . . . I had them doing something totally different, and I thought, "Oh they'd sit down and they'd do all this writing and it'd be wonderful." And they didn't quite do it, and it was not because they didn't want to. It was because they couldn't. They didn't have the tools. I had not broken it down to some steps, so that they understood how to build up to what they needed to say. (Site meeting, Chicago, February 28, 1993)

Davenport mistook her students' enthusiasm for independence.

Later, she did see particularly clear evidence that her students were internalizing strategies for empowerment when, after returning from an absence, she found her class angry with the substitute who had been particularly harsh and controlling. Instead of complaining, they took action. They drafted a letter, which Davenport subsequently included in her instructions for future substitutes:

> Dear Subs:
> Our class is very free. A lot of teachers misunderstand our class. They think our intentions are wrong. Our teacher is very easy going and respects our opinions and thoughts. The things that our teacher lets us do are as follows: 1. If we put things in the desk, we can get them later. 2. We work in groups. 3. We read aloud. 4. We are able to move the chairs and put them back at the end of class. 5. We will be prompt to class 6. We will do the assigned work 7. We are able to go to the bathroom during the break. 8. We will give you respect. The Class called Quest thanks you for being with us. We hope you have a pleasant stay in our class.

In their letter, the students articulated both their belief that their thoughts and actions are worthy of respect and their commitment to acting respectfully themselves. The students showed a mature understanding of how to express their position. This letter shows that Davenport's students were learning ways of acting in the world—they responded to the miscommunication and perceived injustice in their classroom by expressing their position in a balanced and open manner— a significant and impressive rehearsal within school for responding to injustices they may encounter on the outside.

Davenport admitted that students in her classes performed in ways that other teachers found surprising: "I do know that they go beyond what most people think that they can do. I do know that, but I believe that I see something in them that they are able to do. I try to have them believe what it is that I see" (site meeting, Chicago, January 13, 1993). For Davenport, part of what she called "the lesson of faith" of convincing students to believe in themselves was allowing them to see themselves as able to do what they had never done before. The other part involved providing students with structured activities that helped them increase their power to act. Davenport's definition of empowerment required that students would not only come to believe they had the right to take action but that they would know they had a repertoire of strategies and skills they could draw upon as they attempted to achieve the results they desired.

CONCLUSIONS

As Valenti's, O'Malley's and Davenport's research indicates, teachers working in multicultural urban settings cannot always assume that empowering students within the classroom will give them the resources they need to succeed outside the school. Empowering students for the world beyond became their explicit goal, and their classroom curricula and pedagogy grew from this goal. In these classrooms, the academic content of the curriculum and the ways of acting in the class community—such as making choices or interacting with others—are interwoven. The students who fill the M-CLASS teachers' classrooms need access to content knowledge and to literacy skills, but they also need exposure to a wide variety of perspectives, attitudes, and interactional patterns if they are to develop adaptability and resourcefulness.

Teaching about literacy and about life in our society are not separate; they are interrelated in significant, yet often hidden ways. Valenti's, O'Malley's, and Davenport's experiences reveal that students achieve more successfully in the multicultural classroom when teachers acknowledge these relationships and intentionally create opportunities for them to connect school and life. Valenti focused on the ways in which letter writing created a dialogue with the outside world, which supported geography learning. Through developing their ability to evaluate and produce crafted texts, O'Malley offered students a creative and sometimes cathartic outlet through which they could discover a more powerful image of themselves and their families or communities. Davenport emphasized how students develop new strategies that allow them to take action, in school and in society. In the process, all three ensured that the students developed the skills in written communication that they needed to express themselves clearly and confidently, and that would help them succeed in, and ideally, lead in, reshaping the world outside. Stephanie Davenport captured the idea well when she said, "You wish to have this kid see himself [or herself] in the world, and the world in himself [or herself], so that he [or she] sees a connection to everything" (site meeting, Chicago, October 18, 1992). Pursuing an integrated vision of empowerment does not happen naturally; it requires conscious attention to balancing the value of what students are now with the promise of what they can become.

PART V

Implications for Practice and Research

CHAPTER 12

Learning from M-CLASS: Thoughts for the Future

Julie Shalhope Kalnin, Sarah Warshauer Freedman, and Elizabeth Radin Simons

THE CONTRIBUTION OF THE M-CLASS teachers is significant not only because the research was carefully conducted, but also, and especially, because the researchers are teachers. Teachers sit in the hot seat, daily forced to address many of the problems of American society. The M-CLASS teachers show, in specific and clear terms, what can be done—not in the "best" schools, but in those often troubled by social ills and institutional weaknesses. Their re-search—conducted in the scarce free time after papers were graded and les-sons planned—is testimony to the power of their belief that what they learned could not only influence their teaching and their students, but speak to the educational community at large and to other teachers who, like them, are working in particularly challenging environments.

THE IMPORTANCE OF TEACHER RESEARCH FOR THE TEACHERS AND THEIR STUDENTS

In one year, with support from local and site coordinators, the M-CLASS teach-ers formed an effective national research network. Their first task was to shape within this network a local research community that would be a place where they could focus on their own learning. Elyse Eidman-Aadahl (1996) calls this kind of community a "third space," following sociologist Ray Old-enburg. She defines "third spaces" as "places where we can make sense of our lives as teachers by making our teaching public and surrounding it with talk" (p. xi). In this "third space," the M-CLASS teachers came to trust that they could be free to question their decisions, to express their uncertainties, and to admit their failings.

In M-CLASS, the "third space" also became a "research space." The teach-ers all were experienced and effective, and at the outset skilled classroom observers, but they initially found it difficult to assume the detached stance of a researcher, to take on teaching and research roles simultaneously. Over time, as they learned to employ research techniques, daily events gained significance—an essay was no longer only something to be evaluated and entered into the grade book, for instance, but also a piece of data to be analyzed. From their new position, the teacher researchers began to see new aspects of student behavior, new dimensions of student writing, and new implications of their own teaching practices. Although they continued to value their teacher's intuition—the product of years of experience—they found that using research tools helped them to observe the classroom through another lens—to scrutinize their assumptions and articulate what had become unconscious.

Just as the teacher-research group supported teachers in assuming a researcher's stance toward their work, the group played an important role in stimulating the teachers to reconsider and expand their teaching practices. Half of the M-CLASS teachers approached their research effort as a way to structure their own experimentation. The teachers often set out to do something new in their classrooms that they felt was important but that, for a variety of reasons, had been hard for them. For instance, in New Orleans, Pat Ward, though herself a published poet, had avoided teaching poetry—other than asking students to memorize and recite poems. The subject was so personal that she needed support to approach it in a substantive way with her students. For her research, she designed and taught a multicultural poetry unit.

Finding formal ways for the teachers' findings to become part of the research literature was one of the original purposes of M-CLASS. Despite having produced this volume, we consider our success to be only partial. Our original idea was to create a collection capturing all of the diverse voices in the project, but our own voices and points of view have taken a more dominant position than we originally intended. It is our hope that the diverse perspectives offered by the teachers have not been too much altered in the process.

The teachers worked beyond their professional responsibilities to complete their yearlong research projects. Writing for publication was an even more arduous task that stretched, in some cases, over several years, as the teachers stole time for revision from their busy work lives. When working with the teacher researchers to prepare their research pieces for publication, we found that the collaboration changed. Not only were fewer teacher researchers able to continue working with us without continued funding, but we also found ourselves in uncharted territory, as the teachers worked to create a genre that has yet to be fully defined.

As university facilitators, we drew upon our own publishing experiences to advise the teachers as they wrote. This advice was at times useful and at other times counterproductive. The San Francisco teacher-research group, when preparing for a conference presentation in 1995, reflected on this process. Lew described her 2-year process of revision as "entailing a certain loss of ownership" (local meeting, San Francisco, March 9, 1995). Juarez likened it to "having someone correct your grammar as you speak." After the heated discussion in which these comments were made, Simons commented that she had always seen the feedback from the university facilitators as "one way of doing business, not *the* way." Delp explained her perspective:

> I can speak for myself now. [Because of] my own doubts and inexperience I assumed that was *the* answer, and I often heard you say, "This is just a possibility." But then I just thought, "Well that has got to be the right way because I sure as hell don't know how to do it."

Juarez described how she initially believed that she should follow the recommendations of the university facilitators, "even when it felt wrong." Significantly, it took 2 years for this group of teachers, who worked with us the most frequently of all the M-CLASS teams, to reach the point where they could express these frustrations openly. In a collaboration such as this one, participants may find themselves replicating, in unconscious ways, entrenched roles and relations between teachers and university-based educators. Although it was not our intention, the teachers in the project for too long saw setting the course of their revision as primarily the role of the university facilitators.

In spite of their (and our) concerns about ownership, the teachers often appreciated and actively solicited the guidance of the university team. Several years later Delp wrote an extended reflection about the development of her writing, in which she explains, "The university researchers encouraged me to 'keep going and not to worry.'" She elaborates:

> In the final year of my journey, once I had written a draft that had the "beginnings of a publishable piece," I finally learned how to analyze and write about my data. With the support and guidance of a university researcher, I wrote and rewrote my analyses of my students' logs, which simultaneously created a more refined approach to the entire draft. Through this painstaking process, the entire draft took on a new and revised form, until finally it was completed. Just as my students must acquire skills in order to write interpretively, I, too, had to secure the skills I needed to write about my research in a meaningful way.

The M-CLASS collaboration showed us how teachers and university facilitators must together explore and redefine their roles, as teacher researchers move toward participating in knowledge generation about teaching and learning.

Through the process of writing chapters for this book, many of the

M-CLASS teachers, like Delp, felt that they were moving into another professional space as they recycled through their data second, third, and fourth times and refined their writing. With each pass through their data, they learned increasingly more about themselves as teachers and their students as learners. For these teachers, writing generated new insights and advanced their learning. It also provided new levels of professional confidence that often led the teachers to take on stronger and more effective leadership roles at their schools and in their school districts.

A surprisingly large number of the M-CLASS teacher researchers have continued, in spite of much-reduced and in some cases no support—either financial, from the university, or from their colleagues—to conduct research in their classrooms. The San Francisco group has enjoyed the most support, with the Berkeley team still mostly intact and working with those who wish to continue. Several small grants from the Spencer Foundation's Collaborative Research and Mentoring Program and the University of California's Office of the President have allowed three members of the original six-member group of teachers—Delp, Juarez, and Lew—to bring in two new members from each of their schools to create school-based teams. In New Orleans, Williams-Smith independently received a Collaborative Research and Mentoring grant from Spencer to link the New Orleans M-CLASS group with the New Orleans National Writing Project Urban Sites group. Two M-CLASS teachers, Delp from San Francisco and Alford from New Orleans, were awarded individual small grants from Spencer. In Boston, Logan and Shakespear are teaching a course in teacher research at a local university.

Others have continued their teacher research without funding, sometimes by forming a group and sometimes on their own. Yearwood has independently established a teacher-research group at her school in Boston. In Chicago, Diaz-Gemmati, working alone, has consulted with the Berkeley team on her next research project. For some, however, the load of teacher research and teaching proved too demanding to sustain, especially when support was withdrawn. For others, their professional obligations and interests shifted.

HOW TEACHER RESEARCH BENEFITS
THE EDUCATIONAL COMMUNITY

The findings of the M-CLASS teachers and other teacher researchers fill an important niche in the generation of knowledge about teaching. Their findings are important to other educators—fellow teachers and university faculty—because of the particular kinds of questions they ask and the types of answers they find. They add specific cases that bring new perspectives, even to established educational findings. For instance, Kathy Daniels's findings about her adaptations to a reading/writing workshop for her remedial freshman English course enriches our understanding of this popular teaching approach.

The process of teacher research allowed other teacher researchers to bring established research findings to a more meaningful plane. San Francisco teacher researcher George Austin, for example, was aware of research literature indicating the ineffectiveness of tracking. In his own research, he took both a personal look at the impact of tracking on one student and a comparative look at how a challenging classroom activity worked in his "advanced" and his "regular" classes. His two perspectives confirmed the previous findings—but through methods that not only propelled him to work toward changing the practice of tracking at his school, but that also may encourage the many other educators who choose to ignore the research to rethink the consequences of this practice. Although he did not understand this before he did his research, Austin was a participant, implicated, he shows, in the very practice he wished to eradicate.

Several teacher researchers, such as Karen Alford and Elena Valenti, tested theories they had read about but had not previously tried to implement. Alford's findings about the importance of encouraging students to assume voices of people from the past as a way of developing historical empathy and Valenti's findings about the significance of authentic written communication particularize theory by applying it within a complex teaching setting.

Other teacher researchers, such as Verda Delp and Ann Lew, work at the intersection of conflicting educational theories. Their studies reveal their teaching philosophies and document the day-to-day details of how they integrate these theories in order to respond to their students' needs. Their findings suggest ways in which apparently conflictual theories might be augmented and even interwoven.

Teacher research, by setting forth these real and grounded examples, can play a critical role in the generation of theory. Ideally, theory grows from specifics, and is refined when new information supports or contradicts its tenets. Bringing teacher researchers' findings into the literature about teaching is essential, we believe, if educational theory is to grow and thrive. Unless university researchers are seeking out the broadest possible array of examples to drive and enrich their theories, the theory itself becomes limited by its own insularity.

The M-CLASS teacher researchers' experiences may also provide a clue to the thorny issue of dissemination. Their experiences suggest that research findings and the theories that grow from them may be at too general a level for teachers to easily apply in their classrooms, or the applications may require institutional change beyond the level of the classroom. Through the process of teacher research, the teachers in this project were able to bring educational research and theory to life in their individual classrooms and to better understand the institutional constraints that affect them. They also share with others their answers about how these findings and theories could make sense in classrooms and schools where teachers are simultaneously addressing the needs of 30 or more students per class and balancing dozens of other issues. Teacher researchers' findings are important to the educational community in the way that they establish a middle ground between practice and research—in the way that they turn practice into research and the way that they turn research into practice.

In addition to their individual findings, the M-CLASS teacher researchers also make a collective contribution. The teachers' work and transcripts of their research meetings were compiled and analyzed by the Berkeley team, a process that creates the possibility for findings less local and more distanced than an individual teachers' conclusions. Through the analysis of the M-CLASS transcripts, we grouped their research into three major topics, which form the parts of this book: the need for, ways of, and benefits of seeing students and having students see each other across complex boundaries; deciding what to teach, in particular diversifying curricula to suit particular teaching settings; and deciding how to teach, in particular how to uphold high standards that empower students in school and for the world outside the classroom.

"Seeing" was far from a trivial task. Eileen Shakespear once commented, "If our goal is to see each child, we have to know where our sight is weak." Through their teacher research a number of the M-CLASS teachers purposefully tried to figure out ways they could "see better." When they did, they came face to face with the fact that they saw others through themselves—through their personal histories, their beliefs and theories, and even their work environments. By virtue of being in multicultural classrooms, the teachers and many of their students came from different backgrounds and often shared few life experiences. In these settings, the teachers found that they had to teach themselves and their students to see beyond differences in race, ethnicity, social class, or a combination of these. In addition, as is the case in all classrooms, the teachers had to see beyond the school's institutional labels, which promoted unfortunate stereotypes; beyond their students' surface behaviors, which often did not reflect their true intentions; across gender lines; and across inevitable gaps between their generation and their students'.

What did the teacher researchers learn in their classrooms about seeing across boundaries?

- Most students care about doing well in school, even when they give an impression to the contrary.
- Many students have been deeply scarred by school experiences, in particular when their talents and knowledge have not been recognized, or worse yet, demeaned, by institutional structures such as inappropriate ability-group tracking and by teachers who show low expectations and do not teach sufficiently challenging and interesting material.
- Attempting to figure out why students behave as they do and trusting that they deep down care about doing well, rather than blaming students for their failures, can help teachers turn negative interactions into more-positive ones.
- Just as teachers find it difficult to see across boundaries, so do their students. To form effective multicultural academic communities, both teachers and students need to learn to see across boundaries. By designing a curriculum partially to achieve this end, teachers can teach students to explicitly work on such seeing.

Many M-CLASS teachers focused their research on issues surrounding multicultural curriculum. They used their research to experiment with developing new kinds of multicultural curriculum, to articulate the underlying goals that guided their curricular decisions, and to better understand their students' experiences. They show that charting curriculum is a creative process of responding to students' needs by drawing upon a broad range of materials, unusual and traditional, contemporary and canonical. The complex vision of multiculturalism that the M-CLASS teachers offer is fluid and frees teachers from following only one ideological stance. It allows them to respond to the perpetually changing demands of the classroom.

What did the M-CLASS teachers discover in their classrooms about what literature to teach?

- A multicultural curriculum that connects explicitly to the lives of those students who have not been well represented in the traditional curriculum and who have not before shown an interest in the academic content of the school is especially helpful for motivating students to both read and write.
- A curriculum that connects explicitly to students' lives is especially helpful for encouraging students to explore their identities, including their ethnicities, in ways that can expand students' sense of who belongs in school and thus support students in building constructive academic self images.
- Although explicitly discussing issues of race, ethnicity, gender, and social class can be painful and potentially explosive, those teachers who chose to face these issues head on found that students gained a deeper understand-

ing of themselves and others, as well as a complex view of U.S. history and contemporary society. They managed the explosive potential of these discussions by helping students achieve intellectual distance from the issues—often through reading and writing as preparation for talking.

In addition to dealing with questions around multicultural curriculum, the teacher researchers were concerned with how to teach so that students would become empowered. Their research illustrates that literacy skills are fundamentally valuable in helping students counteract the larger social forces that may work to keep them down.

What did the M-CLASS teachers find in their classrooms about how to teach in ways that would allow them to uphold high standards and empower their students?

- Helping students achieve high standards for writing requires explicitly teaching the conventions of standard edited English, especially for non-native speakers of English and speakers of nonstandard dialects. Explicit instruction in broader writing issues, such as structure or style, is equally important.
- Helping students achieve high standards for interpreting literature requires explicitly teaching a range of skills. Students need to be taught to analyze and evaluate external and internal influences on the characters' behavior; to support those analyses with references from the text; to apply knowledge about characters' motivations to those of people in the world; to explore the meanings of imagery and symbolism; and to see and articulate alternate interpretations and points of view.
- Helping students achieve high standards for learning history includes explicitly teaching the skills students need; beyond recounting events, dates, and place-names, students should understand the context and motivations that drove people of the past to act as they did.
- Empowerment does not mean only centering the classroom on students, but rather, carefully balancing students' interests and skills with the standards and expectations they will face when they leave school. In all cases the teachers structured their classrooms in ways that honor students' ideas but that also help them mature through developing new interests, abilities, and ways of thinking.

ON TO THE FUTURE

Through M-CLASS, we saw a range of types of teacher research, all of them valuable. In every case the teachers felt that teacher research allowed them to develop as professionals, in ways that they otherwise could not have. For the M-CLASS teachers, who were highly reflective practitioners to begin with, teacher research offered much more than the "re-seeing" or "re-visioning" that Berthoff (1987) describes. The systematic collection and analysis of data allowed them to reach a metacognitive level that they had not experienced before. It was the insights they gained and their sense of the effects of these on their students that kept them engaged, that made them want to continue a labor-intensive process that offered little in the way of financial reward or job-related recognition.

As the teacher-research movement develops in this country, we feel strongly that it must remain open to various types of teacher research. Some of this will follow the standards set by the academy; some will modify those standards to fit the conditions the teachers work under; other teacher research will ignore those standards in favor of those built to allow the research to lead to action in the teachers' schools or classrooms. Teacher research will necessarily be molded into different shapes depending on whether it is conducted as part of a university-based degree program, a collaboration between researcher and practitioner, or a grass roots effort. It also will differ depending on the kinds of support available to the teachers—both in terms of finances and access to outside expertise. Whatever the form, teacher research has the potential to strengthen the teaching profession and to contribute to the good of our nations' schoolchildren; for this reason, universities, school districts, and schools should do all within their power to promote it.

Original Research Questions:
M-CLASS Teacher Researchers

Karen Alford. In a multicultural social studies class, when students assume the voices of important historical figures in their writing and when they include their personal voices in their writing, what do they learn about history?

George Austin. How does the same activity—oral or written presentation, or both, of current events—compare when done in an advanced and a regular class?

Kathy Daniels. What modifications do I have to make to a reading/writing workshop approach (Atwell, 1987; Rief, 1992) for an inner-city below-level English class? How will my approach affect the students' understandings of one another across cultures? How will it affect their writing across time?

Tom Daniels. What role does talk play as nonnative speakers of English in my freshman Introduction to High School English class learn to write?

Stephanie Davenport. When students write about what they read, how do they learn to make inferences between what they are reading and their personal experiences?

Verda Delp. What are the effects of my mapping and log-writing program on my students' writing and thinking skills?

Griselle Diaz-Gemmati. What happens when adolescent students begin to explore themes of racism and prejudice as they discuss and write about literature? Specifically, how do they separate how they feel from what they've heard from their family, friends, and communities?

Reginald Galley. What kinds of conflicts do children from varied ethnic groups face in a multicultural high school setting? How can talk and writing in a multicultural Louisiana-history curriculum contribute to their dealing with these conflicts?

Sarah Herring. What motivates students in a multicultural classroom to read and write?

Deborah Archuleta Juarez. What happens when race, culture, and class become an ongoing topic of discussion in my classroom?

Ann Lew. How can I help students internalize correctness so it becomes a part of their repertoire?

Brenda Landau McFarland. In a multicultural African American history class, what happens when students are given the opportunity to express their conflicts about multiculturalism and their own cultural identities in their journals? What kind of role does the teacher have to play?

Susanna Merrimee. What is my relationship to my students and how is it redefining my teaching?

Nancy O'Malley. How do students learn to see themselves as writers? How do I teach them to see themselves as writers? How does seeing yourself as a writer empower you as a student?

David O'Neill. How do the varied students in my classroom relate to three pieces of literature, written by authors from different cultural groups: Hurston's *Their Eyes Were Watching God,* Cisneros's *The House on Mango Street,* and Hemingway's *A Farewell to Arms*? Does this writing have special meaning to the students, given their gender, age, ethnicity, and race?

Phil Potestio. How can students learn to justify their opinions in a multicultural classroom? How can students learn to be aware that when they state opinions, they have arrived at them through thought? How can this awareness be used to help them develop arguments in a multicultural social studies class?

Eileen Shakespear. What can we observe about the relationship between Black male students and White female teachers that can enlighten and better inform our class practice? How does the relationship affect the students' literacy learning?

Elena Valenti. What is involved in promoting student dialogue, both written and oral, in my social studies classroom?

Darcelle Walker. How do White students feel if we're covering a book about Malcolm X; and how do Black students react if we're covering a book on Whites?

Pat Ward. What do students reveal in their writings and discussions when they are exposed to multicultural poetry?

Doris Williams-Smith. In an interactive multicultural language arts class-room, how do selected eighth-grade students utilize audience awareness to revise when they share their writing and other language products with their peer audience? In the same interactive multicultural classroom, what is the role of metacognitive awareness in the revision process of these same students?

James Williams. Why do so many Black males in the urban inner city who are competent individuals in the community end up in special needs classes? What's the effect on these students of being placed in lab classes, including the effect on their literacy skills?

Walter Wood. What can I learn about the lives of the students that will help their attendance? or, Why do students fail to come to school? What can I do to help their attendance? How does attendance impact on their work in English class?

Junia Yearwood. Does exposure to heritage study and literature affect the self-perception of students of color and consequently influence their learning?

M-CLASS Data Analysis Procedures

THE SYNTHESIS CHAPTERS (5, 8, and 11) include a focus on a theme central to the project as a whole, as well as the work of several teacher researchers relating to the theme of the part. The Berkeley team members selected the teachers' work for inclusion.

To determine the themes and to select the teachers' work that was focal to the themes, the chapter author analyzed (a) the talk at the M-CLASS site and local meetings, (b) the teachers' writing, both for their research reports and when available, other less formal writing about their classrooms, (c) observational notes of classroom visits, and (d) tape-recorded telephone conversations. The main data sources were the talk at the meetings and the writing, with the observational notes and the telephone conversations serving as supplementary data sources.

Analysis of the meeting talk focused mostly on the transcribed portions of the data. Although the talk at the meetings was always tape-recorded, from the total corpus of nearly 150 tapes, a sample of 97 was selected for transcription. The remainder were summarized. Those transcribed included the three site meetings at each of the four sites, all of which were 6 hours or longer in duration, and three of the 1- to 2-hour local meetings—one held early in the year, one in the middle, and one at the end.

When all transcriptions were complete, one transcript was randomly selected from the full data corpus to begin the process of developing analytical codes which would become the basis for deciding on the dominant themes to be highlighted in this book. Five members of the Berkeley team read the transcript and independently noted themes and possible coding categories. The team then met to discuss the themes and to generate a list of tentative codes. This process was repeated with additional transcripts until no new codes emerged. The final coding guideline categorized each code under broader analytical headings, as shown in Figure B.1.

Additionally, a code book was created to serve as a reference guide. It included notes about the code and a definition of it, as well as illustrations of the codes from the transcripts. An example is shown in Figure B.2.

A coding matrix was then designed that assigned four coders in pairs in a balanced plan across sites, meeting type, time of year, and coding partner (see Figure B.3). For purposes of calibration, each pair of coders first coded

Figure B.1. Transcript coding guidelines.

1.	**Teachers' Issues/Theories of Teaching and Learning**
(1 1)	For multicultural classrooms
(1 2)	For all students
(1 3)	For minority students
(1 4)	For special populations (learning disability, special needs, and troubled students)
(1 5)	About writing
(1 6)	About reading (and interpreting literature)
(1 7)	About learning history
(1 8)	About talking
(1 9)	About empowering and motivating students to learn
(1 10)	About student behavior and self-image
(1 11)	About ability grouping (from remedial to gifted)
(1 12)	Origin of teachers' theories/ideas for curriculum
(1 13)	Change in teachers' theories/ reinterpreting theory
(1 14)	About multicultural curriculum
(1 15)	About teaching style and methodology
(1 16)	About second language/bilingual
(1 17)	About assessment
2.	**Narratives**
(2 1)	About teaching experience
(2 2)	About personal experience
(2 3)	About third person(s)
(2 4)	Reference to past narrative
(2 5)	Student narratives
3.	**Dynamics of the Teacher-Research Group**
(3 1)	Making introductory/social talk
(3 2)	Expressing insecurity
(3 3)	Supporting/praising/agreeing with other(s)
(3 4)	Disagreeing with other(s)
(3 5)	Role of the local coordinator
4.	**Schools and the Politics of Schooling**
(4 1)	In society
(4 2)	In the institution of education
(4 3)	In the community surrounding the school
(4 4)	In the school district
(4 5)	In the school
5.	**Teachers' Issues/Theories of Race, Ethnicity, Class, Culture, Religion, and Gender**
(5 1)	About students
(5 2)	About selves
(5 3)	About interaction between students and selves or other teachers
(5 4)	About teachers' interactions with one another
(5 5)	About schooling/society in general
(5 6)	Students' issues/theories of race, ethnicity, class, culture, religion and gender and school
6.	**Standards**
(6 1)	Academic
(6 2)	Behavioral
7.	**Learning Through Teacher Research**
(7 1)	Learning about themselves (teachers' point of view)
(7 2)	Learning/teaching about their teaching and teaching in general (teachers' point of view)
(7 3)	Learning/teaching/reflecting about research (what it is, how to do it)
(7 4)	Planning/describing specific teacher research projects
(7 5)	Writing about research
(7 6)	Interpreting data
8.	**Issues of Community**
(8 1)	Creating school/classroom community
(8 2)	Making personal connections between teachers and students
(8 3)	Involving parents/the larger community
9.	**Reading**
(9 1)	Reading own writing
(9 2)	Reading others' writing

Figure B.2. Sample code book entry.

(5 4) Teachers' Issues/Theories of Race, Ethnicity, Class, Culture, and Gender: About Teachers' Interactions with One Another

Note(s):　　Including counselors and other school staff

Definition: As stated: teachers' theories about and/or issues surrounding any interaction between themselves and other faculty or staff that involves race, ethnicity, class, culture, and/or gender.

Example:　　Tape 504. SF site mtg. 10/24/92. Proofread, pp. 13–14:

Susanna:　　**That makes me think about how come we don't have <u>dialogue</u> with Black teachers. You know in school they should, uh, maybe we can have different groups of teachers, different you know, ethnic groups, deliberately together. . . . And then talk about different issues, instead of the whole faculty. We (UC talk about the?) the (UC multiculturalcy?) but nobody wants, dares to say anything, / Alex: Hm / Verda: That's right / ya know in front of everybody. / Verda: That's right/ And they're afraid that ya know, our political reason offended you and the group, but if without, you know, really might not, what you're saying is that, ya know, god can we get together? Black teacher, Chinese teacher this week, maybe Hispanic, and uh, American, just take turns meeting in small groups.**

---

an entire transcript together. They discussed areas of agreement and disagreement to establish shared understandings of how each code should be applied to the data. Questions raised by the pair were brought to the weekly meetings of the research group. In light of specific instances from the transcripts, the group would negotiate an agreement about how each code should be used, and, when necessary, would amend the code book. After a pair of coders had coded and reviewed one transcript together, they then independently coded the first 25 codes of the next transcript. If the pair did not reach 80% agreement, they would both code the next 25 codes and compare their results. They continued this procedure until they established 80% agreement. After initial reliability was achieved, only one person coded a transcript, but spot checks were conducted throughout the process to ensure reliability. If on the spot check the pair did not achieve 80% reliability, the first 25 codes of the transcript were recoded, and the pair returned to the initial procedure for establishing reliability.

Transcripts coded at 80% reliability were then entered by code into the NUDIST (Nonnumerical Unstructured Data, Indexing, Searching, and Theorizing) system. This software allowed the Berkeley team to generate reports that included all instances of a specific code. From these reports, the major issues for the book's chapters were identified.

Figure B.3. Project coding matrix.

	Boston	Chicago	New Orleans	San Francisco
Site Meeting 1	10/31/92 201, 202, 203 Liz/Julie	10/18/92 302, 303, 304, 305 Carol/Sarah	10/31/92 403, 404, 405, 406 Liz/Sarah	10/24/92 503, 504, 505, 506, 507, 508 Julie/Carol
Site Meeting 2	3/27/93 215, 216, 217 Liz/Sarah	2/28/93 312, 313, 314, 315, 316, 317 Liz/Carol	2/25/93 414, 415, 416, 417, 418, 419, 420, 421 Julie/Carol	3/13/93 527, 528, 529, 530, 531, 532, 533, 534 Julie/Sarah
Site Meeting 3 (Spot Code)	5/23/93 219, 220, 221 Julie/Carol	5/7/93 320, 322, 323, 324, 325, 326, 327, 328, 329, 330, 331, 332, 333, 334, 335/no 321 Sarah/Liz	4/29/93 425, 426, 427, 428, 429, 430, 431, 432, 433, 434, 435, 436 Liz/Julie	4/29/93, 6/12/93 535, 536, 539, 540, 541, 542, 543, 544, 545, 546, 547 Carol/Sarah
Local Meeting 1	9/22/92 204, 205 Liz/Carol	10/31/92 306 Julie/Carol	10/18/92 401, 402 Julie /Sarah	12/3/92 510 Sarah/Liz
Local Meeting 2	1/21/93 211 Julie/Sarah	1/30/93 310 Liz/Julie	1/9/93 410.1 or 411 Sarah/Carol	1/14/92 512, 513, 514, 515 Carol/Liz
Local Meeting 3	3/16/93 214 Carol/Sarah	5/5/93 336 Julie/Sarah	4/25/93 424 Liz/Carol	6/3/93 537, 538 Liz/Julie

Note: Each box indicates the date the meeting occurred and the tape numbers we assigned to the tape or tapes recorded and transcribed for that meeting.

Structure for M-CLASS

The Opening Conference. At the conference in early September, 1992, the teacher researchers explored multicultural issues, learned about teacher research, and began to think about their research questions. After the panel on multiculturalism moderated by Duster and the follow-up discussion and writing, Mary K. Healy, a well-known teacher educator and a frequent presenter on teacher research for the National Writing Project, led a workshop for the group on formulating research questions. Also on this topic, local teacher researchers and Bay Area Writing Project teacher consultants, Joan Cone, Jane Juska, and Patsy Lockhart led small-group discussions on their own research experiences—explaining both the difficulties and the rewards.

Site Meetings. Three nationally coordinated site meetings introduced substantive research topics sequentially, as well as issues of multiculturalism. These meetings were led by either Freedman or Simons and consisted of a weekend workshop at the site. At the first site meeting in October or November, the teacher researchers continued discussions of multiculturalism, formulated their research questions, and developed a plan for data collection. At the second site meeting in February or March, they began analyzing their data and writing pieces for their research reports. At the third site meeting in May or June, they synthesized themes in the research reports by the 24 teachers from the four sites. The first two site meetings included a discussion of readings. For the first meeting these were about multiculturalism and literacy (Blauner, 1992; Delpit, 1988). For the second meeting they consisted of three teacher-research studies that provided models for the M-CLASS teachers' upcoming writing (Cone, 1992; Juska, 1989; Lew, 1992). All meetings incorporated discussions of each teacher's research project and some time to write.

Local Meetings. Besides attending the nationally organized meetings, the teachers met at least once a month locally to discuss their teaching and their research. Led by the local site coordinators, the local meetings were more relaxed and less formal than the Berkeley-led meetings and provided an essential space for both national and local community building and ongoing local research support. Here, the teachers talked about their teaching, refined their research questions, and discussed how to conduct their studies in their classrooms, schools, and communities.

Additional Support. Intertwining the national and the local, the Berkeley team wrote to every teacher researcher three times during the year: first during the opening conference in response to the teacher researchers' logs, which contained the teachers' preliminary ideas for research questions; second to summarize and make suggestions related to the teachers' research question after the first site visit; and third to respond to midyear progress reports, which every teacher wrote. The Berkeley team wrote additional letters to individual teacher researchers about ongoing drafts of their writing. Also, the Berkeley team kept in touch with individual teacher researchers by telephone and, when possible, by electronic mail. These discussions usually included response to the teachers' ideas and to drafts of their writing. The teachers commonly discussed these letters and conversations during their local research meetings.

Freedman and Simons, along with the site coordinator, visited each teacher researcher's classroom, usually early in the year. The site coordinators sometimes visited the classrooms at other times as well. These classroom visits clarified for the visitors the issues the teacher researchers grappled with in their daily teaching lives and that comprised the substance of their research. Only Roberta Logan, the Boston site coordinator, was unable to visit the Boston teachers' classrooms, because she was herself a teacher and could not get released time for this purpose.

Finally, the Berkeley team kept in touch with the site coordinators to suggest agenda items for local meetings and to discuss issues involving individual teacher researchers.

Evaluation of the Structure. The structure kept the communities at the four sites on roughly the same schedule and allowed the teacher researchers, in spite of their busy schedules, to complete a great deal of high-quality work in a relatively brief time period. The teachers worked extremely hard and felt obligated to meet this schedule, not least because they felt responsible to their colleagues across the country whom they knew were keeping to the same schedule. The M-CLASS teachers had decided on their research questions by October; they collected their data during the year; and they wrote a full report that could be distributed to the national group before the final site meetings in late May and early June. Although the pace of the research year was not relaxed, it was manageable. Those who wanted to publish their work as full chapters in the book continued working beyond the initial research year, as did the university team. Most of us took several years to complete our pieces.

Notes

CHAPTER 1

1. In addition to Freedman and Simons, the Berkeley team included Alex Casareno and Stan Goto in the first phase and Catherine Leak Borella, Julie Kalnin, and Carol Treasure in the second.

2. The conference was funded by CHART, a project of the Rockefeller Foundation. Special guests included Phyllis Franklin, executive director of the Modern Language Association; Miles Myers, then executive director of the National Council of Teachers of English; Judith Renyi, then director of CHART; Richard Sterling, then director of the New York City Writing Project and codirector of the National Writing Project's Urban Sites Network.

3. A few of the teachers worked together and knew each other well. In Chicago, two pairs taught together; one of these was husband and wife. In Boston, two of the teachers had previously taught at the same school, although they currently worked at different schools.

4. The San Francisco Bay Area, unlike the other urban areas, is composed of a number of large urban districts. For this reason, M-CLASS teachers in this region work in four different school districts: San Francisco, Oakland, Berkeley, and West Contra Costa. The only other urban area where we might have had a concentration of teachers not in the main city district is Boston, where other urban districts also surround the city. By chance, however, all of the Boston M-CLASS teachers taught in the Boston city schools. In New Orleans, one of the teachers teaches in St. Bernard Parish, which adjoins Orleans Parish. St. Bernard, although less typically urban, is largely working-class White and is therefore quite unlike the mostly African American population in Orleans Parish. For this reason we included a teacher from this area.

The groupings on this chart obscure important differences within what, according to the labels, appear to be the same ethnic group. Within the Black population, greater numbers of students of Afro-Caribbean and Cape Verdean origin go to school in Boston than in the other areas. The Hispanic populations also differ from one district to another, with mostly Puerto Ricans on the East Coast, mostly Mexican Americans in Chicago and Oakland, and mostly Central Americans in San Francisco.

CHAPTER 2

1. Frequently cited for her work on ability-group tracking and educational equity, Cone has published in *Harvard Educational Review, English Journal, College Board Review,* and *Phi Delta Kappan.* Jane Juska has published in *English Journal,*

Phi Delta Kappan, and *The Quarterly of the National Writing Project and the Center for the Study of Writing and Literacy.* Her article "The Unteachables" first appeared in *The Quarterly* and won an award for the best article in a small publication from the Education Writers Association. An experienced teacher researcher, Lew's writings have appeared in *English Journal* and *Education Week.* She was ready to get feedback on her M-CLASS writings because she began her project with another local teacher-research group the year before M-CLASS began.

2. At this meeting, we also distributed but did not discuss a chapter by British teacher researcher Helen Savva, "Reading Development in a Fifth-year Girl" (Savva, 1982). Fifth year in Britain is the equivalent of 10th grade in the United States. Savva has published her writings in publications for teachers in Great Britain (e.g., *The LINC Reader* and *English Magazine*). She coordinated the Inner London Education Authority (ILEA) Writing Project and the Language in the National Curriculum (LINC) project and has served as an inspector for language teaching. In her article, Savva did a particularly interesting job of tracking a student's growth across time, the task that Lew was in the process of attempting. We recommended that those who were doing case studies of student growth might be especially interested in Savva's chapter. Also, its form and tone were somewhat different from most of the teacher-research pieces we read during our search for models for the group.

CHAPTER 7

Karen Alford left a draft of this manuscript when she died on January 9, 1997. The manuscript was completed by Art Peterson and Sarah Warshauer Freedman. We hope that this version accurately reflects Alford's ideas and feelings about teaching history and her respect for and dedication to her students.

CHAPTER 8

The books referred to in this chapter were taken, as Daniels describes, from various sources, including garage sales, her personal library, and the school book-room. As she was tracing the bibliographic information for these texts, she discovered that some of the texts were inadvertently destroyed when she moved to a new school. As a result, although most of the references were retrievable, full citations are not available for a few of the books.

CHAPTER 9

1. A T-unit is one independent clause with all of its attached and embedded subordinates (Hunt, 1965). The length and complexity of this unit is a better measure of syntactic maturity than is the sentence because it does not count compound senten-ces as mature.

References

Alford, K. (1994, April). *Collaboration with university faculty in doing teacher research in a multicultural classroom.* Paper presented at the annual meeting of the American Educational Research Association, New Orleans.

Atwell, N. M. (1987). *In the middle: Writing, reading, and learning with adolescents.* Portsmouth, NH: Boynton/Cook.

Banks, J. (1979). *Teaching strategies for ethnic studies.* Boston: Allyn & Bacon.

Banks, J. (1992). Multicultural education: Approaches, developments and dimensions. In J. Lynch, C. Modgil, & S. Modgil, (Eds.), *Cultural diversity and the schools: Vol. 1. Education for cultural diversity: Convergence and divergence* (pp. 83–94). London: Falmer Press.

Banks, J. (1995). Multicultural education: Historical development, dimensions, and practice. In J. Banks (Ed.), *Handbook of research on multicultural education* (pp. 3–24). New York: McGraw Hill.

Berthoff, A. (1987). The teacher as researcher. In D. Goswami & P. Stillman (Eds.), *Reclaiming the classroom: Teacher research as an agency for change.* Upper Montclair, NJ: Boynton/Cook.

Bishop, W. (1990). *Released into language: Options for teaching creative writing.* Urbana, IL: National Council of Teachers of English.

Blauner, B. (1992, Summer). Talking past each other: Black and white languages of race. *American Prospect, 10,* 55–64.

Bonham, F. (1965). *Durango Street.* New York: Dutton.

Brown, F., Carter, D., & Harris, J. (1978). Minority students, ability grouping, and career development. *Journal of Black Studies, 8*(4), 477–488.

Check, J. (1997, May/June). Teacher research as powerful professional development. *Harvard Education Letter,* 6–8.

Cisneros, S. (1988). *The house on Mango Street.* Houston, TX: Arte Publico Press.

Cochran-Smith, M., & Lytle, S. L. (1993). *Inside/outside: Teacher research and knowledge.* New York: Teachers College Press.

Cone, J. (1990). Literature, geography, and the untracked English class. *English Journal, 79*(8), 60–67.

Cone, J. (1992). Untracking advanced placement English: Creating opportunity is not enough. *Phi Delta Kappan, 73*(9), 712–717.

Cone, J. (1993, Fall). Learning to teach an untracked class. *College Board Review, 169,* 20–27,31.

Crawford, J. (1995). *Bilingual education: History, politics, theory, and practice* (3rd ed.). Los Angeles: Bilingual Educational Services.

Daniels, T., & Daniels, K. (1994). The value of teacher research: Learning about ourselves and our students. *The Best Practices Newsletter 6,* North Central Regional Educational Laboratory, p. 10.

Danger, P. (1983). *The divorce express.* New York: Dell.

Delpit, L. (1986). Skills and other dilemmas of a progressive Black educator. *Harvard Educational Review, 56,* 379–385

Delpit, L. (1988). The silenced dialogue: Power and pedagogy in educating other people's children. *Harvard Educational Review, 58,* 280–298.

Delpit, L. (1995). *Other peoples' children.* New York: New Press.

Divine, R. (1992). *America, the people and the dream.* Glenview, IL: Scott, Foresman.

Drevitch, G. (1992). Dr Jekyll and Mr. Hyde. *Scholastic Scope, 41*(5), 2–11.

Eidman-Aadahl, E. (1996). My third spaces: From Sharkey's to the Urban Sites Network. In *Cityscapes: Eight views from the urban classroom.* Berkeley, CA: National Writing Project.

Elliott, J. (1981). Foreword. In J. Nixon (Ed.), *A teachers' guide to action research: Evaluation, enquiry and development in the classroom.* London: Grant McIntyre.

England, R., Meier, K., & Fraga, L. (1988). Barriers to equal opportunity: Educational practices and minority students. *Urban Affairs Quarterly, 23*(4), 635–646.

Fast, H. (1961). *April morning.* New York: Bantam Books.

Foster, M. (1997). *Black teachers on teaching.* New York: New Press.

Freedman, S. W., with Simons, E. R., Alford, K., Galley, R., Herring, S., Williams-Smith, D., Valenti, E., & Ward, P. (1994). Teacher researchers together: Delving into the teacher research process. *The Quarterly of the National Writing Project and the National Center for the Study of Writing, 16*(4), 8–17.

Gaines, E. (1971). *The autobiography of Miss Jane Pittman.* New York: Bantam Books.

Gaines, E. (1993). *A lesson before dying.* New York: Alfred A. Knopf.

Galt, M. F. (1992). *The story in history: Writing your way into the American experience.* New York: Teachers & Writers Collaborative.

Gonzalez, N., Moll, L., Floyd-Tenery, M., Rivera, A., Rendon, P., Gonzales, R., & Amanti, C. (1993). *Teacher research on funds of knowledge: Learning from households* (Educational Practice Report No. 6). Santa Cruz, CA: National Center for Research on Cultural Diversity and Second Language Learning.

Goswami, D., & Stillman, P. (Ed.). (1987). *Reclaiming the classroom: Teacher research as an agency for change.* Portsmouth, NH: Boynton/Cook.

Grant, C. (1988). The persistent significance of race in schooling. *Elementary School Journal, 88*(5), 561–570.

Gutierrez, K. (1992). A comparison of instructional contexts in writing process classrooms with Latino children. *Education and Urban Society, 24*(2), 244–262.

Heath, S. B. (1981). English in our language heritage. In C. Ferguson & S. B. Heath (Eds.), *Language in the USA.* Cambridge: Cambridge University Press.

Hemingway, E. (1986). *A farewell to arms.* New York: Collier Books.

Hilliard, A. (1988). Conceptual confusion and the persistence of group oppression through education. *Equity & Excellence, 24,* 36–43.

Hinton, S. E. (1975). *Rumble fish.* New York: Dell.

Huberman, M. (1996). Moving mainstream: Taking a closer look at teacher research. *Language Arts, 73,* 124–140.

Hunt, K. (1965). *Grammatical structures written at three grade levels.* NCTE Research Report No. 3. Urbana, IL: National Council of Teachers of English.

Hurston, Z. N. (1976). *Their eyes were watching god.* New York: Negro Universities Press.

Juska, J. (1989). The unteachables. *Quarterly of the National Writing Project and the National Center for the Study of Writing, 11*(1), 1–3, 26–27.

Khanga, Yelena, with Susan Jacoby. (1992). *Soul to soul: A Black Russian American family 1865–1992.* New York: W. W. Norton

Ladson-Billings, G. (1994). *The dreamkeepers: Successful teachers of African American children.* San Francisco: Jossey-Bass.

Latino Eligibility Task Force. (1993, March). *Myths and realities about Latino students* (Report No. 1). Oakland, CA: University of California, Office of the President.

Lee, C. (1993). *Signifying as a scaffold for literary interpretation: The pedagogical implications of an African American discourse genre.* Urbana, IL: National Council of Teachers of English.

Lee, C. (1995). A culturally based cognitive apprenticeship: Teaching African American high school students skills in literary interpretation. *Reading Research Quarterly, 30*(4), 608–630.

Lee, H. (1960). *To kill a mockingbird.* Philadelphia: Lippincott.

Lew, A. (1992). Raw fish or steamed? Unpublished manuscript, University of California, Berkeley.

McKernan, J. (1991). *Curriculum action research: A handbook of methods and resources for the reflective practitioner.* New York: St. Martin's Press.

Melville, Herman. (1979) *Moby Dick.* New York: Dodd, Mead.

Mohr, M., & MacLean, M. (1987). *Working together: A guide for teacher-researchers.* Urbana, IL: National Council of Teachers of English.

Natriello, G. (1994). Coming together and breaking apart: Unifying and differentiating processes in schools and classrooms. *Research in Sociology of Education and Socialization, 10,* 111–145.

Nickerson, M. (1992, October 14). Sniper kills Cabrini kid steps from school. *Chicago Tribune,* pp. 1, 13.

Nieto, S. (1992). *Affirming diversity.* New York: Longman.

Nixon, J. (Ed.). (1981). *A teachers' guide to action research: Evaluation, enquiry and development in the classroom.* London: Grant McIntyre.

Oakes, J. (1985). *Keeping track: How schools structure inequality.* New Haven: Yale University Press.

Oakes, J. (1995). Two cities' tracking and within-school segregation. *Teachers College Record, 96*(4), 681–690.

Okada, J. (1976). *No-no boy.* Seattle: University of Washington Press.

Richter, C. (1953). *A light in the forest.* New York: Bantam Books.

Rief, L. (1992). *Seeking diversity: Language arts with adolescents.* Portsmouth, NH: Heinemann.

Rosenblatt, L. (1994). Transactional theory of reading and writing. In R. B. Ruddell, M. R. Ruddell, & H. Singer (Eds.), *Theoretical models and processes of reading.* Newark, DE: International Reading Association.

Savva, H. (1982). Reading development in a fifth-year girl. In *Becoming our own experts: The Vauxhall papers of the Vauxhall Manor School Talk Workshop Group* (pp. 159–195). London: Inner London Education Authority English Centre.

Sietsema, J., & Bose, J. (1995). *Characteristics of the 100 largest public elementary and secondary school districts in the United States: 1992–93.* Statistical analysis report. ERIC document. (No. ED 392850).

Slavin, R. E. (1990). *Achievement effects of ability grouping in secondary schools: A best-evidence synthesis.* Madison, WI: National Center for Effective Secondary Schools.

Sleeter, C. (1989). Multicultural education as a form of resistance to oppression. *Journal of Education, 171*(3), 51–72.

Sleeter, C. E., & Grant, C. A. (1987). An analysis of multicultural education in the United States. *Harvard Educational Review, 57,* 421–444.

Spradley, J. P. (1980). *Participant observation.* New York: Holt, Reinhart, & Winston.

Stenhouse, L. (1985). What counts as research. In J. Rudduck & D. Hopkins (Eds.), *Research as a basis for teaching: Readings from the work of Lawrence Stenhouse.* Portsmouth, NH: Heinemann Books.

Tafel, L. S., & Fischer, J. C. (1996). Lives of inquiry: Communities of learning and caring. In G. Burnaford, J. Fischer, & D. Hobson (Eds.), *Teachers doing research: Practical possibilities.* Mahwah, NJ: Lawrence Erlbaum.

Tatum, B. (1992). Talking about race, learning about racism: The application of racial identity development theory in the classroom. *Harvard Educational Review, 62*(1), 1–24.

Taylor, M. (1978). *Roll of thunder, hear my cry.* New York: Bantam Books.

Uchida, Y. (1987). *Picture bride: A novel.* Flagstaff, AZ: Northland Press.

Valdés, G. (1996). *Con respeto: Bridging the distances between culturally diverse families and schools, An ethnographic portrait.* New York: Teachers College Press.

West, C. (1994). *Race matters.* New York: Vintage Books.

Wiesel, E. (1985, April 22). Facing history and ourselves, Speech at Boston University.

Winter, R. (1989). *Learning from experience: Principles and practice in action-research.* London: Falmer Press.

Wong, W. (1993, January 3). The complex issue of immigration. *Oakland Tribune,* p. B4.

Wright, R. (1945a). *Black boy, a record of childhood and youth.* New York: Harper.

Wright. R. (1945b). The living ethics of Jim Crow: An autobiographical sketch. In B. Moon (Ed.), *Primer for white folks.* Garden City, NY: Doubleday, Doran.

X, Malcolm. (1970). *Malcolm X on Afro-American history.* New York: Pathfinder Press.

About the Authors

Sarah Warshauer Freedman, a former secondary English teacher, is professor of education at the University of California, Berkeley, where she also directed the National Center for the Study of Writing and Literacy from 1985–1996. She is the author of *Exchanging Writing, Exchanging Cultures: Lessons in School Reform from the United States and Great Britain* (Harvard University Press) and *Response to Student Writing* (National Council of Teachers of English), and edited *The Acquisition of Written Language* (Ablex). She has also published numerous journal articles and book chapters and has won several national awards for her books. In April 1997, she was a resident at the Rockefeller Foundation's Bellagio Study and Conference Center, where she worked on this book.

    Elizabeth Radin Simons, codirector of M-CLASS, is the English teacher coordinator of the Puente High School Project of the University of California's Office of the President. Puente targets underserved students, helping them matriculate into four-year colleges and universities. She was a history and English teacher in New York City; Newton, Massachusetts; and Bay Area schools and has worked as codirector of the Minority Education Project at the University of California, Berkeley. Simons holds a PhD in folklore and education from Berkeley and conducts workshops in folklore and writing in the United States and abroad. She is the author of *Student Worlds, Student Words: Teaching Writing Through Folklore* (Heinemann) and articles on folklore and writing. Along with Freedman, Simons was a resident at the Rockefeller Foundation's Bellagio Study and Conference Center, where she worked on this book.

    Julie Shalhope Kalnin is a doctoral candidate in language, literacy and culture at UC Berkeley. Previously a high school English teacher, she continues to pursue her interest in how teachers can best facilitate their students' writing development. She is the author of "Walking on the Commons: Genre as a Tool in Supporting Adolescent Literacy " published in *Reconceptualizing the Literacies in Adolescents' Lives* (Erlbaum). With the support of a Spencer Foundation Dissertation Fellowship, she is currently studying how teachers' theories about literacy and about the teaching of literacy are influenced by their participation in teacher research.

    Alex Casareno is assistant professor of education at the University of Portland in Portland, Oregon, where he teaches undergraduate and graduate classes in reading and language arts education for elementary and secondary preservice teachers. Before that he was an assistant professor at the University of Alabama, where he served as chair of the Multiple Abilities Program (MAP), an inclusive teacher-education program for K–6 teachers. Along with MAP colleagues, he received the Career Development Award in Inclusive Teacher Education from the Joseph P. Kennedy, Jr., Foundation, and an award in Inclusive Teacher Preparation from the Coca-Cola Foundation. His research is on the impact of reflectivity on teachers in multicultural contexts. Casareno received his PhD in language and literacy education from UC Berkeley, and taught for 7 years in a wide variety of public and private elementary school settings.

THE M-CLASS TEAMS

Boston

Site leader **Roberta Logan,** a sixth-grade social studies teacher at the Martin Luther King Middle School, has been teaching in Boston for more than 20 years. A Philadelphia native and graduate of that city's public schools, Logan maintains an active interest in African American history and recently served as group leader for a summer course on using primary-source documents to teach that subject. She came to M-CLASS with experience as a teacher researcher through the National Writing Project's Urban Sites Network.

Supporting site leader **Joseph W. Check** is Director of the Leadership in Urban Schools Doctoral Program of the Graduate College of Education at the University of Massachusetts Boston, as well as director of the Boston Writing Project. He has worked closely with practitioners on reading and writing issues in urban schools since 1979, with a particular interest in teachers as researchers. He acts as codirector of the Urban Sites Network of the National Writing Project and of the Writing Within School Reform project of the Annenberg Institute for School Reform. His current research interests include the ways in which practitioners can become creators of knowledge, leadership for change in urban settings, and the interface between practitioners as writers and school reform. He recently published a piece in the *Harvard Education Letter* on teacher research.

Nancy O'Malley, an English teacher since 1970, now teaches at Boston Latin School. Previously, she taught at middle and high schools in Boston, including O'Bryant, where she conducted her M-CLASS research. Active in the Boston School District on curriculum and standards committees, she also leads district workshops for teachers on these topics. Most recently she worked to ensure that a new and inclusive canon of literature for teaching in the Boston schools consisted of high-quality literature. She was awarded a 2-year Conant Fellowship to study at Harvard University from 1994 to 1996 and received a Certificate of Advanced Graduate Study. She has an MA from Harvard and since her involvement with M-CLASS has given many talks at conferences and presentations on teaching in multicultural classrooms. Since 1991 she has directed, in collaboration with the Boston Writing Project, a Student Writer's Workshop, which enrolls more than 60 Boston high school students each summer.

Eileen Shakespear has taught for more than 25 years, all of them in the Boston public schools. She is co-chair of the humanities department and teaches English as part of an interdisciplinary team at the Fenway Middle College High School. Fenway is part of the Coalition for Essential Schools, and Shakespear serves as a lead teacher for the coalition for the city of Boston, frequently giving presentations on portfolios and expositions to other teachers and to students and faculty at local universities. She serves as a mentor teacher for the interns in her school and as a university supervisor for preservice teachers through Harvard University and the University of Massachusetts, Boston. Her current interests are in both preservice and in-service site-based teacher education.

Darcelle Walker is a 20-year veteran teacher in the Boston public schools. She also brings a master's degree in educational administration to her work at McCormick Middle School. Through work on the School Improvement Task Force, Walker is currently involved both in designing ways for teachers to bring theories of multiple intelligences to bear in their practice and in conducting a study of the effectiveness of the approaches teachers employ. In addition to her teaching responsibilities, she is writing a semi-autobiographical novel.

James Williams is an economics and history teacher at Boston Latin Academy. He has taught for 15 years in the Boston system. For eight of those years, he taught at the Thompson Middle School, where he conducted his research. In 1991, Williams was named a Golden Apple Teacher by the Boston School District. In 1992 he was featured in a Boston television special as a New England Spirit Award recipient. In his search for new ways to enrich his students' learning, Williams is currently pursuing a Master's in Creative Arts that emphasizes integrating the arts into all subject areas. Williams has also been a coach and an administrator and has a special professional interest in how African American adolescent males learn.

Walter Wood, a former English teacher and current assistant headmaster at South Boston High School—the scene of nationally televised confrontations during the mid-1970s—has worked in the Boston school system for almost 30 years. During Boston's desegregation, Wood was a member of a specialized Instructional Support Team that worked with school faculties to better address their students' needs. A secondary teacher for 25 years, Wood has extended his involvement in the district's schools beyond his own classroom. He was active on the parent councils of his children's schools. He was, for 12 years, a member of the Boston Teacher's Union's Executive Board, and, in that role, was part of a committee to design staff development schools in the district. Wood, a teacher at heart, brings the results of his M-CLASS research to his current position, where he emphasizes the need to approach education one person at a time, by attempting to give individuals the attention and support they need.

Junia Yearwood, originally from the West Indies, is a humanities and English teacher at Boston English High School. Inspired by her desire to help her students develop positive identities through learning about their cultural history, Yearwood established a multicultural library at her school and is designing a Black history course that will be taught through literature. Yearwood, who has in the past led a study group at her school exploring multicultural teaching, learning, and curriculum issues as they affect English High's diverse urban population, is currently leading a teacher's reading group, where 25 of her colleagues will join her in reading, writing about, and discussing professional literature. She hopes that this reading group will provide the necessary groundwork for establishing a teacher-research team at her school.

Chicago

Site coordinator **Betty Jane Wagner** is a professor in the College of Education at Roosevelt University and director of the Chicago Area Writing Project. She is an internationally recognized authority in the educational uses of drama in the classroom and in composition instruction. Her most recent publications are *Educational Drama and Language Arts: What Research Shows* (1998); *Situations: A Case Book of Virtual Realities for the English Teacher* (1995), coauthored with Mark Larson; and the fourth edition of *Student-Centered Language Arts, K–12* (1992), coauthored with the late James Moffett. She also published *Dorothy Heathcote: Drama as a Learning Medium* as well as several sets of curriculum materials, including *Books at Play* (1997), a dramatic approach to language arts.

Kathy Daniels has been teaching English since 1968 and her husband, **Tom Daniels,** has been teaching this subject since 1961. They work together on most projects, having co-led staff development workshops for the Illinois Writing Project since 1984. One of their workshops was featured in a PBS documentary, *Teach Me,* which won an Emmy in 1991. They also have written a number of articles for the *Best Practice* newspaper and, after working with other teachers and Writing Project leaders, have established a new and very small public high school, designed to model best practices. Both are lead teachers; Kathy Daniels teaches English, and Tom Daniels is in charge of the computer program.

In 1996, **Stephanie Davenport** completed her doctorate in educational administration at Roosevelt University. An English teacher in Chicago public schools since 1967, Davenport has participated in several national curriculum development projects on educational diversity and the arts. Since 1994, she has collaborated with Professor Carol Lee at Northwestern University on a multimedia research project focused on developing curriculum in English literature for inner-city African American students. Davenport also has taught English methods courses at Loyola University, authored an article on travel to be published in an anthology of Black women's travel stories, and dances with the Trinity United Church of Christ Adult Dance Ministry.

Griselle M. Diaz-Gemmati is a fourth-generation teacher. She started her career in 1986 in bilingual education at Norwood Park and has been there ever since. Currently, she teaches language arts, social studies, and literature. In 1993, she received one of the city of Chicago's coveted Golden Apple awards for excellence in education and has had work published by *Kappa Delta Pi.* She has consulted for the Illinois State Board of Education and for the National Board for Professional Teaching Standards. She received her MA in education from National-Louis University in 1997.

Brenda Landau McFarland recently retired after 20 years in the classroom. Besides teaching secondary social studies, she taught public finance at the university level. For much of her career she worked in special education and child protection, on a Title I project; on an implementation plan for the Day Crisis Nursery and Family Support Center, designed to prevent the abuse of children; and as a social worker. Landau McFarland has published numerous curriculum guides as well as a book chapter, "The Abused Student," in B. J. Wagner's *Situations: A Casebook of Virtual Realities for the English Teacher.*

David O'Neill began teaching English in 1959 at Kingsdale Comprehensive School in London, England, where he was part of the then new British plan to democratize their schools. Upon his return to the United States the next year, he taught for 11 years in private schools. After a 4-year stint in textbook publishing, O'Neill returned to the classroom, first teaching English to new immigrants and then teaching English for 7 years at Clemente in the Puerto Rican barrio and for one year at Juarez before coming to Lane, where he has taught since 1984. He attended two National Endowment for the Humanities summer programs in the 1980s and spent one summer at a National Institute for the Humanities program in 1991.

New Orleans

Cynthia Roy is an associate professor in the English Department at the University of New Orleans and director of the Greater New Orleans Writing Project. She is a sociolinguist whose research is in language and gender, discourse analysis, and composition. She began her career as an interpreter for the deaf and has authored the forthcoming book *Interpreting as a Discourse Process* (Oxford University Press).

In 1996, her final year of teaching, **Karen Alford** received a grant from the Spencer Foundation to complete her M-CLASS research. At Audubon she served as president of the Parent Teacher Association and in 1994 was elected Teacher of the Year. Always dedicated to her students and their success and persistent about completing her teacher research, she leaves a lasting legacy.

Before teaching in the New Orleans schools, **Reginald Galley,** who holds a law degree and an MBA from Texas Southern University and an MA in education from Xavier, has taught business courses in the community colleges since 1977. He has taught social studies in the New Orleans schools since 1990 and during the M-CLASS research year also served as an assistant to the principal. He currently also has his own educational consulting firm and specializes in programs to develop critical thinking, reasoning, and motivation.

Sarah Herring began teaching English in 1970 and currently serves as department chair at Edna Karr Magnet and is active in professional organizations. In 1993–1994 she was named District Teacher of the Year, a major honor. Since participating in M-CLASS, she initiated a multicultural assembly series to provide yearround cultural programs at her school.

Elena Valenti has been teaching social studies since 1984 and in 1996 was named assistant principal at Andrew Jackson. Known for her curriculum innovations, she has forged partnerships linking Stennis Space Center with geography students at her school and has participated in a computerized geography program that allowed students to use and interact with global positioning data transmitted from satellites.

A published poet and a teacher in New Orleans schools since 1964, **Patricia Ward** teaches at McMain. She just received her MA in poetry from the University of New Orleans. She has attended numerous National Endowment for the Humanities and Louisiana Endowment for the Humanities summer institutes and in 1994 traveled to Senegal and Ghana on a Fulbright award.

Doris Williams-Smith taught in New Orleans schools for almost 20 years before leaving the classroom in 1993 to direct teacher education and to complete her doctorate in education at the University of New Orleans. After receiving her degree in 1996, she became an assistant professor and assistant dean at the University of New Orleans. She recently received a grant from the Spencer Foundation to work with teachers from the New Orleans M-CLASS group and the National Writing Project's Urban Sites Network on writing for publication and designing professional development activities based on their research.

San Francisco Bay Area

Site coordinator **Carol Tateishi** taught English at the middle school level for 14 years in the San Francisco Bay Area and for 2 years at the elementary level in London, England. Currently, she directs the Bay Area Writing Project at the Graduate School of Education, University of California at Berkeley, and is an associate director of the National Writing Project. She has conducted workshops on the teaching of writing in California, Japan, Korea, and Puerto Rico. She helped develop the first statewide writing assessment in California and is coeditor of *Meeting the Challenges: Stories from Today's Classrooms.*

George Austin attended Kent State University on a football scholarship, served a stint of military duty during the Vietnam War, and then completed his education at the University of California, Berkeley. He began his teaching career in 1986 at Oakland High School, after a career as a health-care field administrator. Austin currently teaches history and government and serves as a football and track coach at El Cerrito High School in El Cerrito, California, where he has taught since 1989 and where he conducted his teacher research for M-CLASS.

Verda Delp has taught in the Berkeley schools since 1973. With credentials in elementary education and secondary English, she has taught across the grade levels. Delp has led a number of summer institutes for teachers at the University of California, Berkeley, and offers many workshops throughout the year. In 1996 she received a grant from the Spencer Foundation for her teacher research and currently serves as a school-site leader for the M-CLASS Site-Based Network.

A secondary English teacher in the Oakland Unified School District since 1989, **Deborah Archuleta Juarez** had led textbook adoption planning for her district and curriculum development activities. She also helped the district develop content and performance standards for English language arts. She has served as a reader for Educational Testing Service, is a task force member for the California Subject Matter Projects, and serves as a school-site leader for a teacher research group at Calvin Simmons Junior High for the M-CLASS Site-Based Network. The summer of 1997 brought Juarez to the Berkeley campus to participate in a National Endowment for the Humanities summer institute titled "Making American Literatures."

Ann Lew has been a teacher in the San Francisco Unified School district since 1972. She is involved in local school reform efforts through the Annenberg Foundation and regularly presents in-service workshops for her colleagues in the Bay Area. As a mentor teacher for the San Francisco District, she planned and implemented a series of workshops in 1997. She has published in *English Journal* and *Education Week.* Her article "In Praise of the Red Pen" (*Education Week,* 1993) has been reprinted several times. Like Juarez, Lew serves as her school-site leader for the M-CLASS Site-Based Network and spent the summer of 1997 at UC Berkeley as a participant in the National Endowment for the Humanities summer institute, "Making American Literatures."

Born in China and raised in Hong Kong, **Susanna Merrimee** began her teaching career in a Hong Kong elementary school in 1967. She came to the United States 2 years later, when she enrolled at Louisiana State University at New Orleans to study to become a social science teacher. After teaching in New Orleans for a year, she moved to San Francisco, where she has spent most of her teaching career. She holds a bilingual specialist teaching credential in Cantonese and English, and a state single-subject credential in social studies. She currently teaches sheltered-English social studies and English as a Second Language (ESL).

Phil Potestio has been teaching junior high school social studies in Oakland, California, since 1986, at Havenscourt Junior High, where he began his teaching career. In 1993 he completed requirements for a certificate to teach sheltered-English and ESL. He has chaired his school's Site-Based Development Team since 1992. In that role, he helped direct whole-school change and also promoted site-based governance throughout the district and the region. In addition, at the district level, he has been involved in projects to develop curriculum and standards and to support new teachers. He is a mentor teacher and has worked with student teachers through credential programs at Mills College and California State University at Hayward. He has presented his ideas on instructional strategies to motivate students at the annual California League of Middle Schools Conference. He also enjoys writing poetry.

OTHER MAJOR CONTRIBUTORS

Catherine Borella is the lead teacher and coordinator of the gifted programs at Maplebrook Elementary, in Naperville, Illinois. She teaches language arts and mathematics classes to gifted fourth- and fifth-grade students, and develops enrichment curriculum for kindergarten through third-grade students.

She received her master's degree in educational psychology from UC Berkeley. Her research interests include literacy development and gifted education.

Carol Treasure, a fifth-grade teacher, is pursuing a PhD in education at UC Berkeley. She is interested in issues related to technology and literacy and will focus her dissertation studies on how teachers and students use computers in their classrooms.

Index